# IMAGES
## of America
# KAPA'A

ON THE COVER: A local fisherman is caught in a pensive moment as he scans the Kapaʻa shoreline checking the tides and looking for the perfect spot to cast his line. (Courtesy of Diane Ferry.)

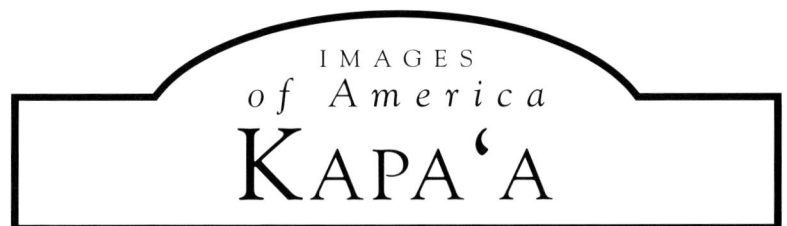

# IMAGES of America
# KAPA'A

Marta Miller Hulsman, Wilma Chandler,
Bill and Judie Fernandez, Linda Kaialoa,
Linda Moriarty, and Herman Texeira

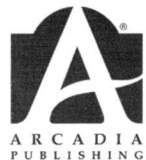

Copyright © 2015 by Marta Miller Hulsman, Wilma Chandler, Bill and Judie Fernandez,
  Linda Kaialoa, Linda Moriarty, and Herman Texeira
ISBN 978-1-4671-3337-1

Published by Arcadia Publishing
Charleston, South Carolina

Printed in the United States of America

Library of Congress Control Number: 2015937853

For all general information, please contact Arcadia Publishing:
Telephone 843-853-2070
Fax 843-853-0044
E-mail sales@arcadiapublishing.com
For customer service and orders:
Toll-Free 1-888-313-2665

Visit us on the Internet at www.arcadiapublishing.com

*This book is dedicated with aloha to the people of Kapaʻa,
then and now, and to all who hold it dear.*

# Contents

| | | |
|---|---|---|
| Acknowledgments | | 6 |
| Introduction | | 7 |
| 1. | Early History | 9 |
| 2. | Plantations and Immigration | 23 |
| 3. | Commerce and Town Development | 33 |
| 4. | The Pineapple Industry | 51 |
| 5. | War Years 1941–1945 | 61 |
| 6. | Churches | 71 |
| 7. | Schools | 83 |
| 8. | Community Life | 91 |
| 9. | Kapaʻa Today | 111 |

# Acknowledgments

We express our heartfelt *mahalo* to Kapaʻa Senior Center for sponsoring this tribute to Kapaʻa town. We are grateful to the following institutions that contributed time and resources to this project: The Church of Jesus Christ of Latter-Day Saints, *The Garden Island* newspaper, Grove Farm Homestead Museum, Honolulu Army Museum, *Honolulu Star Advertiser*, Kapaʻa First Hawaiian Church, Kapaʻa High School, Kapaʻa Hongwanji Mission, Kapaʻa Jodo Mission, Kapaʻa Library, Kauaʻi Historical Society (KHS), Kauaʻi Museum, Kauaʻi Veteran's Museum, and St. Catherine's Church.

We would like to express our sincere gratitude to the staff and volunteers of Kauaʻi Historical Society, especially Mary Requilman, Keith Holderman, Laraine Moriguchi, and Ruth Ann Jackson, for their countless hours of assistance. In addition, we thank Father Anthony Rapozo, Carmen Nakasone, Bob Schleck, Moises Madayag, Liza Capazzi, Lani Kawahara, Lyah Kama-Drake, Chris Faye, Vanessa Owens, and Beth Pemberton. The original illustrations that appear in the first chapter are by Kapaʻa High School student artists Anuhea Lizarraga, Raven-Brittaney Langagora, Rhandie Fernandez, Kahiwahiwa Davis, Jodi A. Reis, Justin Franklin, Elia Leone, Alohilani Chun, and Cadance Keaweamahi-Kahokuloa.

Finally, *mahalo nui loa* to the following Kapaʻa residents past and present who generously contributed their time, stories, and photographs to help us tell Kapaʻa's story: Kalei Arinaga, Danita Aiu, Helene Kahaunaele-Akiona, Philip Boiser, Andy Bushnell, Doris Chang, Diane Ferry, Gary Furugen, Clyde Furumoto, Doreen Vilela Geiger, Marilyn Suzuki Haugh, Clay Hiramoto, Winston and Reggie Kawamoto, Dolores Kaauwai, Josephine Ornellas, Ken and Bobby Kubota, Lyle Kuboyama, Kathy Matayoshi, Bonnie Matsumura, Ronnie Matsumura, Amelia McGregor, Mary Moriarty Jones, Paul Nakamura, Barbara Nishida, Gladys Padre, Robert Paik, Ernest Palmeira, Valerie Wong Poai, Janice Padre Plumer, Richard Sheldon, Moke' Smith, Dennis Thomas, Miles and Karen Tone, Marissa Valencia, Carrie Bettencourt Vilela, Laraine Okano Yamashita, Ruben and Florence Yoshida, and Avery Youn.

Albert Fukushima, born and raised in Kapaʻa, shepherded this project by providing steadfast guidance and a deep historical perspective of the town's history.

Please forgive any errors found; they were unintentional. If there are omissions of the *okina* and *kahako*, they were unintentional.

# Introduction

Bounded by the Pacific Ocean on the east and swampland to the west, an undesirable cigar-shaped sliver of land on the east coast of Kauaʻi provided a home in pre–Western contact time to poor Hawaiian commoners. In ancient times, the choice locations for the ruling class of the island were on the leeward side with its mild sunny weather and at Wailua, where the great temple complexes of the island were built. Probably because it was the only arable hard ground by the shoreline, this sliver of land was called Kapaʻa, meaning "the solid."

There is little early history of this area. Kapaʻa is barely mentioned in legends. There is no existing *heiau* (temple) in its vicinity nor is there evidence of fishponds, a common construction in other populated parts of Hawaiʻi. But this remoteness would be important. Those who dwelt in the solid enjoyed a modicum of freedom from war and *aliʻi* authority.

When the missionaries came in the 1820s, Kapaʻa was mentioned in the writings of Hiram Bingham as a rest stop on the way to Hanalei. Its founding date as a modern community can be traced to the arrival of two people in 1877, King David Kalākaua and a Chinese entrepreneur, Wong Aloiau.

Kalākaua had successfully concluded a reciprocity treaty with the United States that took effect in 1876. This agreement allowed Hawaiian sugar to be imported to America duty free. It meant that those in the plantation business could become wealthy. Kapaʻa and the land around it were crown lands, which meant that the monarch could use it without rental payments. The king and his cronies formed the Hui Kawaihau and entered into a partnership with Capt. James Makee, a man knowledgeable in sugar growing. The king's group came to Kapaʻa intent on starting a plantation.

Wong Aloiau was an immigrant Chinese who had knowledge of rice growing. He saw in the swampland to the west of town the opportunity to grow rice. He acquired property from a Hawaiian *kalo* (taro) farmer and began planting. Rice growing was a successful industry in Hawaiʻi due to the demand for it by Chinese laborers both in the islands and in California.

The Hui Kawaihau constructed residences, warehouses, and a mill. Aloiau did likewise for his enterprise of rice growing. Unfortunately for the king, Makee died early in the sugar venture. By 1881, the Hui's plantation efforts had failed, and what it had built in Kapaʻa reverted to the Chinese rice growers.

Meanwhile, Col. Zephaniah Spalding, son-in-law to Makee, purchased the sugar company. He moved the mill and plantation operation to Keālia, a location two miles north of Kapaʻa.

But, rice growing alone did not develop the Chinese town into a thriving community. A glimmer of opportunity for growth occurred when Hawaiʻi became a territory of the United States, and the government subdivided the former crown lands into lots for purchase in 1906. It is an axiom in real estate that if land is cheap enough, buyers will come. Soon, former plantation laborers, Japanese, Portuguese, and Europeans, acquired land in Kapaʻa and made it a bedroom community for skilled laborers working at the Keālia sugar mill.

Kapaʻa grew into a thriving town when the cannery opened for business during World War I. This enterprise meant that there was money to be earned in growing, harvesting, and processing pineapple. Hundreds, perhaps thousands, of laborers came to work in the fields and in the cannery, which created a need for services. Soon, small businesses flourished: general-goods stores, markets, barber shops, cafés, bakeries, fish mongers, slop gatherers, a kaleidoscope of enterprises that transformed the Chinese settlement into a town.

During the plantation era, the sugar companies throughout Hawaiʻi fostered the concept of plantation camps. Each sugar mill had satellite housing areas for its workers, and living arrangements were segregated by ethnicity: Japanese, Chinese, Filipinos, Koreans, and so forth each lived in their own camp. There were strict rules: wake up at 4:30 a.m., arrive at work before dawn, and lights out at night by 8:30 p.m. Fraternization between camps was discouraged.

Kapaʻa was never a regulated plantation town. During its growth, it retained its ancient characteristic of being a community where people lived in freedom. It was a town that fostered the aloha spirit of sharing and caring for each other. This Hawaiian concept of *kokua* helped all who lived in Kapaʻa make it through the hardest of times.

The rickety, ramshackle construction in the town had an unexpected facelift in 1923. A negligently placed kerosene lantern caused a major fire that destroyed 28 of the town's buildings. It was from this rebuilding effort that Kapaʻa developed the basic configuration of buildings and streets that exists today. Several buildings are marked with dates in the 1920s.

There have been changes in the last 50 years. Pono Cannery ended its business in 1963. This closure was followed by the termination of the second major cannery in the district in 1971.

Kapaʻa is no longer a laborer's town. It has become a tourist destination on the Coconut Coast of Kauaʻi. This transition is reflected in the large hotel complex known as the Pono Kai Resort, built where the cannery once stood, and smaller hotels like the Coral Reef. Chinese and Portuguese no longer have businesses in the town. Instead, there has been an influx of young people from the US mainland and Mexico who have revitalized the community. Several businesses are still run by the second and third generations of the original families, including the Japanese.

*Forbes* magazine named Kapaʻa as one of the 15 prettiest towns in America.

# One

# EARLY HISTORY

Hawaiian history usually focuses on the powerful ruling class—chiefs and priests—and their traditional practices. Kapaʻa, an *ahupuaʻa,* a land division stretching from the mountains to the sea, was located several miles north of Wailua. In ancient time, Kapaʻa was not the political or religious center. It was populated primarily by commoners, *makaʻainana*. This chapter focuses on the commoners—how they lived, worked, and played.

Prior to Western contact, Hawaiʻi had an oral history. Stories, chants, poems, and proverbs, *olelo noʻeau*, were committed to memory. Their traditions emphasized respect for leaders and family and the land and sea that nourished them. These values defined who they were and what was expected of them. This system of rules, *kapu*, affected all life from birth to death.

Most of the Kapaʻa makaʻainana would have lived along the seashore, their primary source of food. Some were farmers growing canoe crops along the edges of a large wetland between the ocean and the mountains. This was the original self-sustaining society. Kapaʻa is mentioned in only a few stories. A story about Pakaʻa and stories about Moʻikeha are exceptions. Kapaʻa was on the fringe of the Wailua Complex, which was the largest in the area. This allowed life in Kapaʻa to be more relaxed.

The makaʻainana were industrious people who depended on each other for food, clothing, spirituality, and comradeship. They believed in the principles of humility, hospitality, generosity, and all that sustained harmony. The extended family was their foundation. No task was considered too challenging when done together. All skills were valued, as was subordination of individual needs to those of the family and community. This proverb expresses those values:

*Ike aku, Ike mai, kokua mai, Pela iho laka nohana ohana*. "Recognize others, be recognized, help others, be helped. Such is the family relationship."

Kapaʻa High School art students illustrated this chapter. It was an opportunity for them to share what they have learned, encourage their interest in history, and acknowledge that lives are enriched when people understand their past.

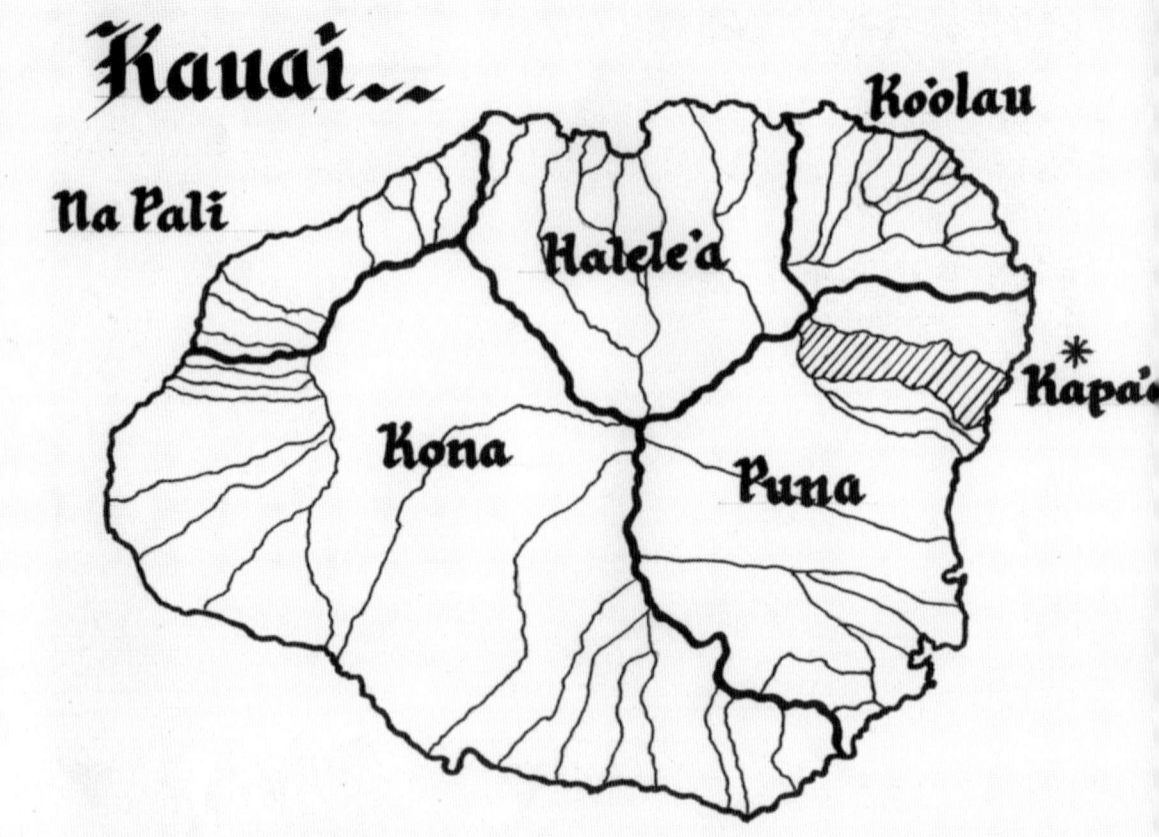

This sketch of Kauaʻi's land division by *moku* and ahupuaʻa is based on information from the US Geologic Survey Map of 1912. Each moku established by the aliʻi, chief of the island, divided the island into sections that covered three essential regions—mountains, valleys, and seashore. This system allowed communities equal access to natural resources. The entire island, or *mokupuni*, was divided into smaller sections, ahupuaʻa, and smaller still, *kuleana*, land tracts used by commoners. The size of these tracts was determined by the natural resources of the area. Commoners had no private ownership. They bartered with each other and paid weekly taxes to the *konohiki*, overseer, who collected all goods to support the aliʻi and his court. All land was controlled by the highest aliʻi, who supervised it through a complex system based on social standing. Through sharing resources and a strict work ethic, Hawaiians enjoyed life with time for music, dance, sports, and crafts. (Courtesy of Clyde Furumoto.)

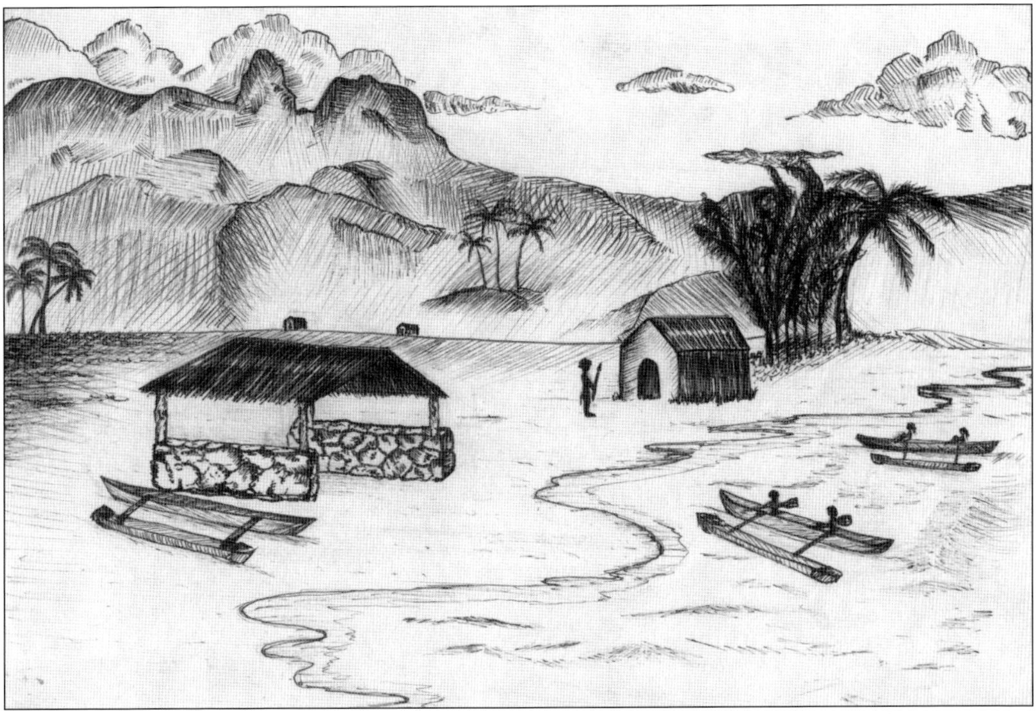

Hawaiians had several kinds of huts; a dining hut for men and boys, a hut for women and girls, a canoe hut, and sleeping shelters for families. The comfortable weather allowed many activities to occur outside. (Illustrated by Anuhea Lizarraga.)

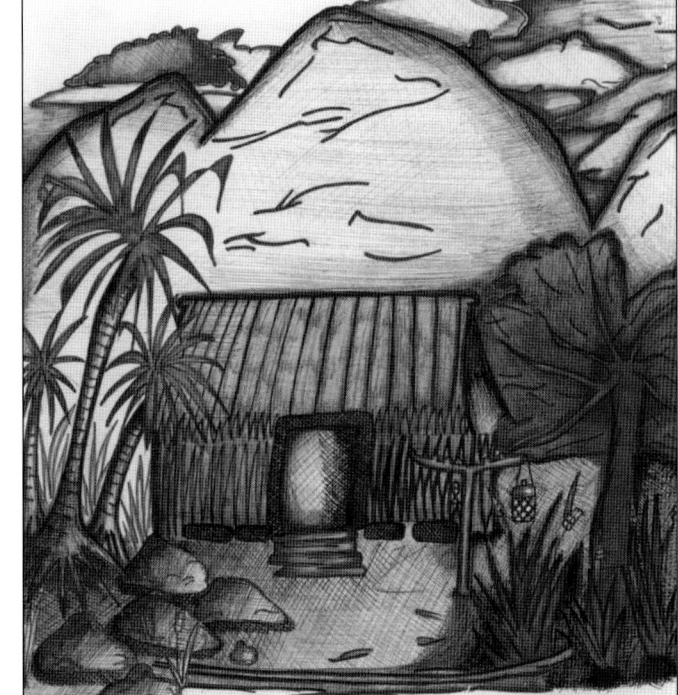

Huts were framed with native timber and thatched with *pili* grass. Many rules and superstitions controlled the construction of a hut. The location was determined by the priest, who had knowledge of the wind, rain, ocean, and seasonal changes. A blessing ritual and feast marked the completion of each new shelter. (Illustrated by Raven-Brittney Landagora.)

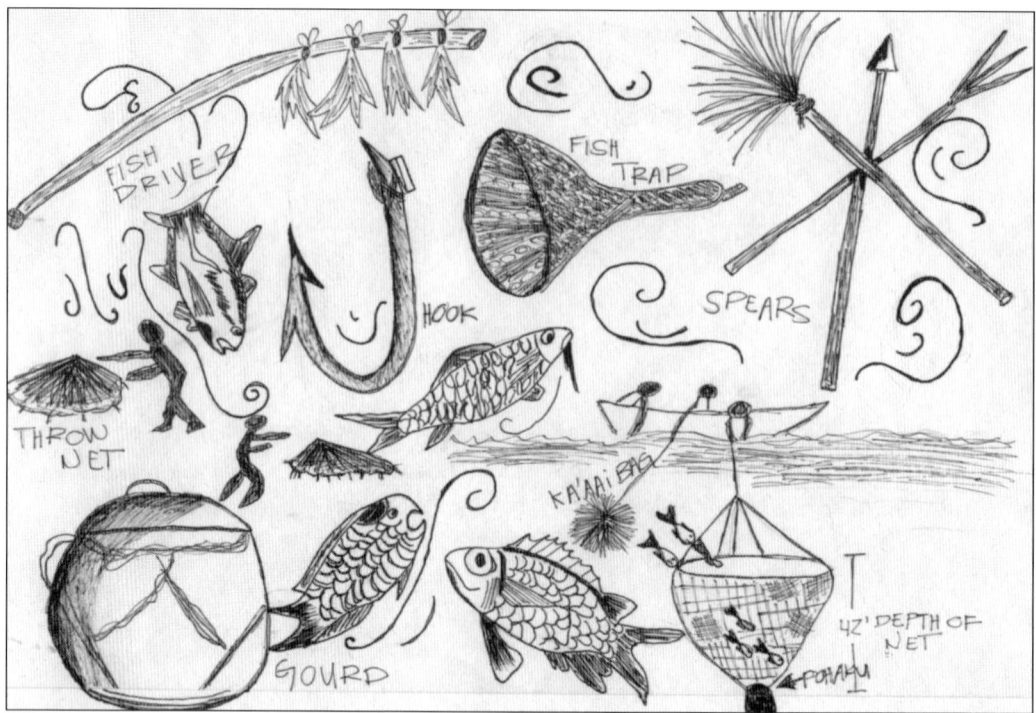

The skilled fisherman was well respected for his important contribution to the community. As in all arts, Hawaiians believed that one must study diligently and practice the skills of the family unit until it became a part of one's identity. Fishermen had their own gods and religious ceremonies. Kapu, seasonal restrictions, determined what could be caught. This early conservation method protected the area from over-fishing. (Illustrated by Rhandie Fernandez.)

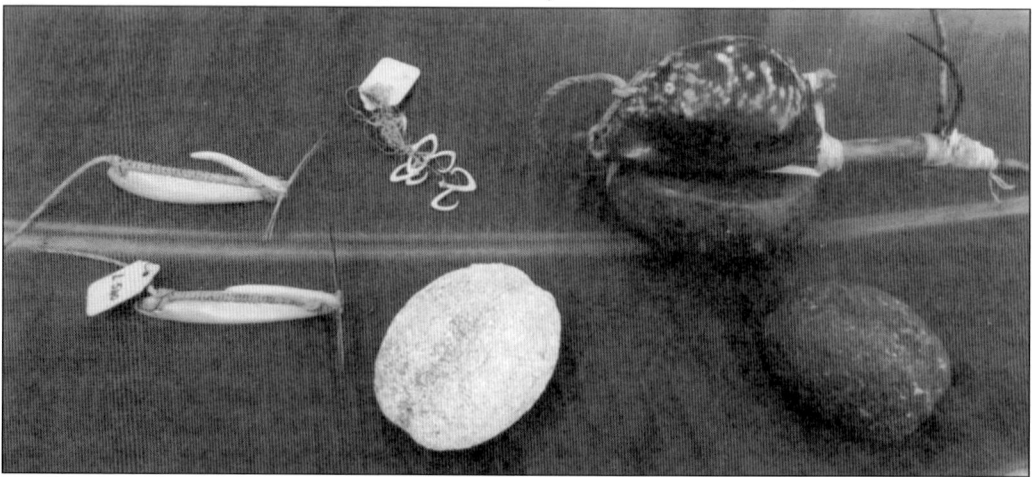

The two hooks on the left are bonita hooks, used to catch *aku*. They are made of bone, pearl, and fiber. The shell hook, in the middle, is made from pearl shells, *uhi*, and fiber. This type of hook was made in different sizes. The smaller ones were used to catch *opelu*. The squid lure is a cowrie lashed to a stone sinker. The lure was attached to a long cord and shaken to attract the squid. The two sinkers at the bottom are grooved, the most common type of sinker. The grooves were used to secure nets, lines, and lures. The light sinker is made from reef rock, and the dark sinker is basalt rock. (Courtesy of the Grove Farm Homestead Museum.)

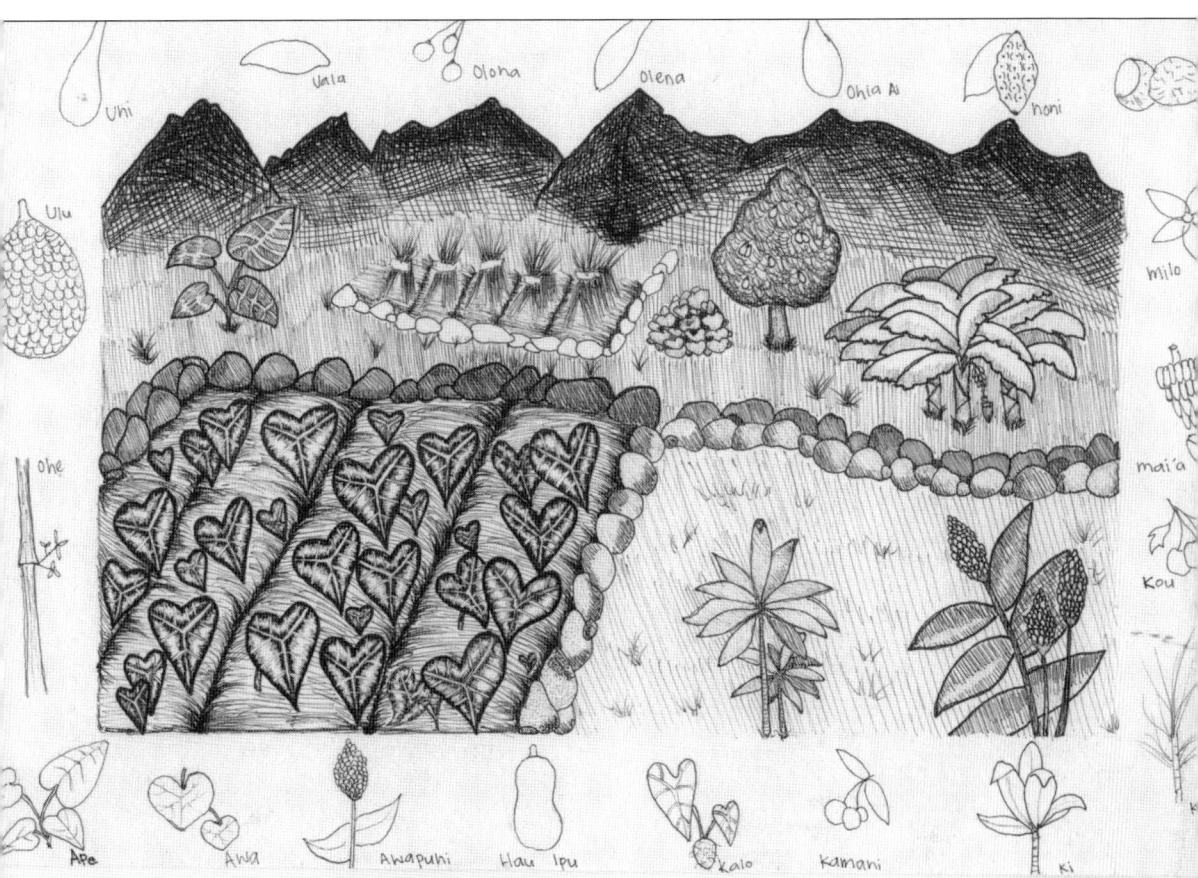

Hawai'i's culture evolved over thousands of years of migratory Polynesians. There is strong evidence that the first settlers were from the Marquesas Islands (300–700 CE), ending with the Tahitians in the 12th century. The early settlers came prepared with the skills and traditions necessary to establish a society. They brought pigs, chickens, dogs, rats, *ape* (elephant ear), *kawa*, shampoo ginger, gourds, taro, *kamani*, *ti* leaf, sugarcane, *kukui* nut, banana, *milo*, coconut, *noni*, bamboo, mountain apple, turmeric, arrowroot, sweet potato, yam, breadfruit, and paper mulberry. The natural resources of the area determined what they raised. Stone walls were constructed to protect crops, create wetlands, and pen animals. (Illustrated by Alohilani Chun.)

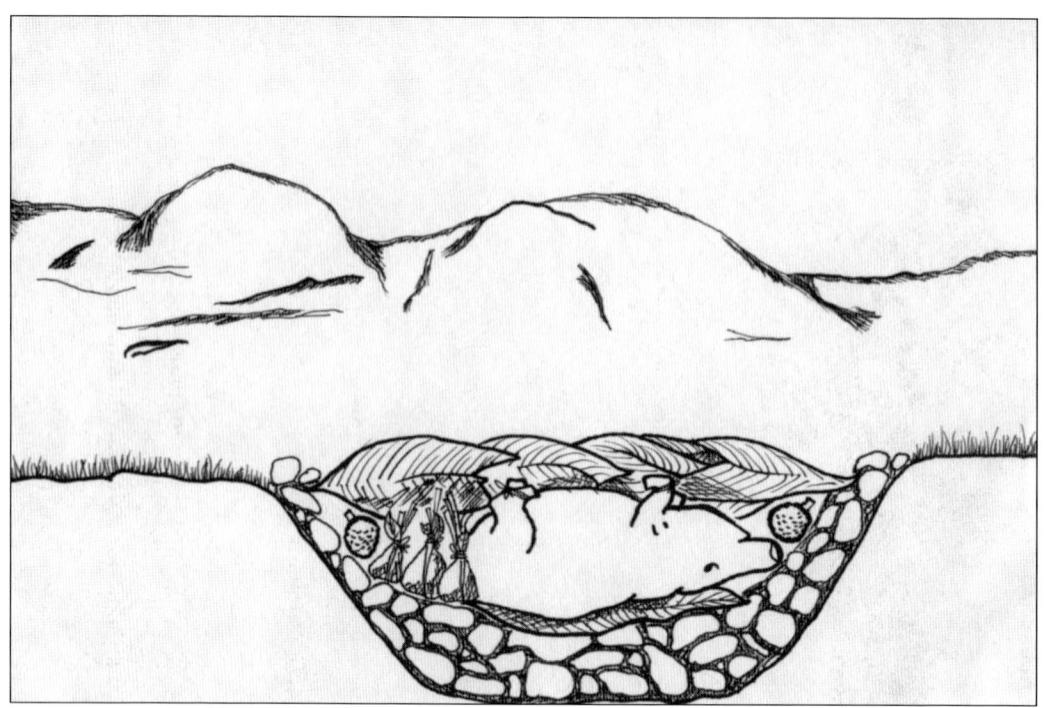

Traditional methods of cooking were boiling, steaming, salting, drying, and roasting in an *imu*, underground oven. They used wooden bowls and tools made from stone, sticks, bamboo, shells, shark teeth, coconut shells, and fibers. Food was wrapped in ti leaves for cooking and serving. (Illustrated by Kahiwahiwa Davis.)

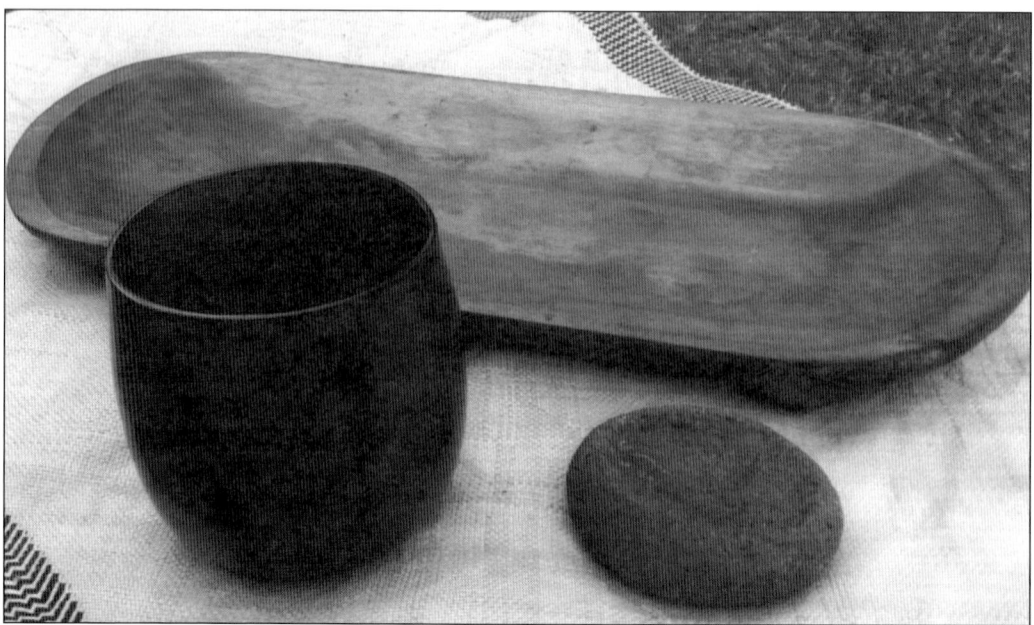

Hawaiians had no fireproof pots; heated stones were dropped into wooden bowls of water to boil food. Bowls and boards like this pig board were used for serving. Salt was served in a stone. (Courtesy of the Grove Farm Homestead Museum.)

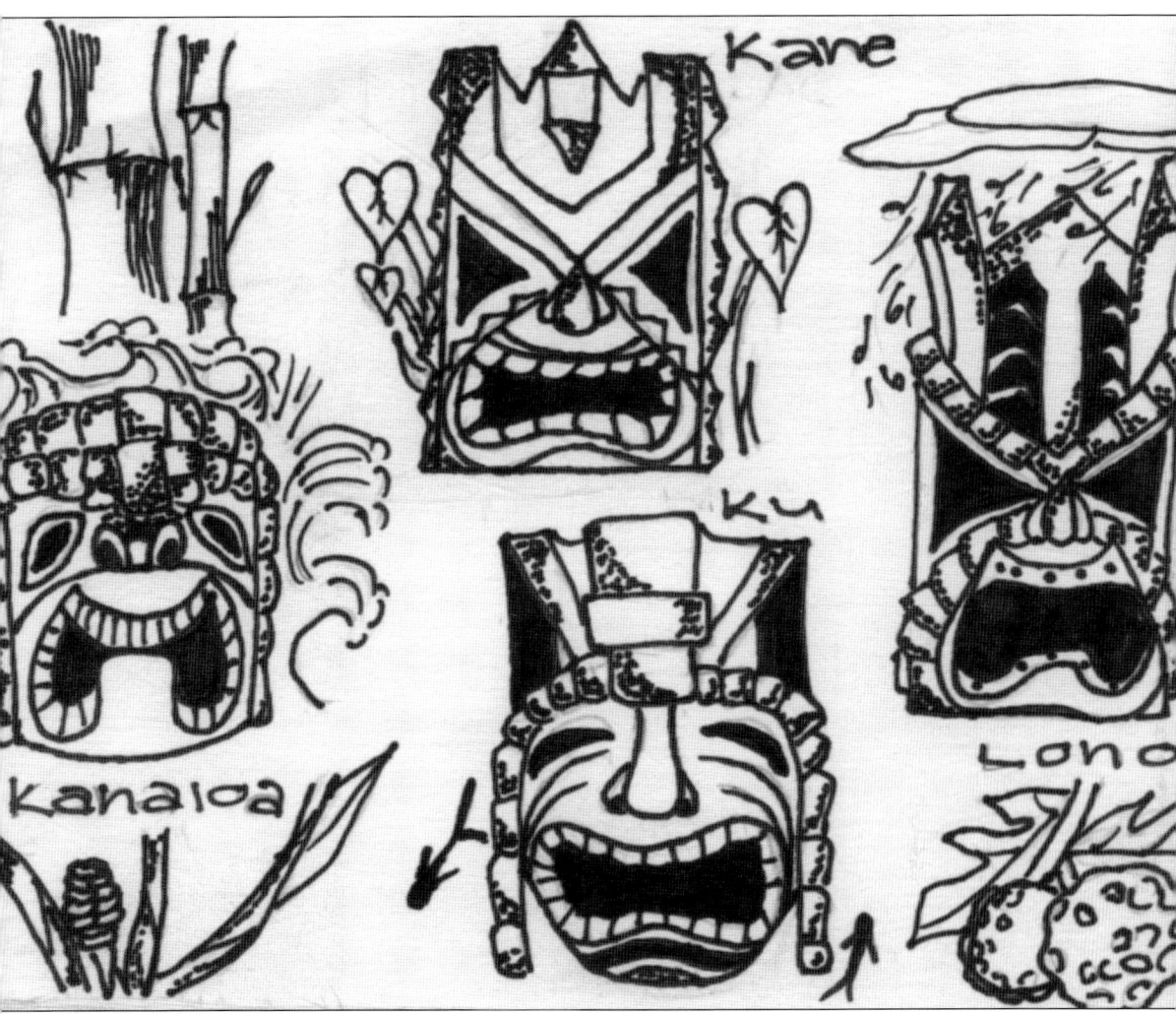

The Hawaiians were very spiritual. Their four main gods were Ku, Kane, Lono, and Kanaloa. Ku represented masculine power and was prayed to for rain, growth, fishing, and sorcery. He was the fierce image carried into battle. Kane was the life-giving creator—a leader among gods—the god of sunlight, air, and forest. Lono was the god of agriculture, the sea, clouds, wind, and thunder. He had as many as 50 different forms. His image was honored during the annual Makahiki season and carried on tax-collection tours. Kanaloa was the god of the ocean, sea breeze, and healing. He was often the companion of Kane. (Illustrated by Jodi A. Reis.)

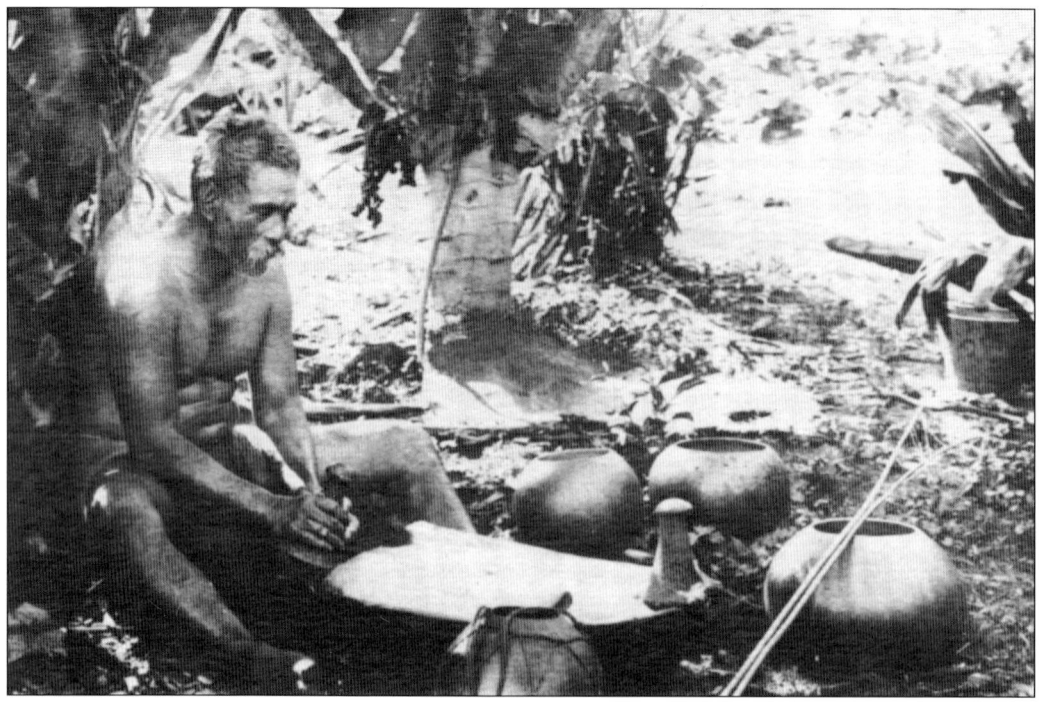

Taro was pounded, usually by men, with a stone pounder on a board. The product, *poi*, was a staple for Hawaiians of all classes. There were three types of pounders. The pestle shape, pictured above, also called knobbed or conical, was common throughout the islands. The stirrup and ring pounders pictured below were found only on Kaua'i, where women also used them to make poi. Grove Farm Homestead Museum has an impressive collection of 44 pounders. Researchers believe that the stirrup form was the oldest type found on Kaua'i. On Kaua'i and Ni'ihau, residents still referred to the ring type as a *wahine* pounder well into the late 1920s. (Above, courtesy of Linda Paik Moriarty; below, courtesy of Grove Farm Homestead Museum.)

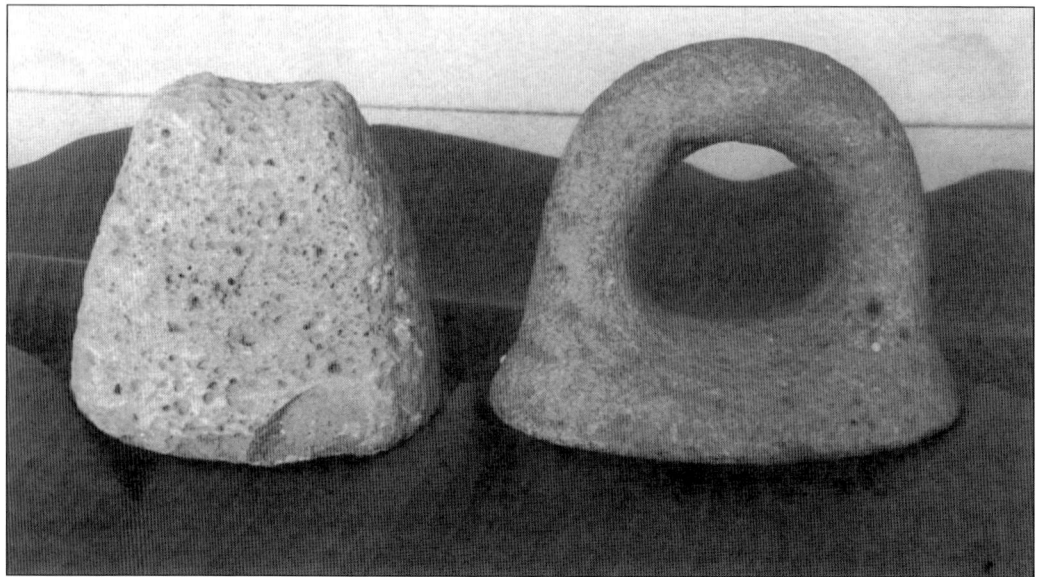

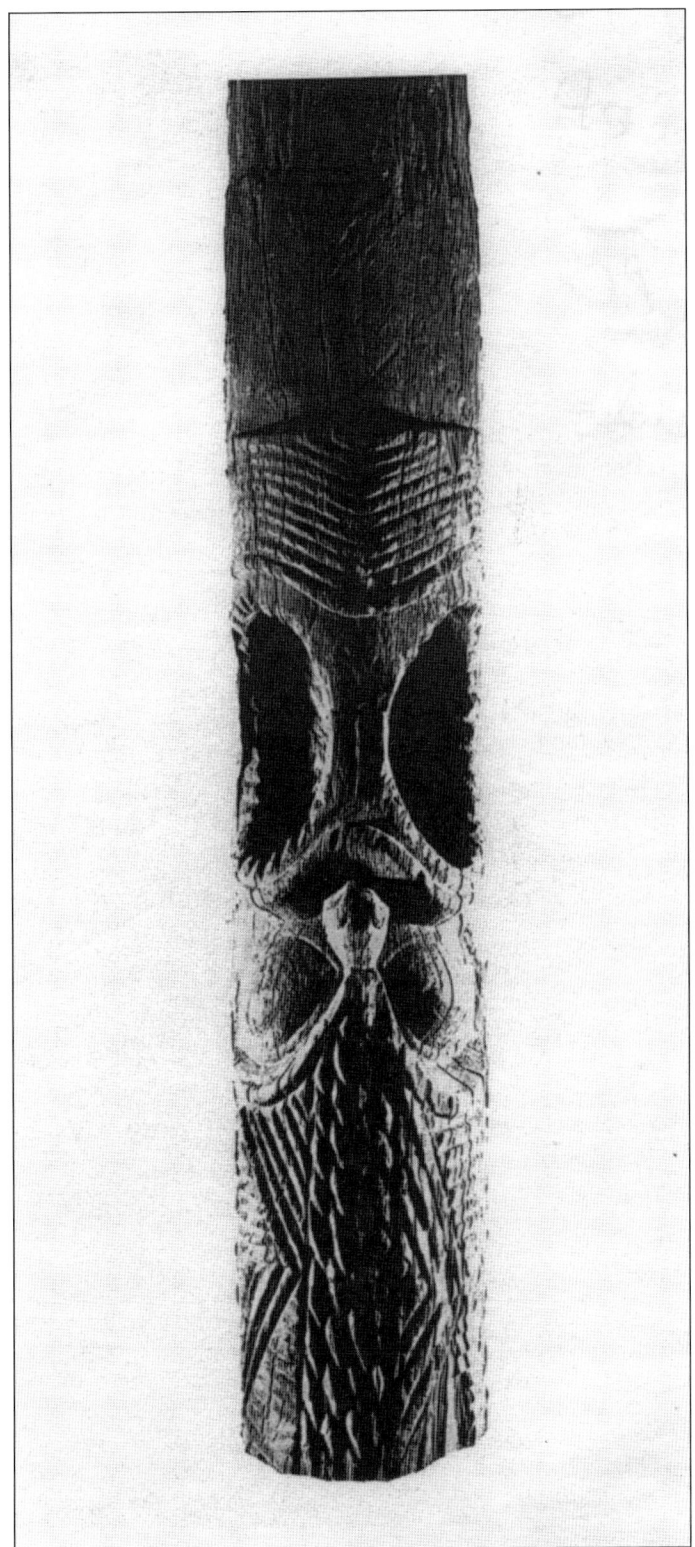

This large wooden image was found by Edward Morgan Sr., a construction engineer for the Makee Sugar Company. It was found while the men were working on the Waianuenue Bridge near Hee Fat's rice mill, about a mile from Kapa'a town. Morgan discovered it in the mud, dug it up, and brought it home. The family donated it to the Bishop Museum in 1911. This image would have been attached to a post in a heiau. (Courtesy of Linda Paik Moriarty.)

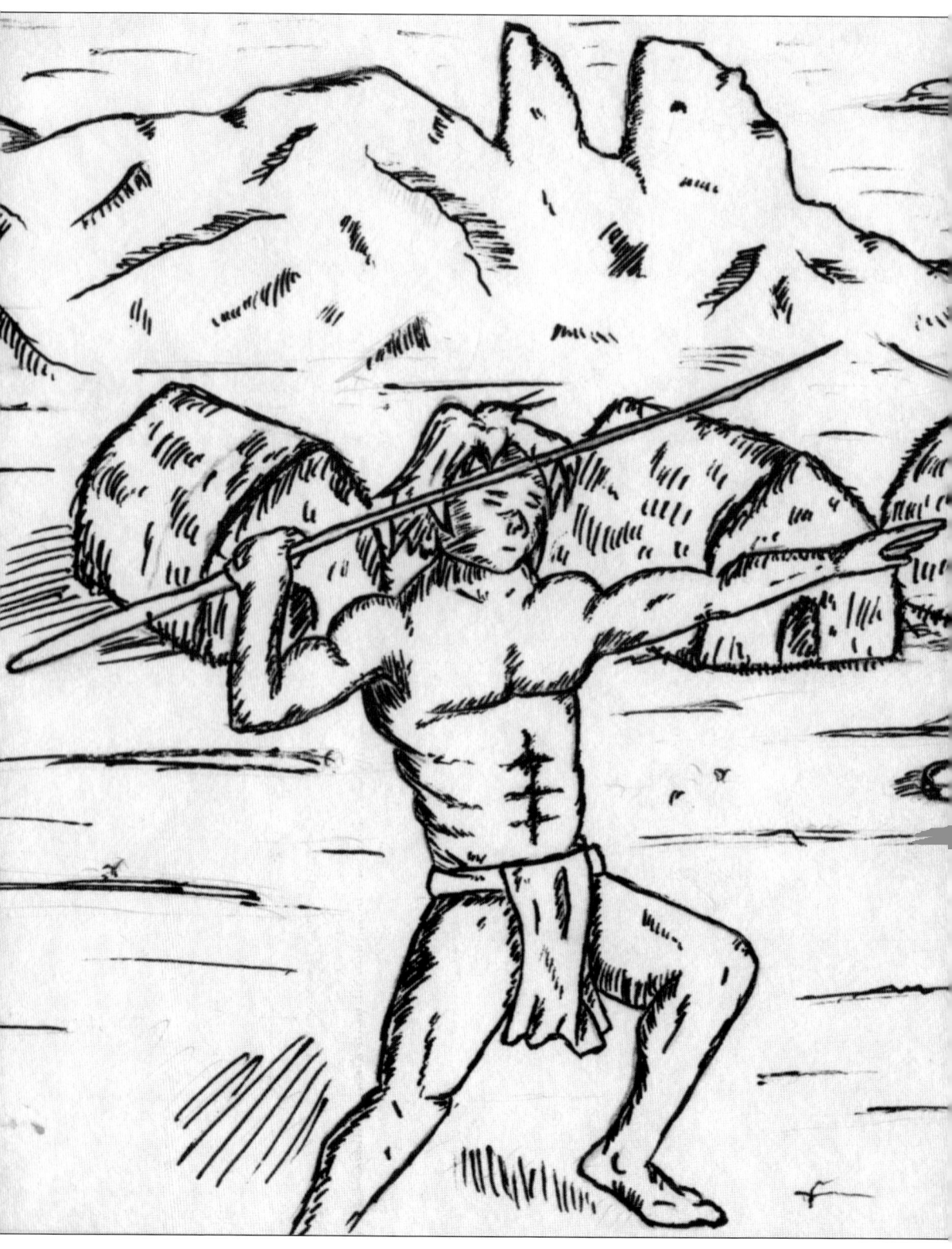

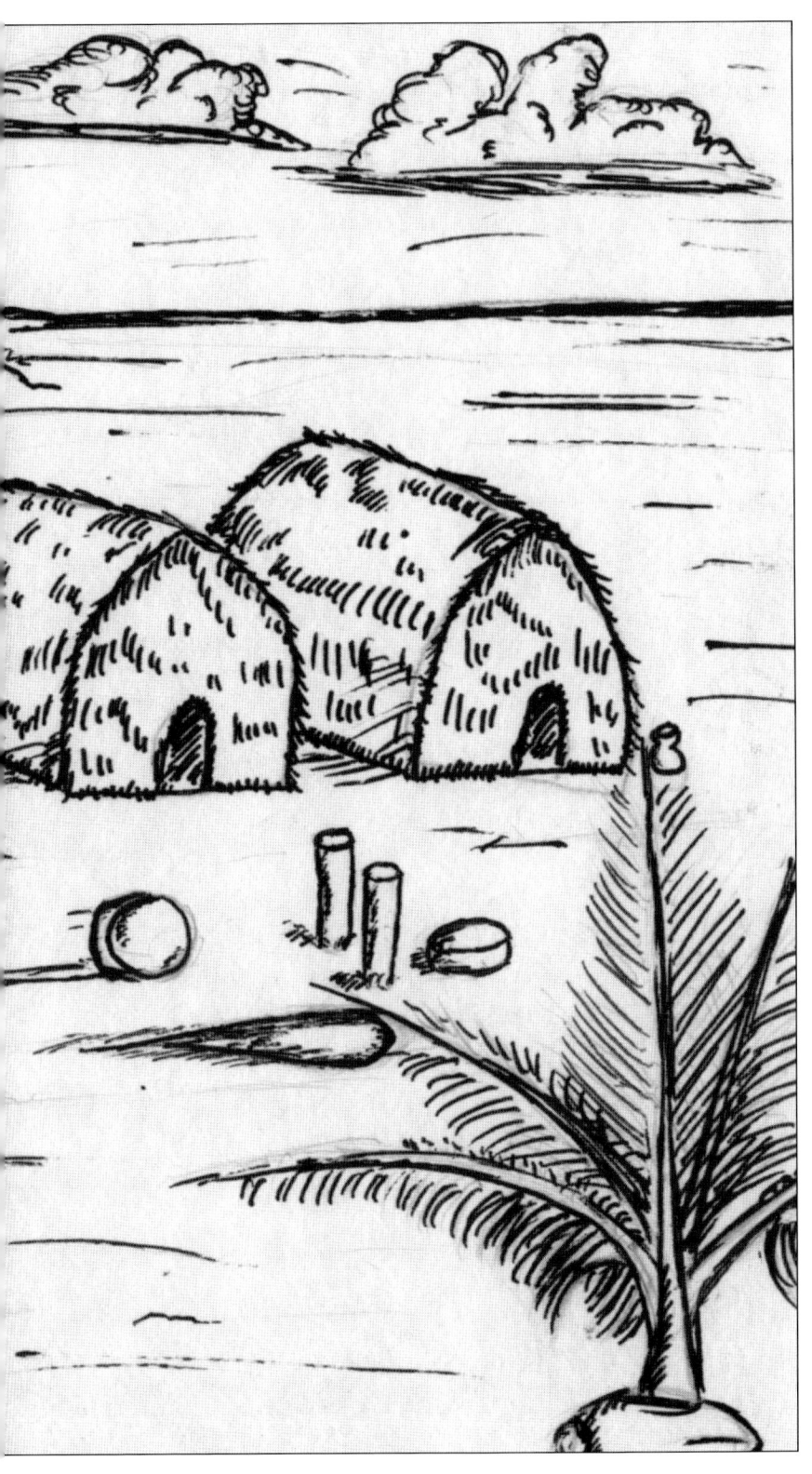

Hawaiians enjoyed a variety of games and sports. Some, like the Makahiki games, were seasonal. Makahiki, October through January, was strictly enforced as a time of complete rest and recreation. Many games involved betting, and some sports were for only the ruling class. Popular activities were *heʻe nalu* (surfing), *holua* (toboggan sled), *lupe* (flying large kites), *kukini* (foot racing), *pahee* (javelin throwing), *hei hei waʻi* (canoe racing), and *hula*. (Illustrated by Justin Franklin.)

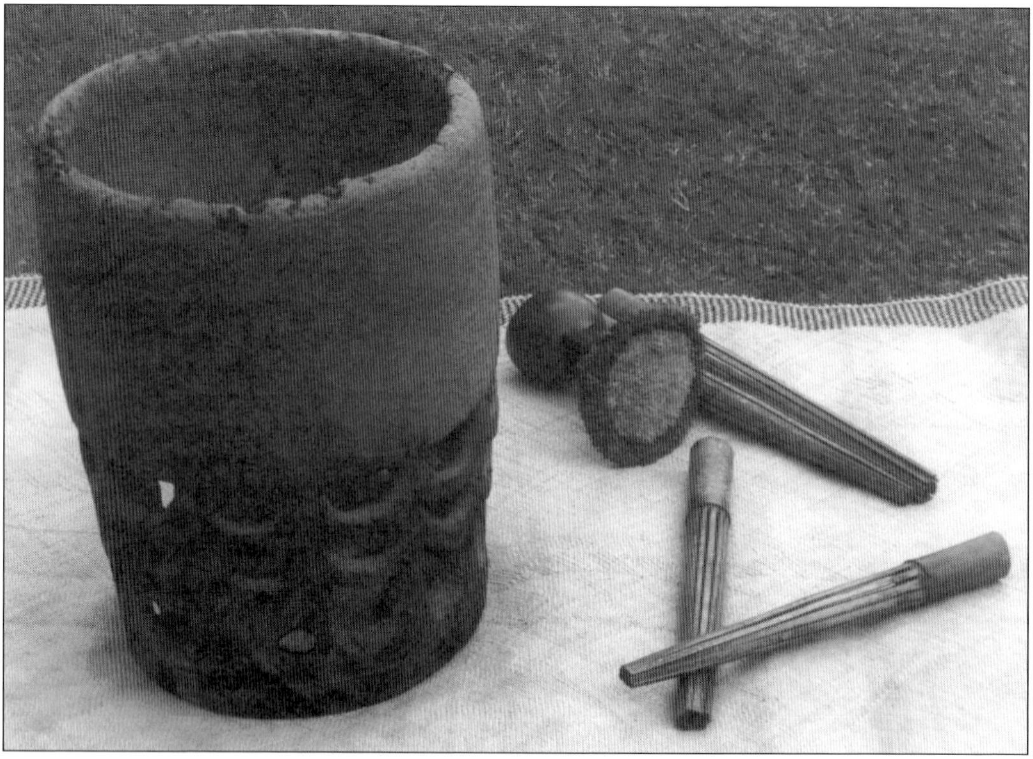

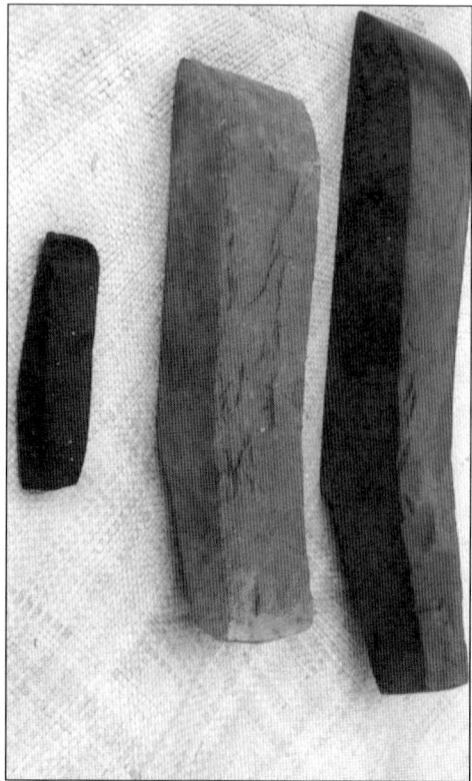

Hawaiians had several types of drums—wooden, knee, calabash, and bamboo pipes. The wooden drum in this photograph was carved from a coconut tree trunk. Wooden drums like this were either short or tall. The short *pahu hula* drum was used to beat the time for hula dancers. The tall *pahu heiau* drum was for religious ceremonies. Drumheads had lashed-down shark-skin covers. The *puʻili* bamboo rattles were used by partner dancers, sitting facing each other. They created music by tapping each other and the ground between them. (Courtesy of the Grove Farm Homestead Museum.)

These adzes, essential tools, were made by skilled and respected craftsmen. Many had favorite basalt quarries and special methods of shaping adzes with hammer stones. Adzes were used as hand tools or lashed to wooden handles. They were used to make other tools, hollow out canoes and bowls, shape poles for hut construction, and in a variety of wood carving. (Courtesy of the Grove Farm Homestead Museum.)

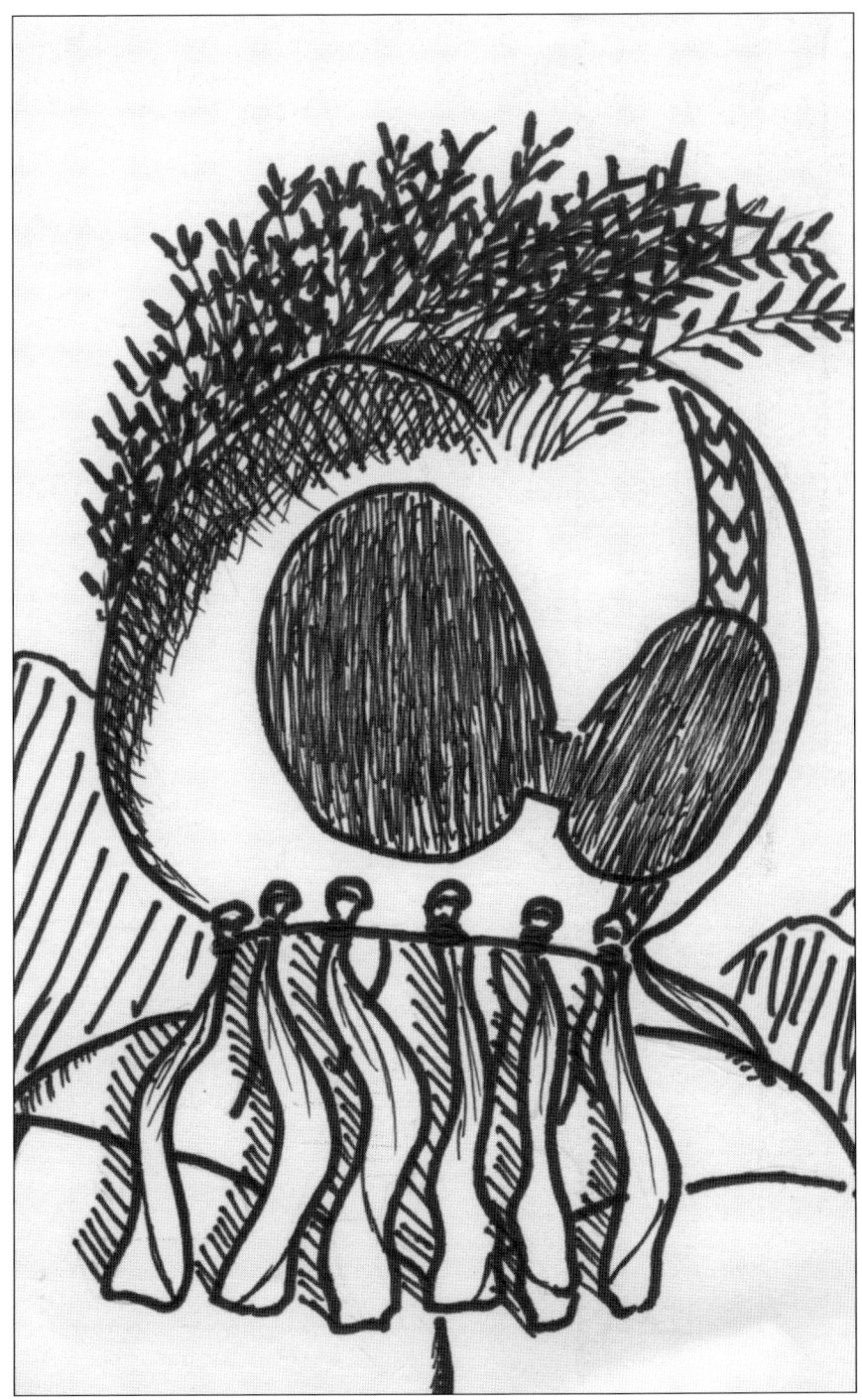

Popular legends about Pakaʻa can be found in chants, Hawaiian antiquities, and a newspaper serial from 1869–1871. His legends were very popular. Pakaʻa traveled with the chief of Kauaʻi. One story tells of how he created a sail to capture the wind and win a fishing contest in Kapaʻa. The gourd mask of Lono is associated with Pakaʻa, for it controlled the wind. Hawaiians had dozens of words for specific types of winds. (Illustrated by Elia Leone.)

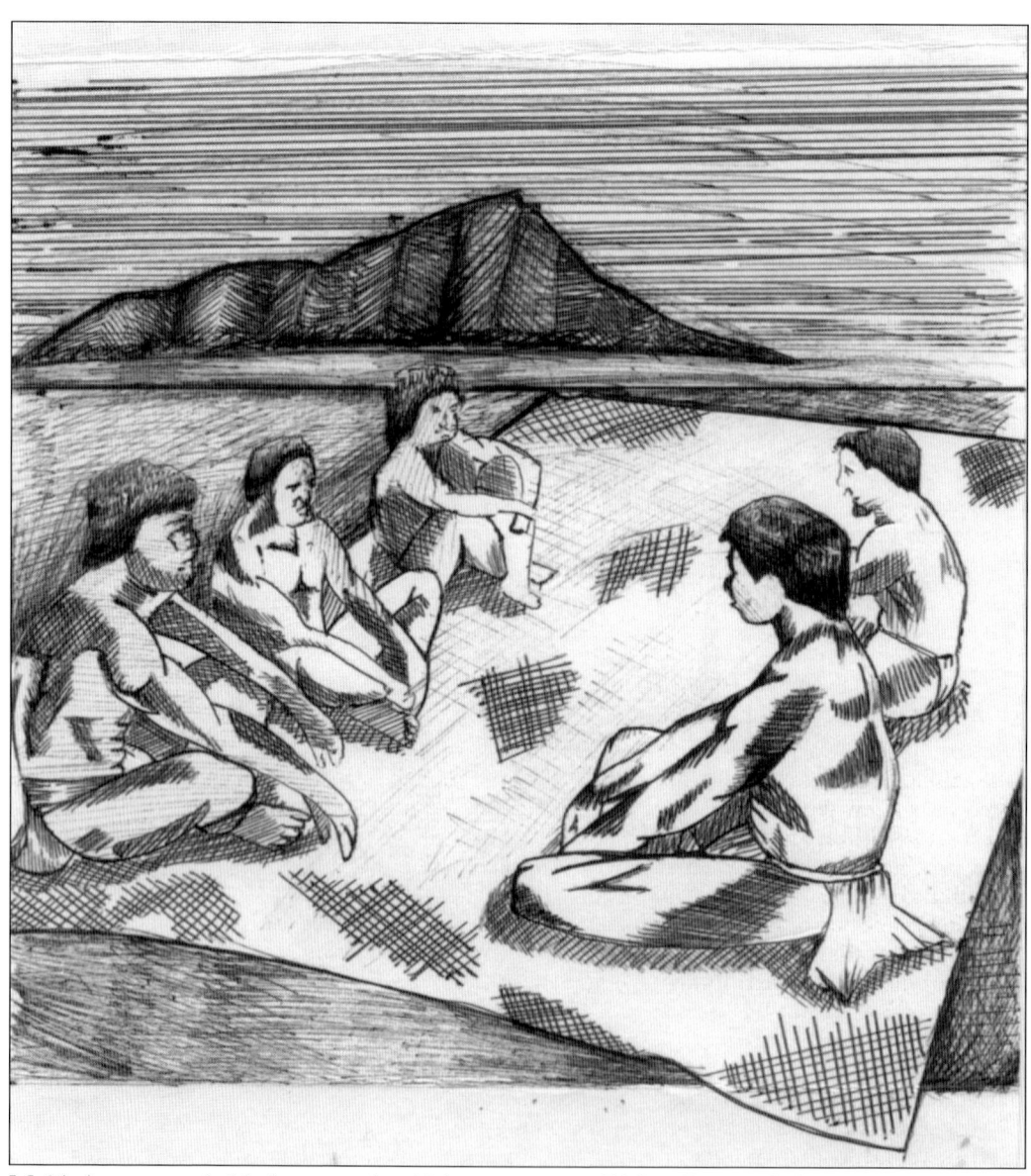

Mo'ikeha was probably born in the 13th century on O'ahu. Descended from a long line of chiefs, he was an adventurer. Many stories tell of his trips throughout the islands and back to Tahiti. His son Kila was believed to have been on the last Hawaiian voyage to other Polynesian islands. On one of his visits to Kauai, he won the hand of Chief Puna's daughter Hooipo. They settled in Wailua and had many sons. Mo'ikeha's reign, after Puna, was peaceful, and he was respected throughout the islands. Late in his life, he passed his responsibilities to Kila and retired to Kapa'a. (Illustrated by Cadance Keaweamahi Kahokuloa.)

# Two

# Plantations and Immigration

The town of Kapaʻa has its roots in Hawaiʻi's plantation era with King David Kalākaua's efforts to organize a sugar plantation in the ahupuaʻa, giving birth to the town in 1877. The enterprise lasted only a few years in Kapaʻa, as the plantation and mill moved to the next valley, Keālia, and flourished over the next half century and more. The Makee Sugar Co., as it was known, provided Kapaʻa both its customers and its population.

From its beginnings, Makee Sugar Company was run by white men, but labor was needed to make it a viable business. With a limited native population, the need for immigrant workers was apparent. Hawaiians and Chinese immigrants were the earliest workers. Portuguese, including many families, came next, followed by Japanese and later, from the 1910s, Filipinos. Smaller numbers of Koreans and Puerto Ricans also came to work here. The immigrant workers were male, and most came without a spouse or family, leaving behind their home countries for various political and economic reasons. Many eventually sent for brides from their home countries and started families.

Workers lived in camps that were segregated by race, and heavy plantation control left most of them to spend their money in stores run by the plantation. There were also women who worked in the fields and did side jobs such as laundry and cooking to supplement their income. Plantation life was a challenge for the immigrants as they adjusted to being away from home, a new culture, language barriers, and hard physical labor.

Over time and as their work contracts expired, some returned to their home countries or moved away, but many of the immigrants settled in Kapaʻa and the homestead land to establish themselves as merchants and farmers. The predominantly single men who came as immigrants frequented the goods and services of Kapaʻa not available in a plantation town, such as liquor, alcohol, opium, and women.

The opening of a pineapple cannery in Kapaʻa in 1915 offered new jobs and new customers for Kapaʻa merchants. Laborers, especially Filipinos, came to work in the pineapple fields. A second cannery in the hills above Kapaʻa offered more jobs and more customers.

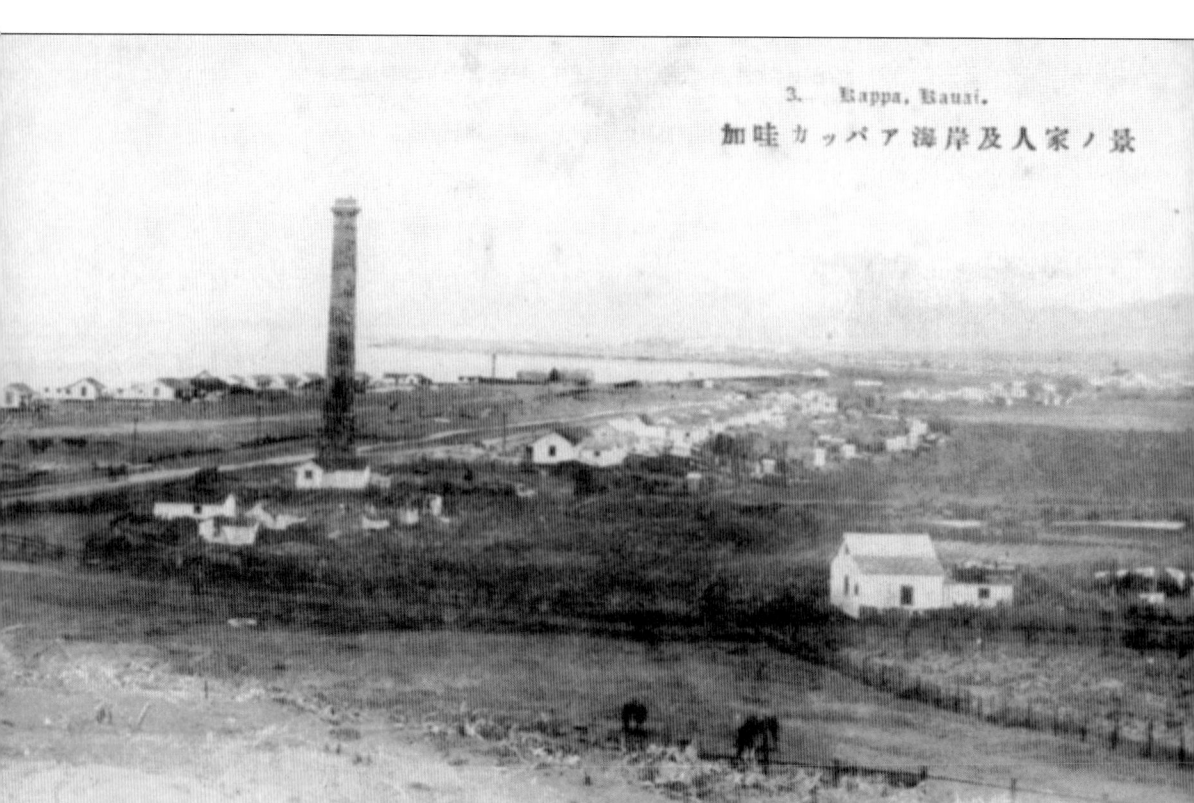

An early postcard of Kapa'a from around 1910 shows the original Makee mill stack in the foreground. It is no longer there. In the background, just to the right of the stack, the courthouse can be seen, site of the present-day Kapa'a Neighborhood Center, along with the Kapa'a Landing where sugar was loaded onto ships. (Courtesy of Clay Hiramoto.)

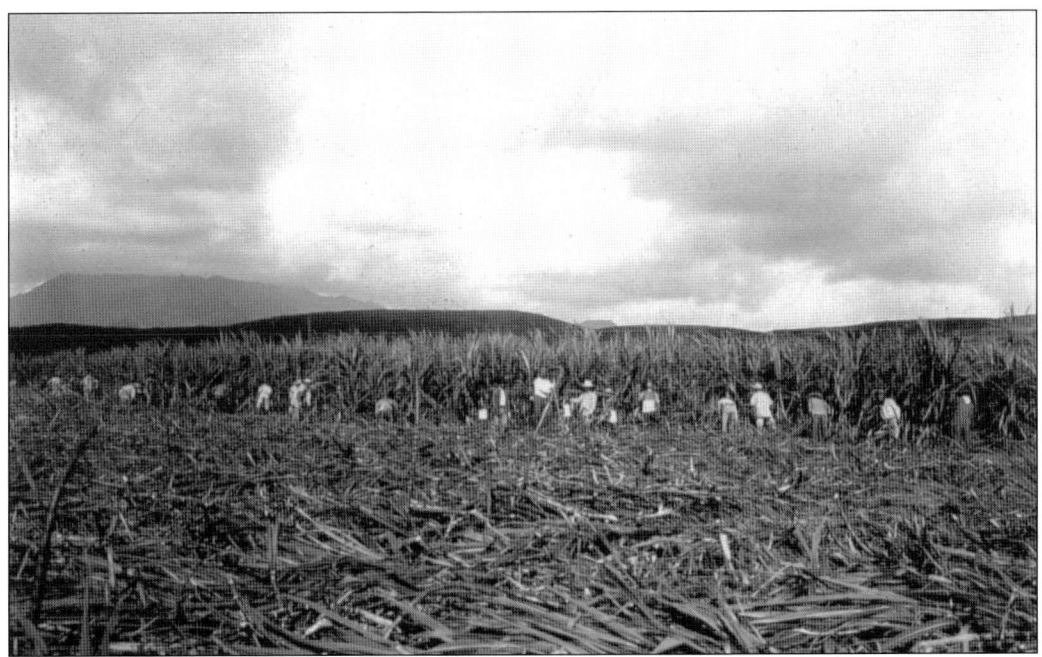

In the mid-1850s, sugarcane was harvested by hand. It was difficult work that required protective clothing not only from the hot sun but from the sharp cane leaves. Chinese and Hawaiian men were the first field workers. The Chinese immigrated with the intention of making money and then returning to China. Consequently, they came without wives or families. By 1884, after the 1876 Reciprocity Treaty, more than one third of those in the Kawaihau District were Chinese. Most were planting and harvesting cane for the Makee Sugar Company. (Courtesy of Kaua'i Museum.)

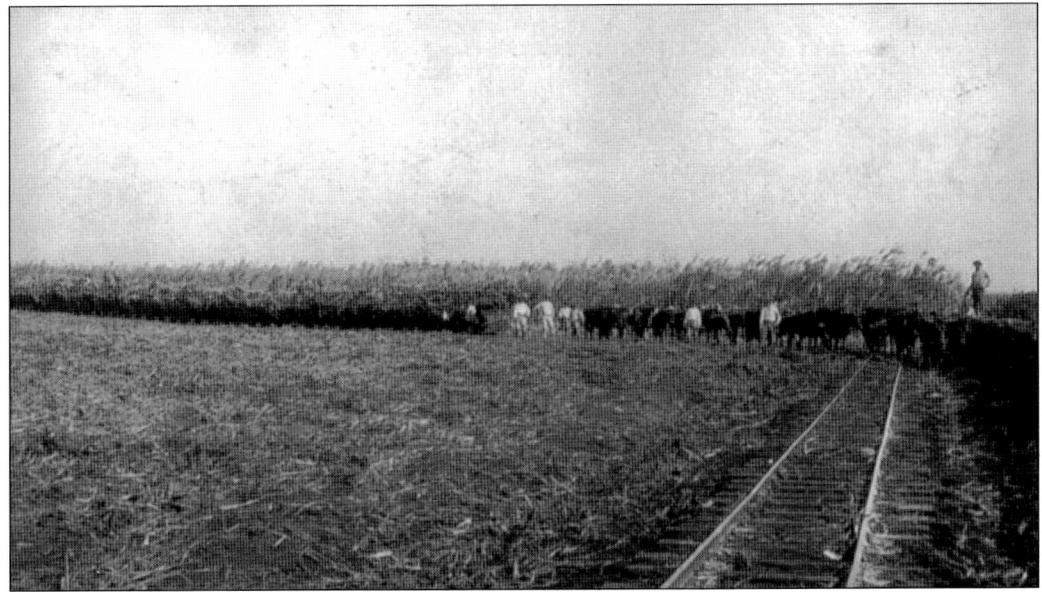

These immigrant workers were brought to Kaua'i to work in the fields and mill operations side by side with the few Hawaiian families that survived the diseases brought in by foreigners. (Courtesy of Kaua'i Museum.)

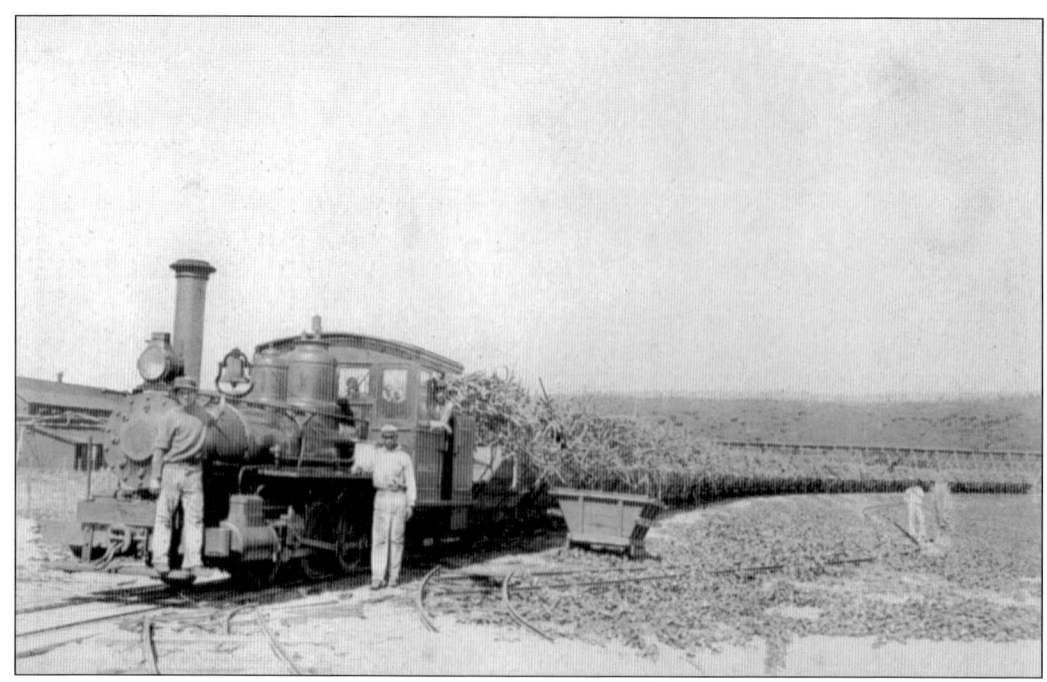

Pictured here are cane cars hitched to a locomotive getting ready to be transported by rail to the mill. Nicknamed the "Makee," this locomotive regularly pulled heavy loads of sugarcane from the cane fields above Keālia. (Courtesy of Kauaʻi Museum.)

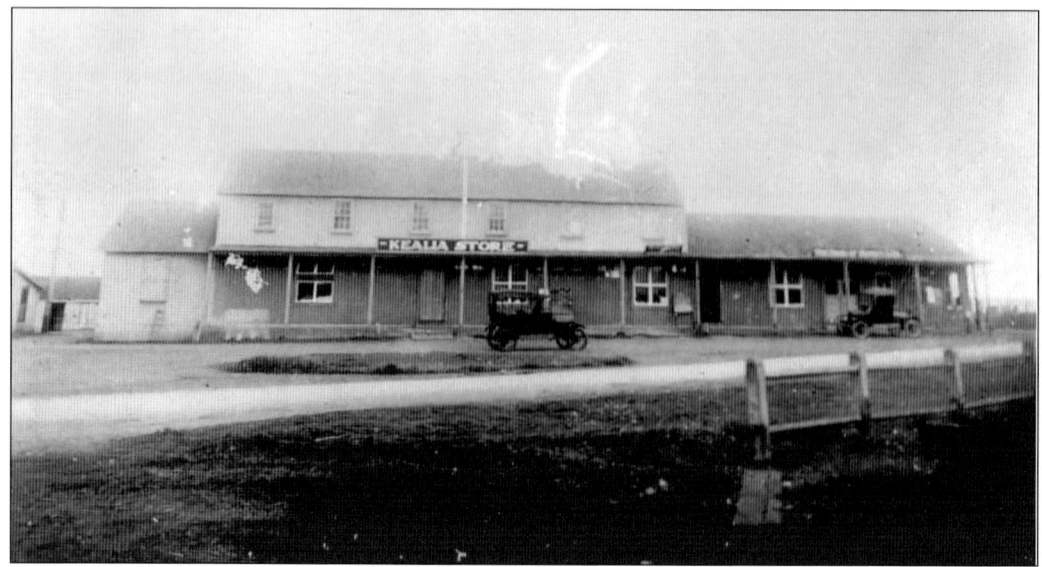

Kealia Store, owned and operated by Makee Sugar Company, opened in the 1920s. It made shopping convenient for the mill camp employees. The plantation store flourished because credit was extended to the families, who paid when they picked up their monthly checks. This building was first built in the 1880s and included a hotel; Queen Liliʻuokalani stayed here during her tour in 1881. (Courtesy of Kauaʻi Museum.)

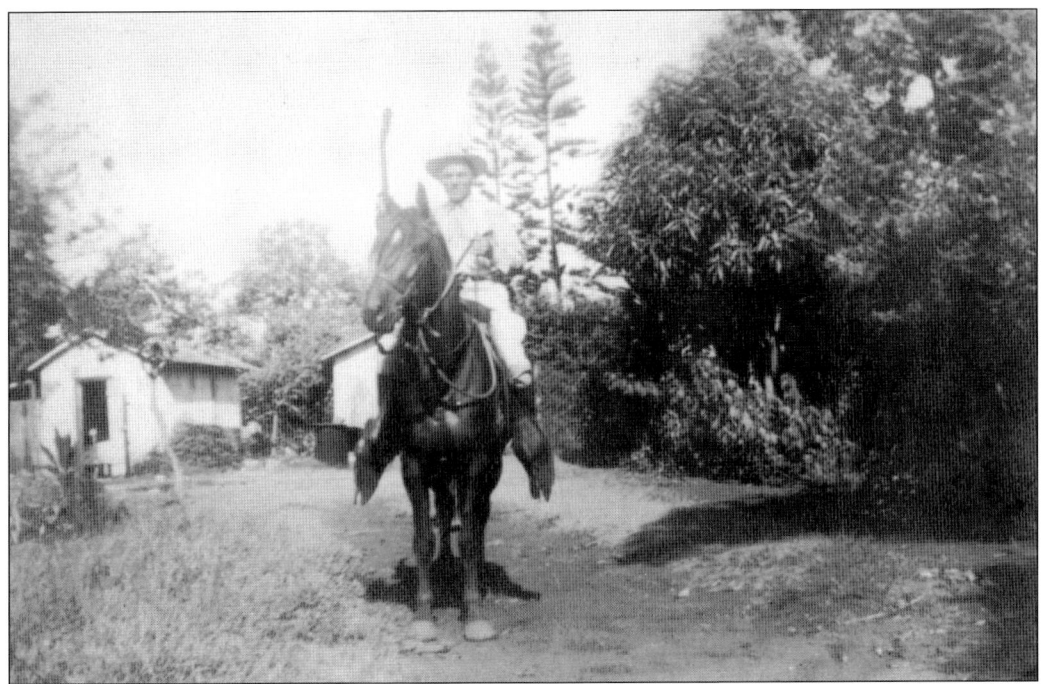

These photographs represent three generations of a Kapa'a Portugese immigrant family that worked on a plantation ranch. Manuel Ornellas, above, was born on Kaua'i. His grandfather Joao came in 1883 on the *Hankow* from Madeira with his wife, Maria, and three young children. Not all plantation employees were involved in cultivating sugar. Many plantations, including Makee, raised cattle to provide beef, sheep, and dairy products for their company store as well as for personal use. (Both, courtesy of Josephine Ornellas.)

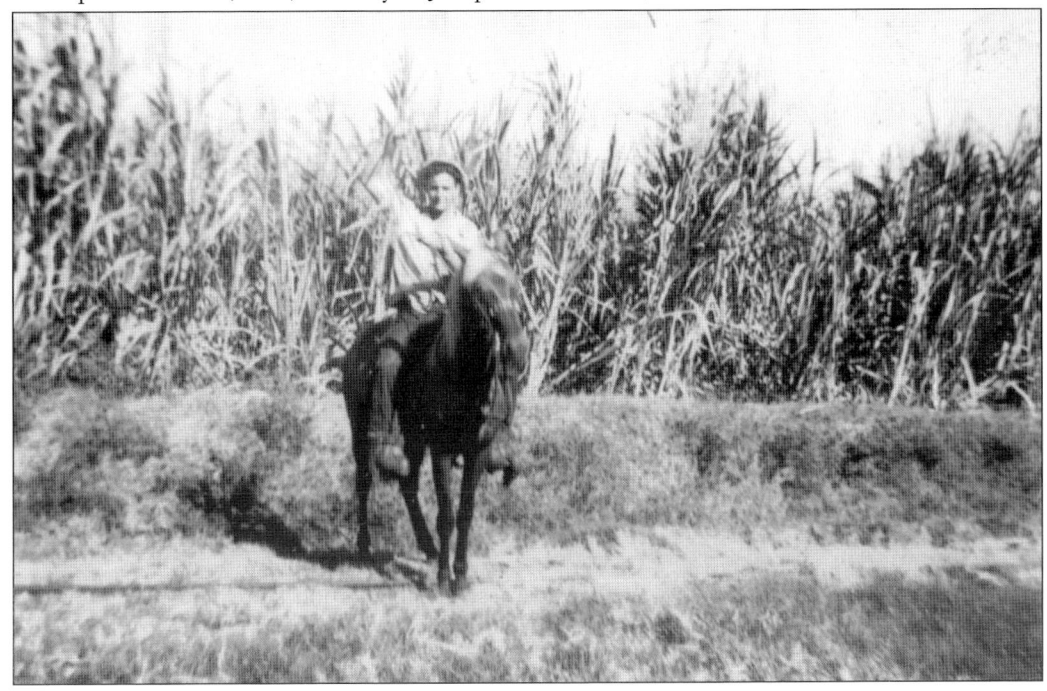

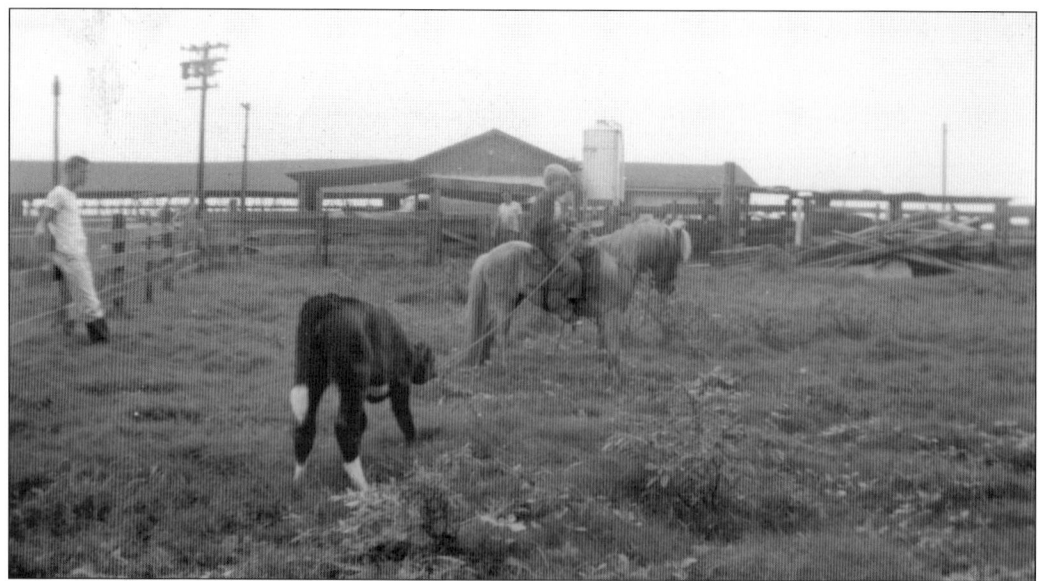

Ranching was an important part of the community. It also supplied the plantation with oxen, horses, and mules, which were necessary before the introduction of machines. Grazing animals also made good use of fallow and other unproductive fields. As political issues impacted the sugar industry and land became available to immigrants, ranching was appealing for its solid local market. Working the land became a way of life and developed its unique Hawai'i culture. Manuel Ornellas's son and grandsons left plantation employment to establish their own family ranches and dairy farm. (Courtesy of Josephine Ornellas.)

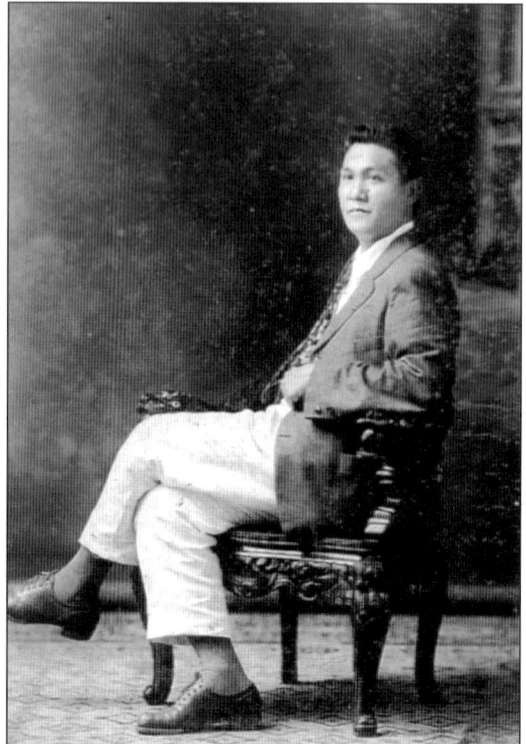

This photograph shows a young Chu Wai of Kaua'i around 1900. He is dressed in a finely tailored, western-style suit. Chu Wai was born in China in 1881 and came to Kaua'i in 1898. Instead of finding work in the sugar plantations, he went to work in a tailor shop owned by his cousin, where he developed his fine skills in tailoring. Eventually he moved to Kapa'a to open his own store, called Mau Wo Lung. (Courtesy of Janice Lee Santos.)

Most Spanish immigrants arrived in Hawai'i on six ships between 1907 and 1913. Importation of Spanish laborers with their families continued until 1913. In all, 9,000 came to work for the sugar plantations. Although, like the Vasquez family members in these photographs, some came earlier, sailing with the Portuguese immigrants on small wooden ships of less than 1,000 gross tonnage capacity. Jose and Emilia Vasquez traveled from Celanova, Spain, to Madeira to sail to Hawai'i on the SS *Victoria* in 1899. They were one of two Spanish families that joined the Portuguese immigrants aboard the ship. (Both, courtesy of Josephine Ornellas.)

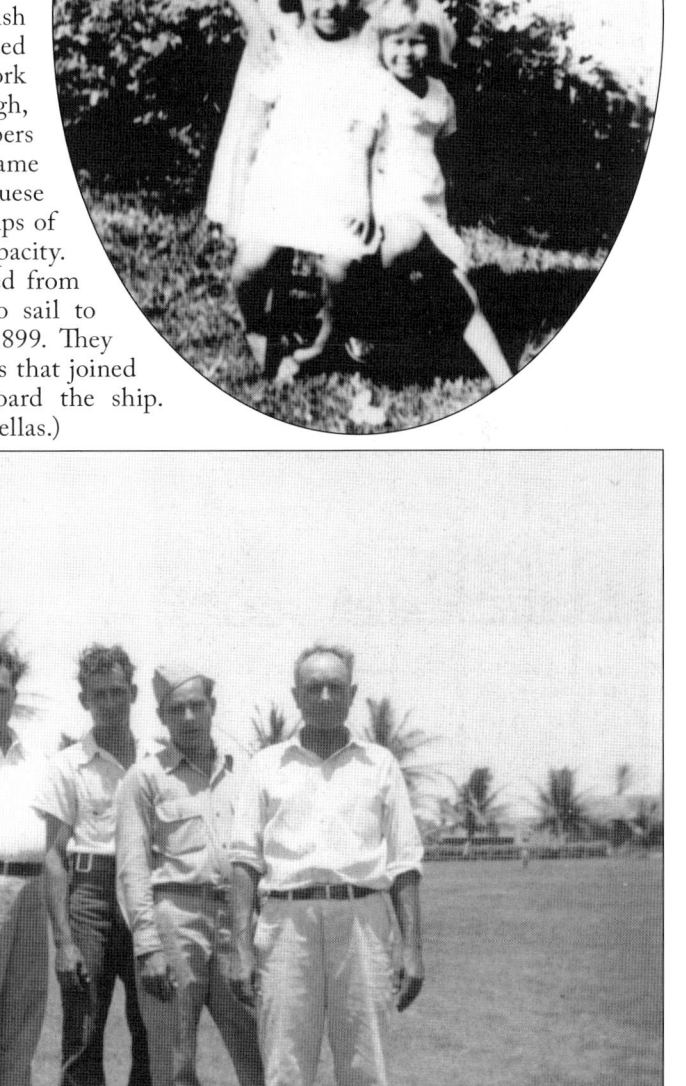

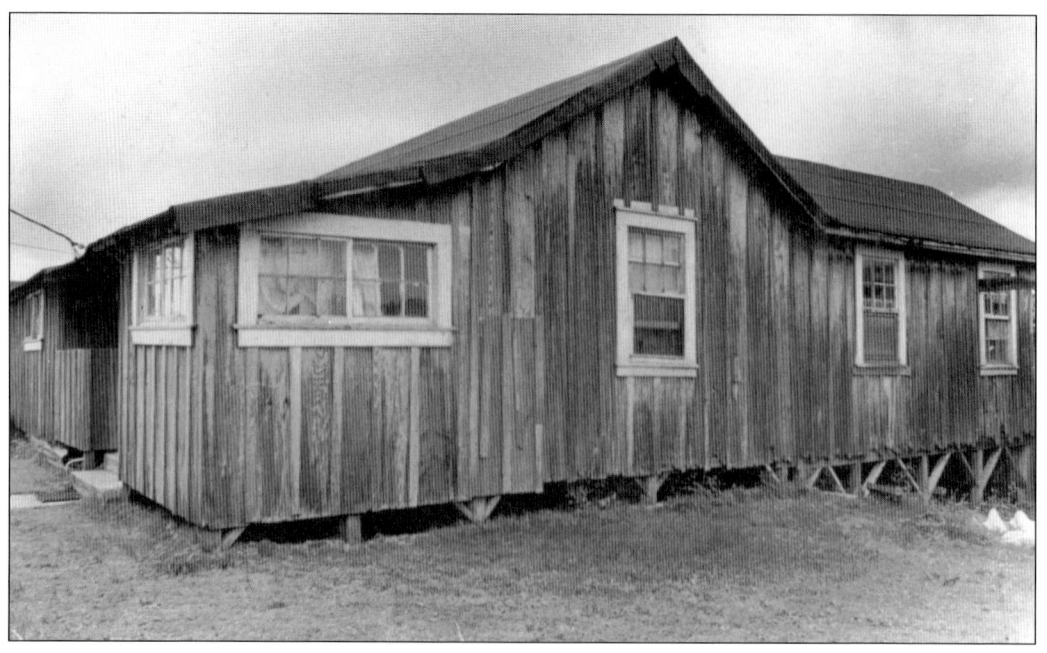

Pictured here is a typical Japanese immigrants' family home in Kapaʻa in the early 1900s. Life was difficult, and the homes were spartan. Below left is the *furo* traditional Japanese bath and to the right is the latrine—a two-seater. This was usually in a separate building away from the main house. (All, courtesy of Laraine Okano Yamashita.)

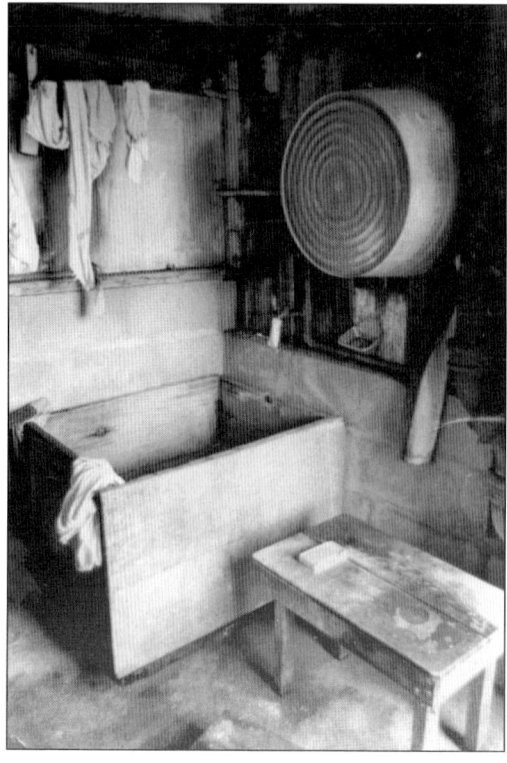
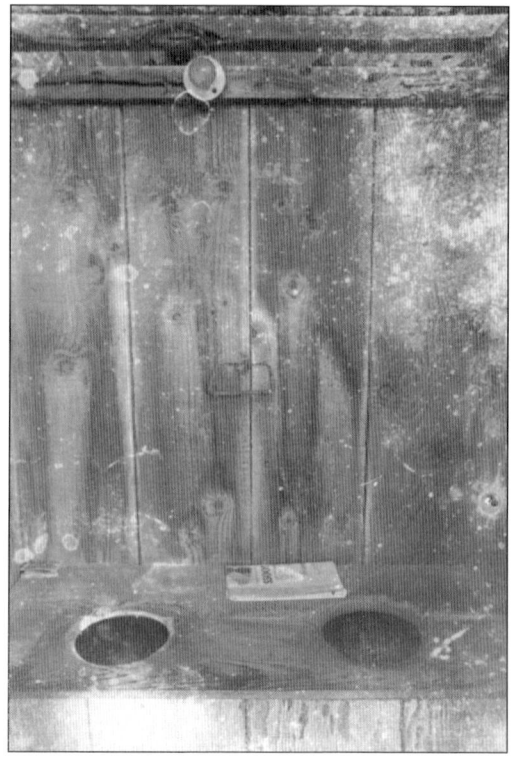

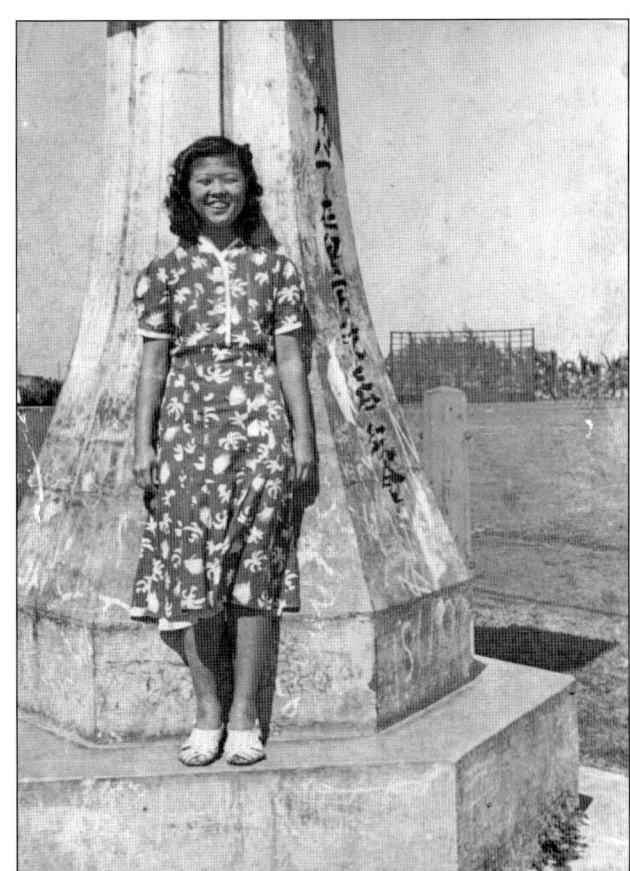

These photographs are of second-generation Japanese women. The one at right is standing in front of the stone lantern (*ishidoro*) in Kapaʻa Park. The sisters below stand in front of the Kapaʻa Café. By the second generation, some of the immigrants had left the plantations to start businesses in town. (Both, courtesy of Laraine Okano Yamashita)

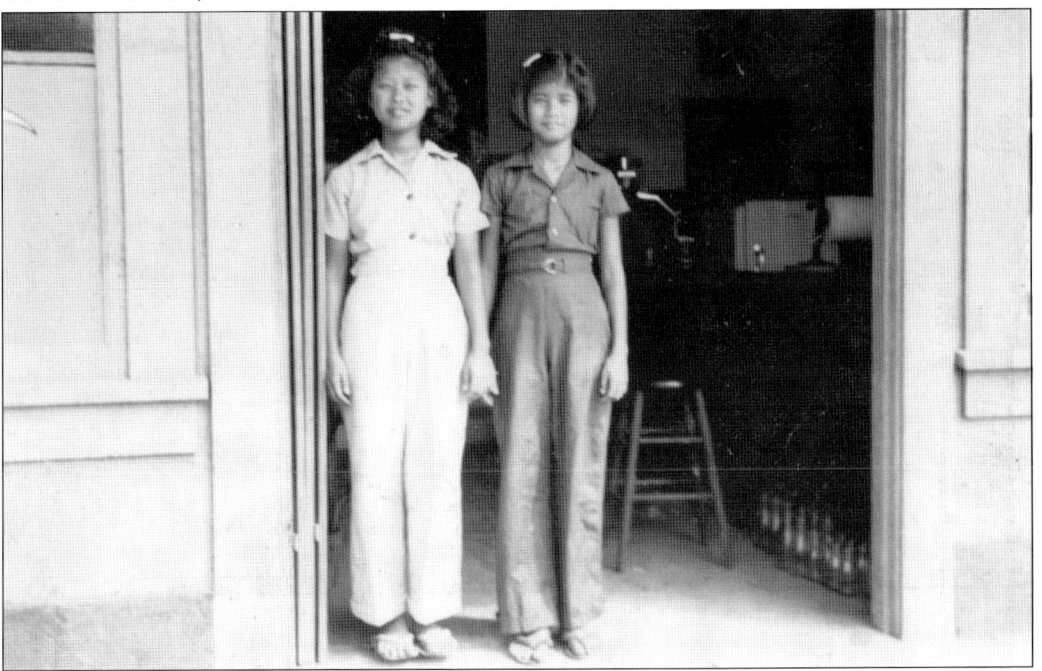

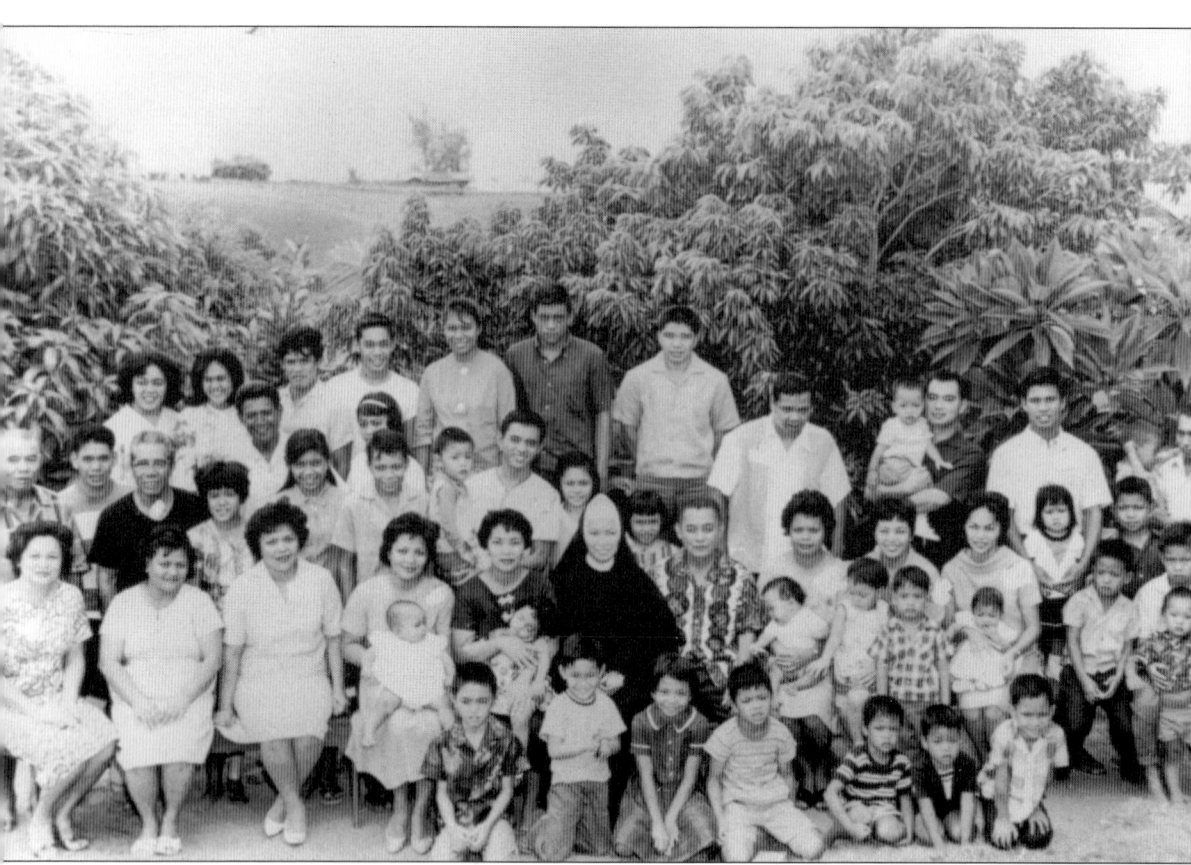

Josephine Maglinte, Sister Mary Marcelia (center), is pictured with her extended family in the early 1960s. The Maglintes are descendants of Filipino immigrants who settled in Kealia and worked for the Makee Sugar Company. At first, Filipino immigrants were overwhelmingly male, expecting to return to their native land. As they settled into plantation life, some sent for wives and brides from their villages. They were industrious, religious, and had strong family values. (Courtesy of St. Catherine Church.)

# Three

# COMMERCE AND TOWN DEVELOPMENT

Kapaʻa town was founded as a result of the Reciprocity Treaty King Kalakaua signed with the United States in 1876. This agreement spurred a boom for the sugar industry in the islands. Kalakaua, capitalizing on this emerging industry, organized a group of friends in Honolulu into the Hui Kawaihau with the intent to grow sugar on his crown lands in Kapaʻa in 1877. The inexperienced group, including James Makee, who was experienced, set up a mill on the north end of Kapaʻa town to process the cane.

Eventually, the Hui floundered, and the plantation was taken over by Zephaniah Spalding, the son-in-law of James Makee. In addition to the lands of the Hui Kawaihau, he purchased land in Kealia and moved Makee Sugar Company there in 1885. As the Makee Sugar Company and other plantations on the island grew, so did the population of workers from abroad and the need for services to support them. Kapaʻa slowly evolved as the commercial and recreational center for the north and east sides of Kauaʻi.

The Chinese were the first immigrants to complete their plantation-work contracts and establish businesses. The Portuguese, Japanese, Filipino, and other ethnic groups quickly followed as both proprietors and customers. When government lands became available for homesteading at the turn of the 20th century, plots of fee-simple land were purchased for cattle ranching, farming, and eventually, pineapple cultivation by independent growers. In 1913, Hawaiian canneries opened in Kapaʻa, further expanding the farm and factory industry. Kapaʻa became known as Kapaʻa Pono, or "Kapaʻa, Town of Opportunity." The expansion of the economy resulted in the further development of the town with the opening of more stores, banks, churches, theaters, pool halls, and restaurants.

Tourism development in the 1960s slowly replaced the waning pineapple and sugar industries. The site of Hawaiian Canneries became the Pono Kai Resort in the mid-1970s. Kapaʻa town is now known as Historic Kapaʻa town, with many of its original buildings standing. Where once there were markets, theaters, pool halls, and everyday household commerce, there are now more tourist-oriented shops, restaurants, and activity centers. Kapaʻa continues as a town of opportunity today.

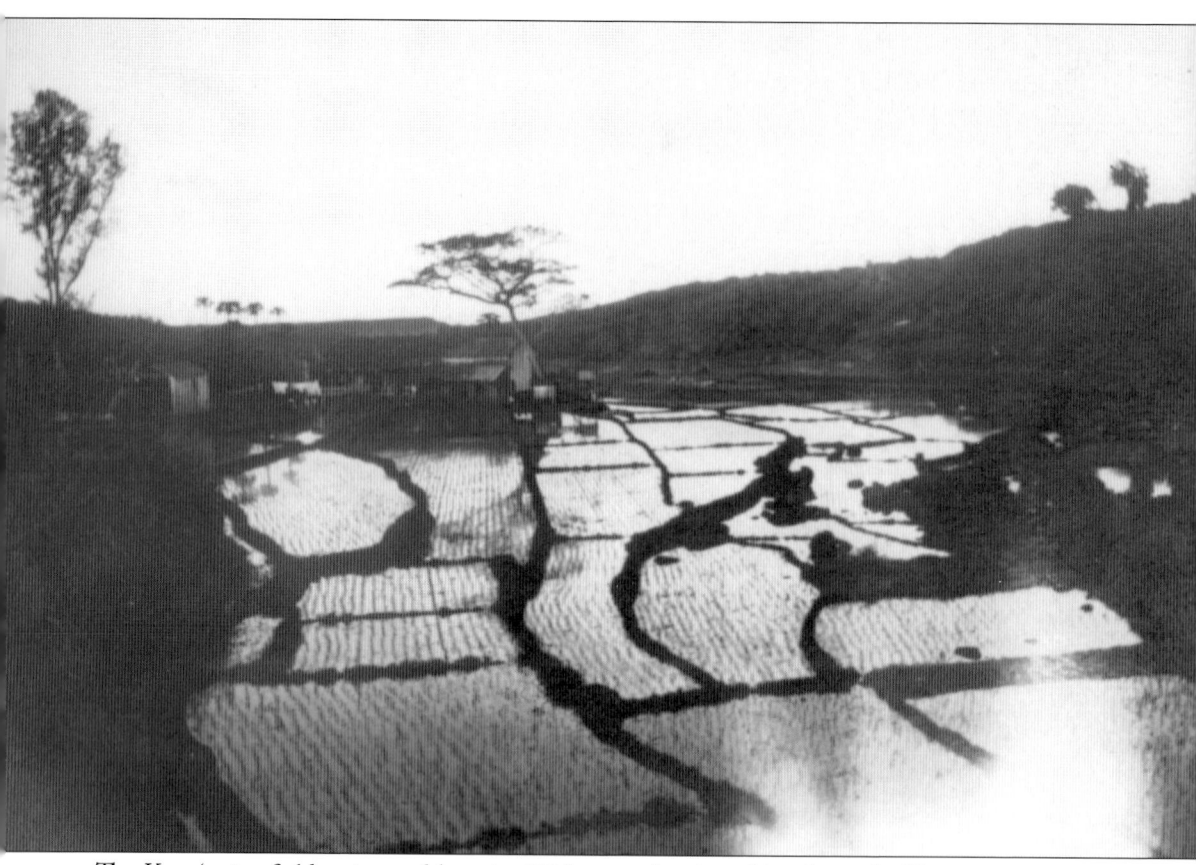

The Kapa'a rice fields, pictured here in 1925, were developed by the early Chinese immigrants in the mid-1800s. Prior to the Chinese, Hawaiians grew taro in these wetlands. The rice was consumed locally by the large Asian immigrant population and exported to California to meet the demands of the Chinese railroad workers in the West. As a result, Chinese accrued wealth, bought land, and established businesses in town. (Courtesy of KHS.)

In 1924, the Chinese-American Bank Ltd. was the first bank established in Kapaʻa. It was started by the Chinese community and reflected their economic prosperity and prominence. It also was a clear sign of their confidence in establishing Hawaii as their permanent home. The bank building is now occupied by Java Kai Coffee Shop, with a kitchen in the original bank vault. (Courtesy of Doris Chang.)

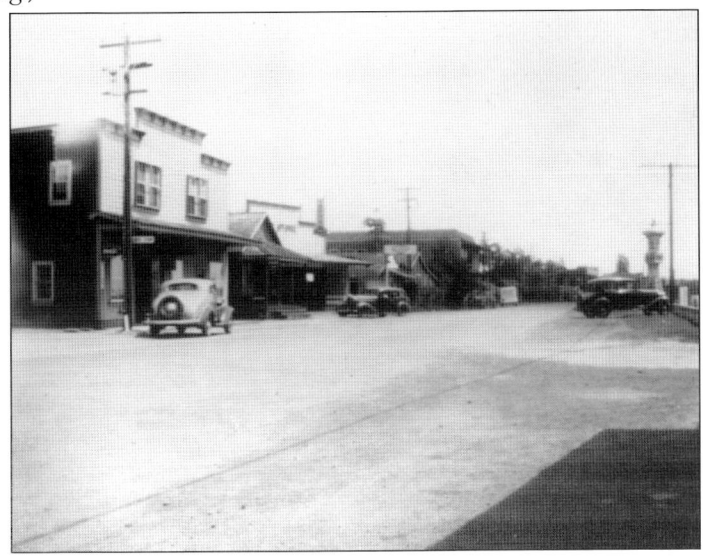

Pictured here in the 1930s are several businesses on Kuhio Highway, fronting the Kapaʻa Ball Park. The historic Japanese stone lantern sits prominently on the far right edge of the park. From left to right are Izumi Hotel, Higashi Store, Miura Store, and the Seto Building. All of the establishments were owned and operated by Japanese families except for the Seto Store, which was Chinese-owned. (Courtesy of St. Catherine's Church.)

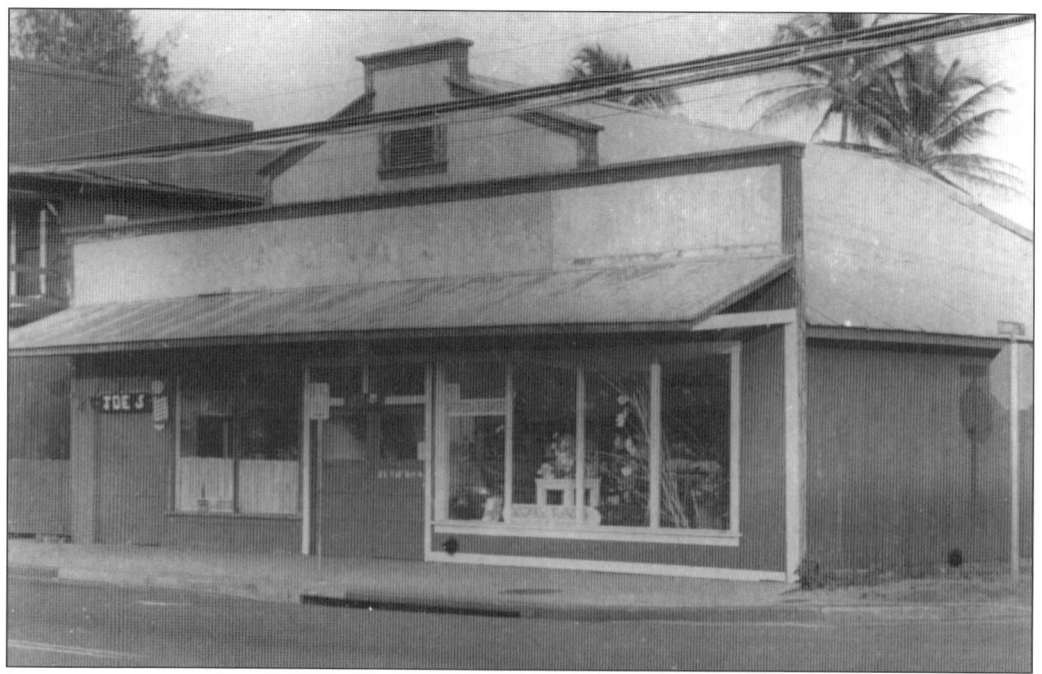

This 1970s photograph of Kawamura Store, built in 1924, shows the general dry-goods section of the building and the adjacent Joe's Barbershop. Joe Alayvilla started cutting hair before World War II and had a shop in different locations in town until the early 1990s. Kawamura store had many incarnations, from dry goods and produce to fish market and a feed store. (Courtesy of Diane Ferry.)

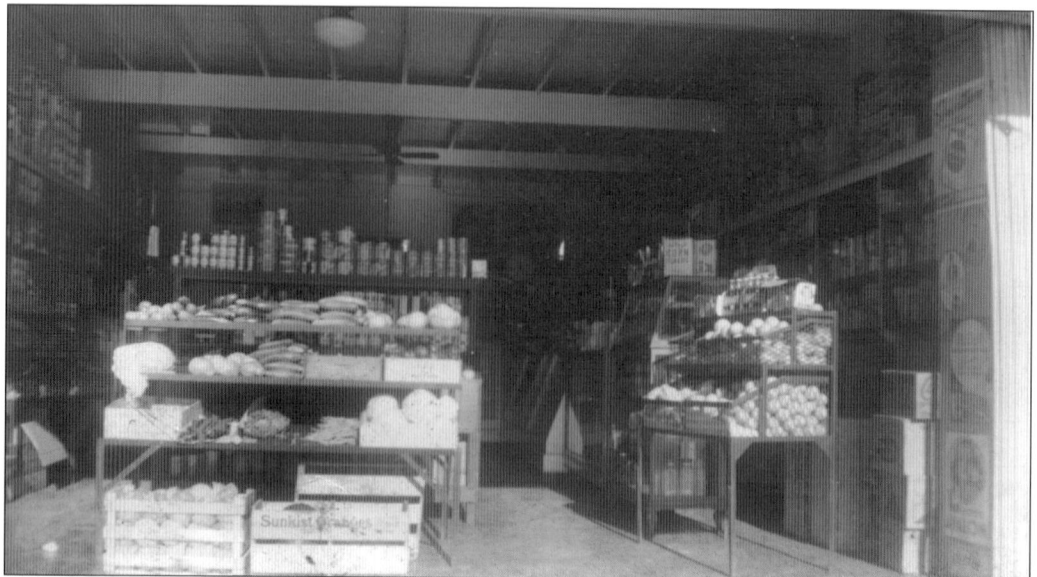

Wakumoto Market was located on the ground floor of the Hee Fat Building, which was built in 1924. The market sold fresh produce and canned goods and had a butcher shop in the back. Typically, the front of the store was open onto the sidewalk for easy pedestrian access. Later, the market was run by Mr. and Mrs. Hirata as Hirata Market. (Courtesy of the Kawamoto family.)

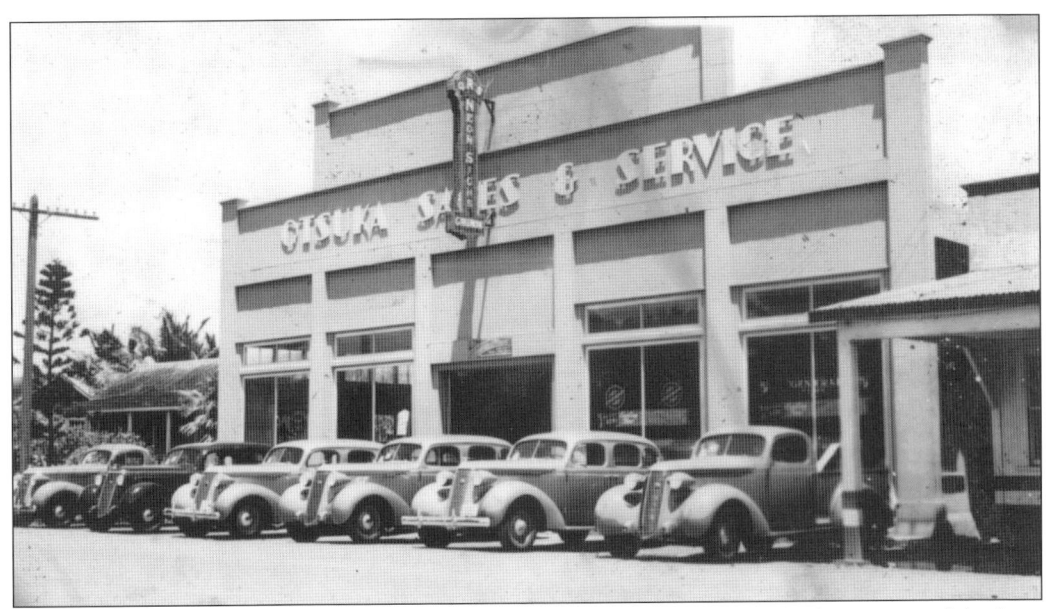

Otsuka Sales and Service, pictured above in the 1930s, sold Studebaker cars and had an attached gas/service station. It was one of many businesses started by Suekichi Otsuka, born in Hiroshima, Japan, in 1884. He immigrated to Kaua'i in 1899 at the age of 15 as an independent worker, not a labor contract worker. He worked various jobs, including cultivating rice and cutting and selling firewood. He married Shige Takitini, a daughter of a rice grower in Koolau district, and together they built a thriving family business, which evolved from sales of cars, appliances, and furniture to real-estate development. Today, Otsuka Furniture Store is on the original store site. Pictured below are the children of Suekichi and Shige Otsuka. From left to right are (first row) Suekichi Otsuka, Harry Otsuka, and Shige Otsuka; (second row) Florence Otsuka Hishibata, Eiko Otsuka Watanabe, Jay Otsuka, Wallace Otsuka, Jitsuo Otsuka, Masayo Otsuka Tone, and Sadako Otsuka Kawamoto. (Courtesy of Kawamoto family.)

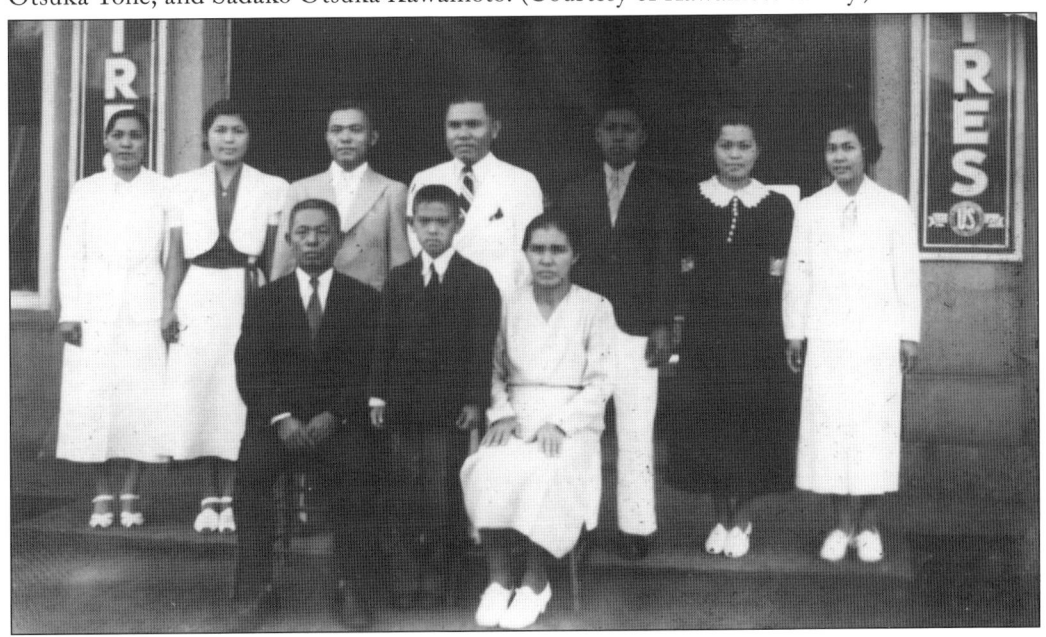

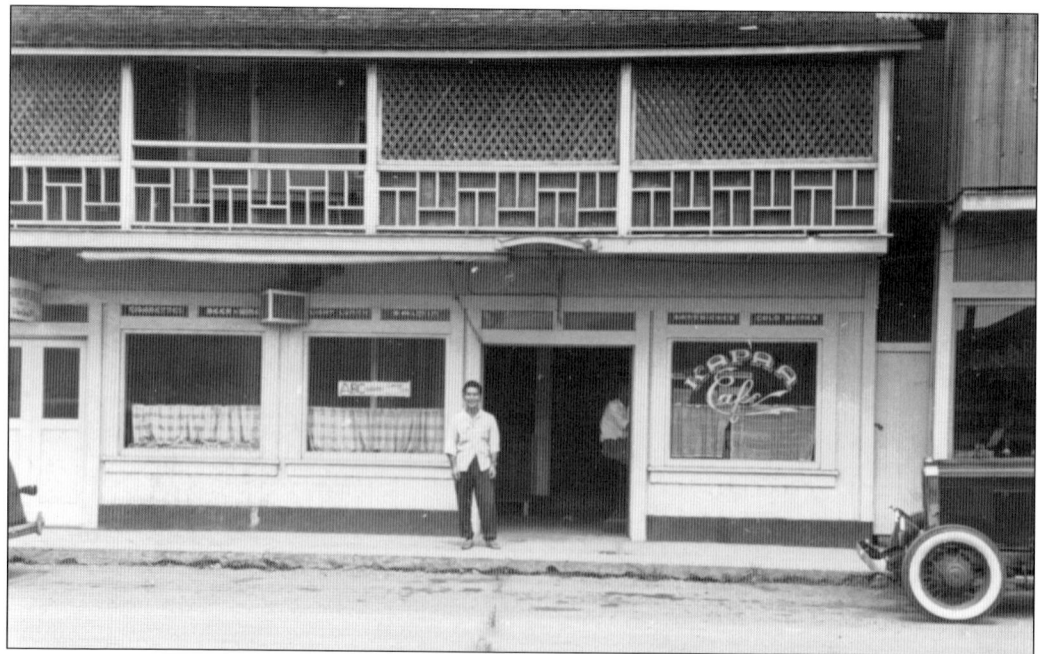

Kapa'a Café was started by Masato Nishimitsu in 1938. The café and bar was located on Kuhio Highway. The clientele were mostly plantation and pineapple cannery employees. During the war, this changed to a dance hall, and the service men frequented the bar, as did the taxi dancers and their clients. It served as an after-game hangout for the Hawaiian Cannery's football team and other local sports teams. Pictured here is Joe Nakamura. (Courtesy of Laraine Okano Yamashita.)

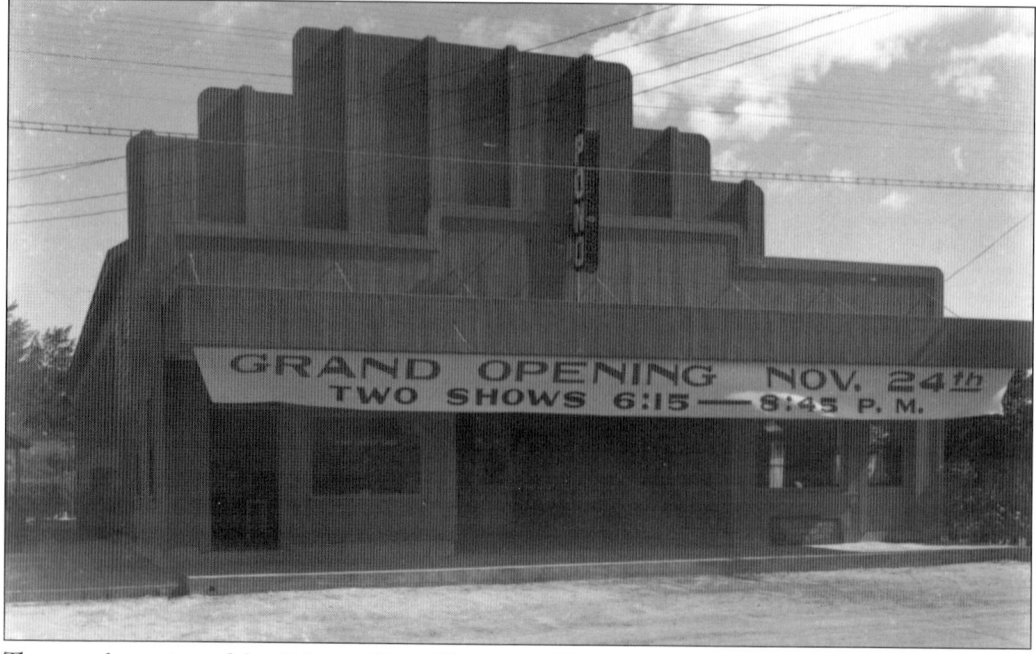

The grand opening of the 420-seat Pono Theatre on November 24, 1938, heralded the popularity of movies as entertainment in Kapa'a in an era when there was no television. A ticket for a show cost 5¢. The former theater is now the site of Ono Family Restaurant. (Courtesy of KHS.)

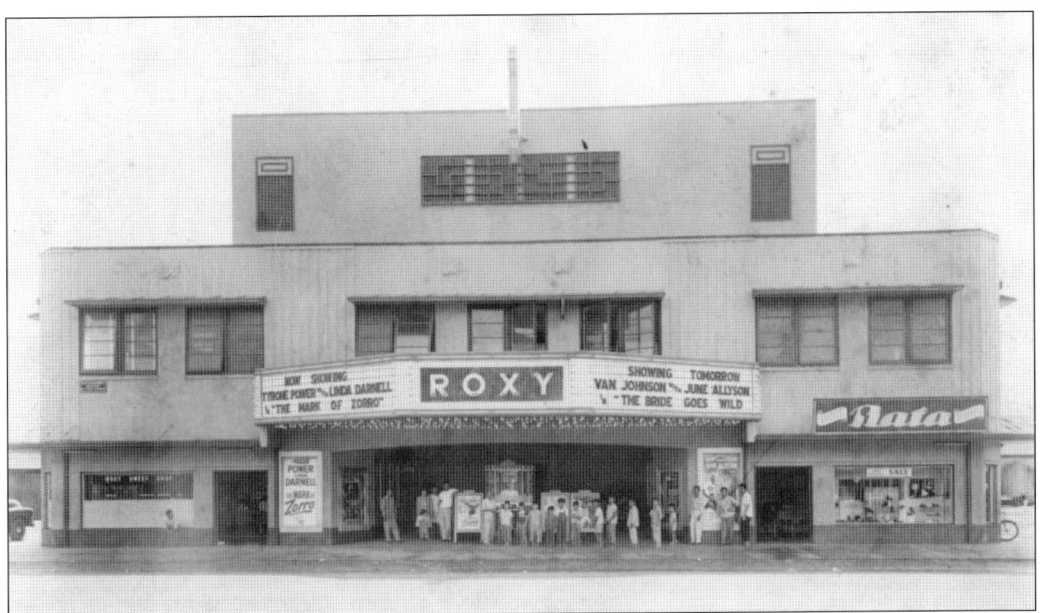

Roxy Theatre, opened in 1939, was built by William and Agnes Scharsch Fernandez. It was the largest movie theater in Hawaii at the time, seating 1,050, and was designed by C.W. Dickey, a well-known island architect. The theater showed movies seven days a week, including matinees and an evening show. Monday was Filipino movie night, and Japanese-language features were screened on Tuesdays and Thursdays. The ground floor housed the Ilima Restaurant and BATA Shoe Store. The second floor featured a dentist and attorney's offices. After Hurricane Iniki in 1992, it was demolished. (Courtesy of Linda Paik Moriarty.)

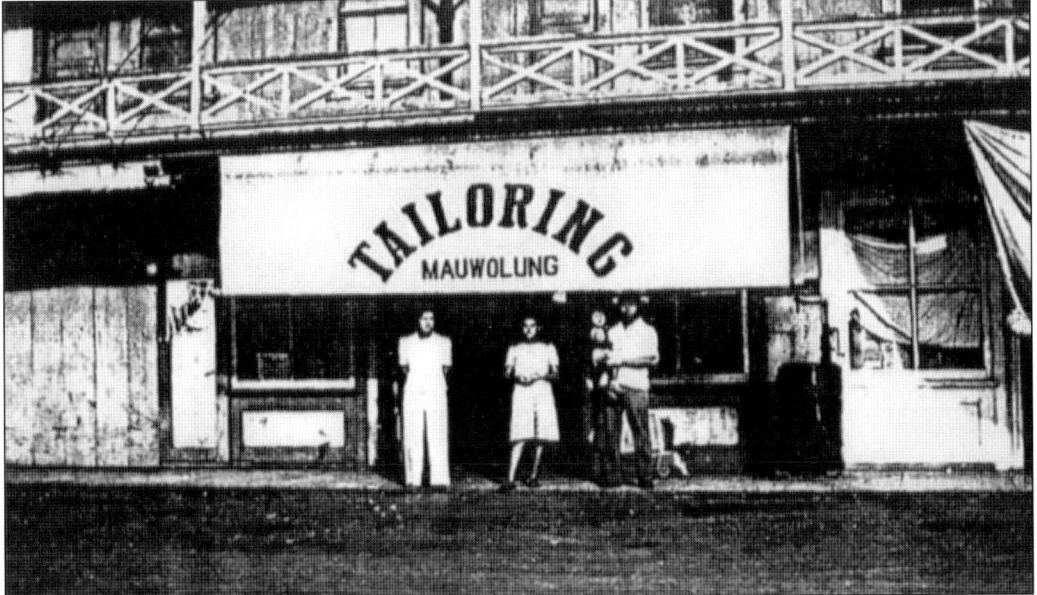

Mau Wo Lung Tailor Shop was located on the ground floor of the Hee Fat Building. Chu Wai, the proprietor and tailor, was erroneously called Mr. Mau by some of his customers. The tailor shop stocked serge palaka, wool, and gabardine yardage for custom-made suits, jackets, and trousers. (Courtesy of Janice Lee Santos.)

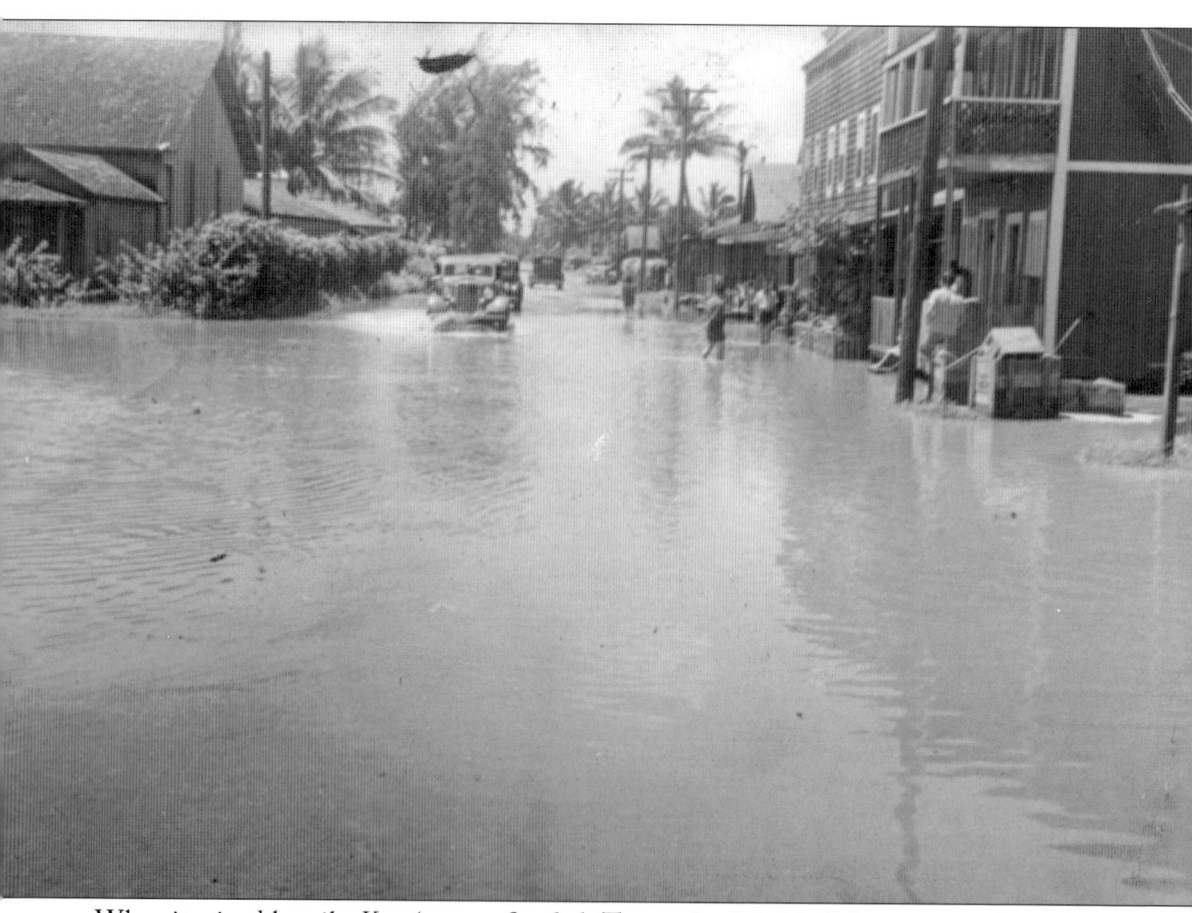

When it rained heavily, Kapaʻa town flooded. The wetlands behind the town overflowed, and the streets became rivers, some navigable only by rowboat. This scene in 1940 depicts Ulu Street with the Congregational church on the left and Urabe Store on the right. To alleviate this problem, three canals were dredged in the 1940s: the Moʻikeha, the Waiakea, and the Uhelekawawa. (Courtesy of the Kawamoto family.)

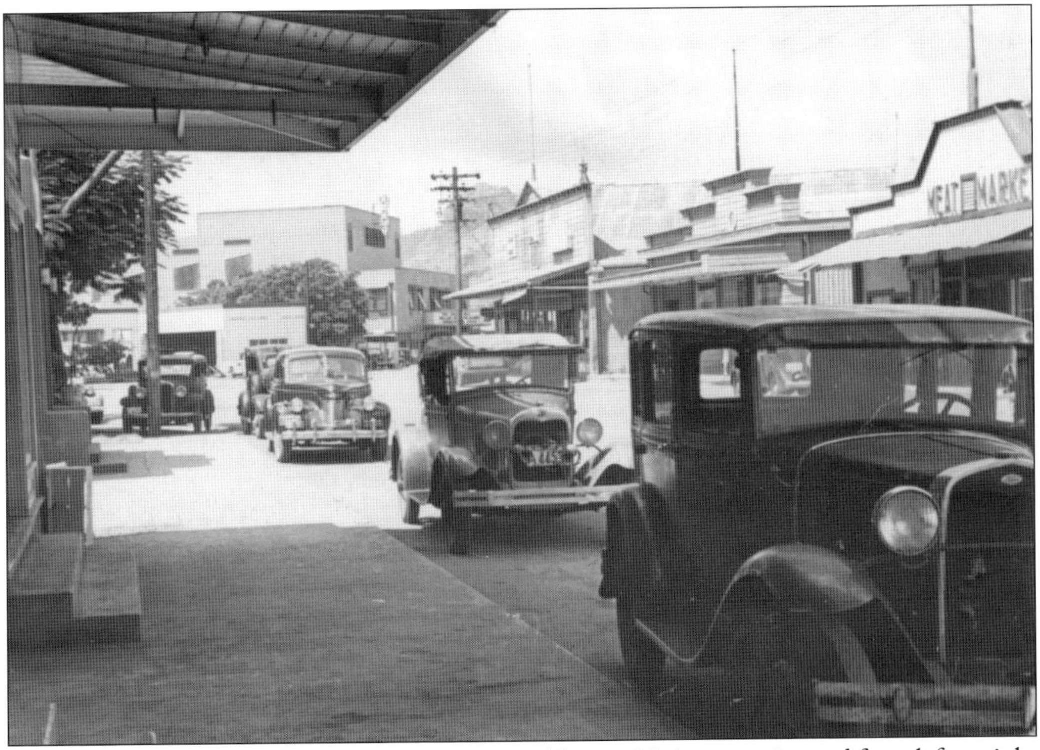

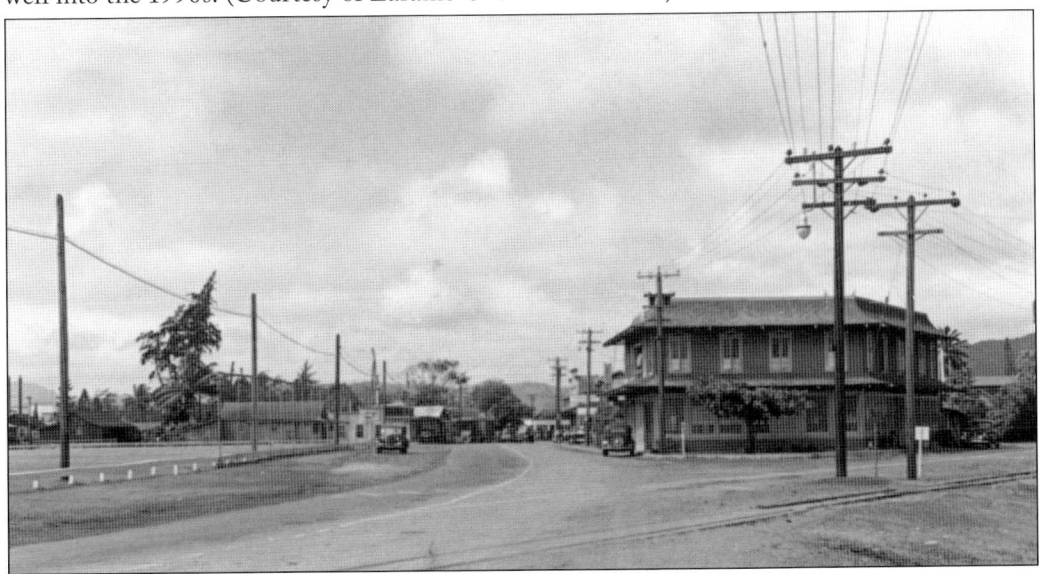

This is an early 1940s street scene of Kapaʻa town. The establishments pictured from left to right are Roxy Theatre, Town Furniture, Shido Store, and Lai Family Meat Market. Shido Store specialized in fabrics, and since most women made their own clothes, they remained in business well into the 1990s. (Courtesy of Laraine Okano Yamashita.)

The Seto Building, built in 1929, housed the Seto Market, which featured "refrigeration for meat, fish and produce." Robert Brooks Taylor, the engineer at the Hawaiian Canneries, designed the building. It was restored in the 1980s by its present owners, Jack and Diana Seto, and is listed in the National Register of Historic Places. (Courtesy of Laraine Okano Yamashita.)

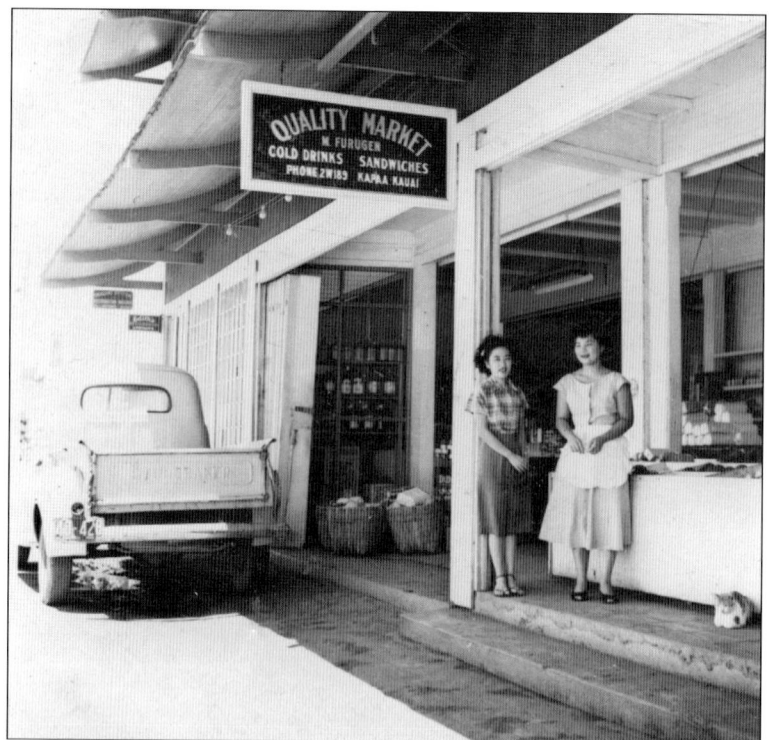

For 20 years, Quality Market rented the Seto Building. Founded in 1942 by Minoru and Sosei Furugen, they sold local meat, pork from the family farm, canned goods, groceries, liquor, and general produce. They closed the market in 1961 and moved to Big Save in Waipouli. Pictured here in the 1950s is Masako Furugen and a friend in the front entrance to the store across from the Kapaʻa Ball Park. (Courtesy of Gary Furugen.)

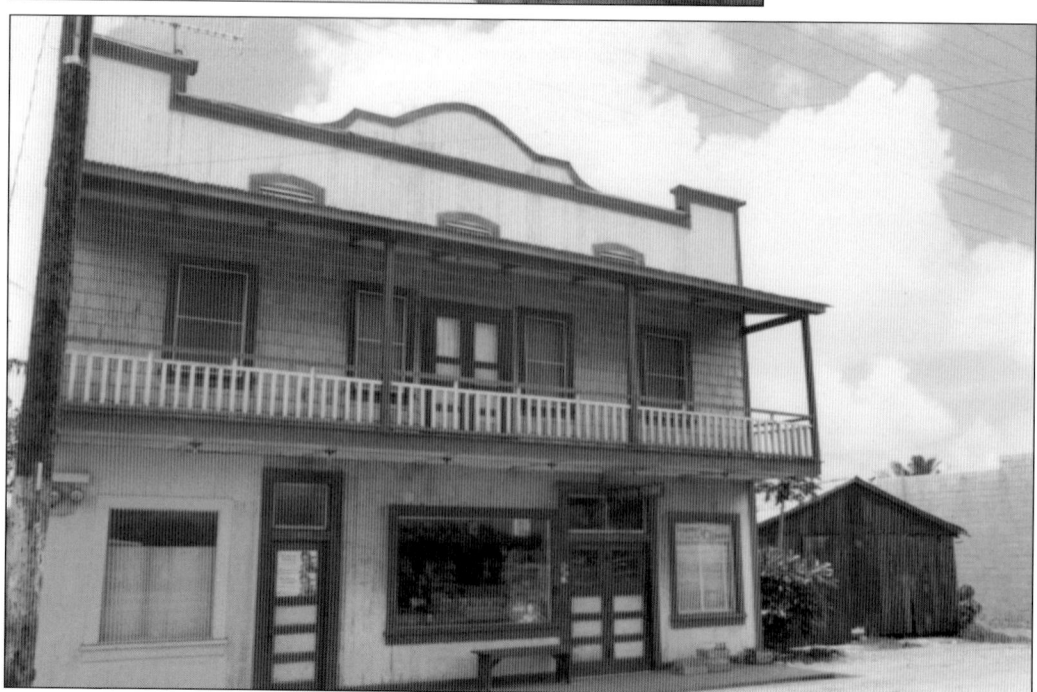

Tokigawa Store was built in 1946 in a classic Western style, with the storefront on the ground floor and living quarters upstairs. It started as a mom-and-pop store and early convenience store that sold soft drinks, magazines, and comics. The building is currently leased to a tourist curio store. (Courtesy of KHS.)

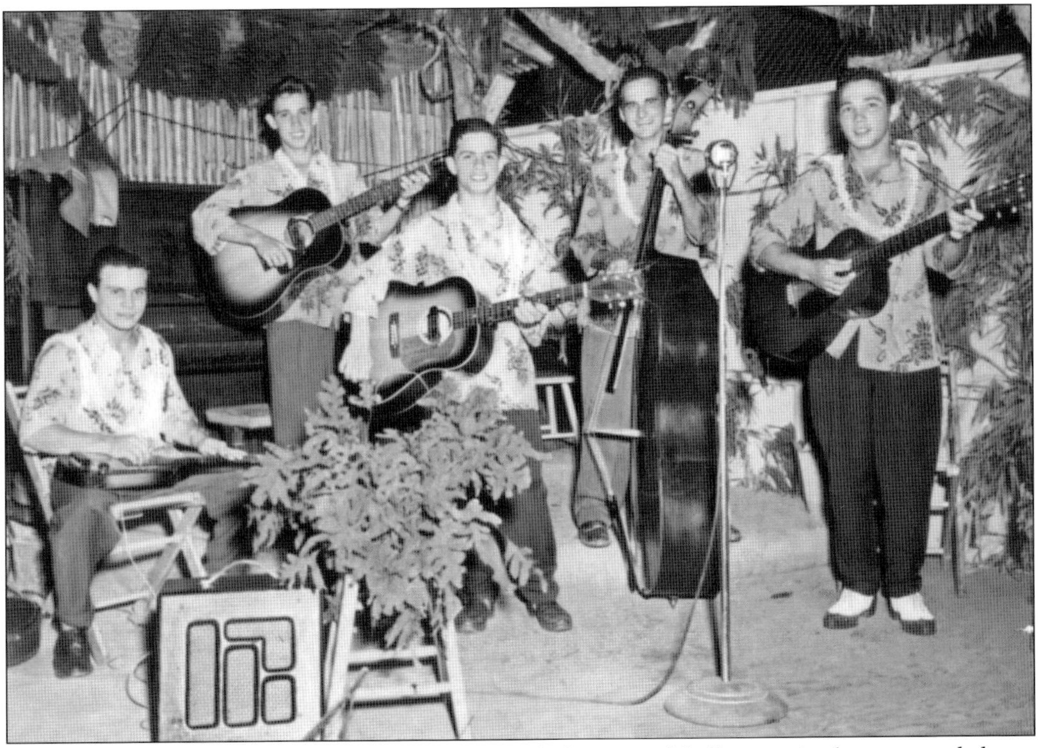

Kapaʻa had an island-wide reputation for its lively bars, pool halls, movie theaters, and dance halls. One of the legendary establishments was the Blue Lei, a popular bar featuring island music. In the 1940s, the Palmeira brothers and friends were regular musicians. Pictured from left to right are Ernest, Wally, and Jimmy Palmeria, Joaquin Ornellas, and Raymond Mendes. As most of them were in their teens and too young to drink, they had to enter through the back door. Wally and Ernest entertained on Kauaʻi throughout their lives. (Courtesy of Ernest Palmeria.)

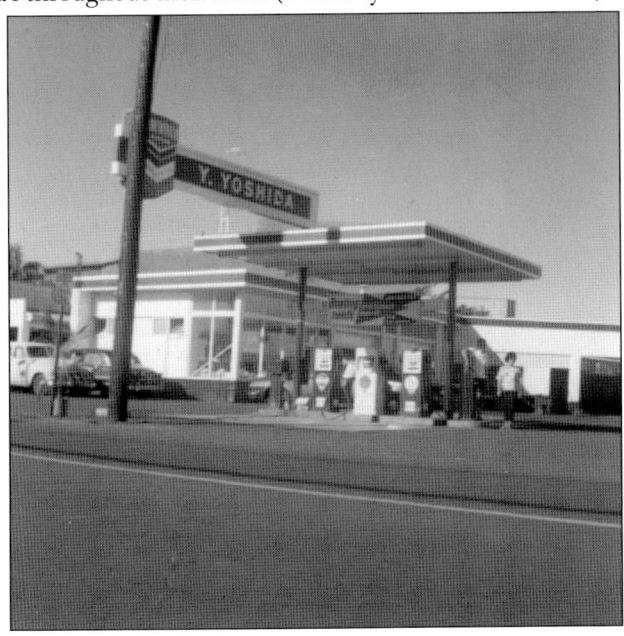

Y. Yoshida Service Station was opened by Yoshiichi "Big Mice" Yoshida and rebuilt in the 1950s. Big Mice ran the station with his brother Isami "Small Mice" Yoshida, whom he sent to Detroit, Michigan, to become an automobile mechanic. The brothers ran the service station and had the contract for the school bus. They were listed in the telephone book respectively as Big Mice Yoshida and Small Mice Yoshida. (Courtesy of the Yoshida family.)

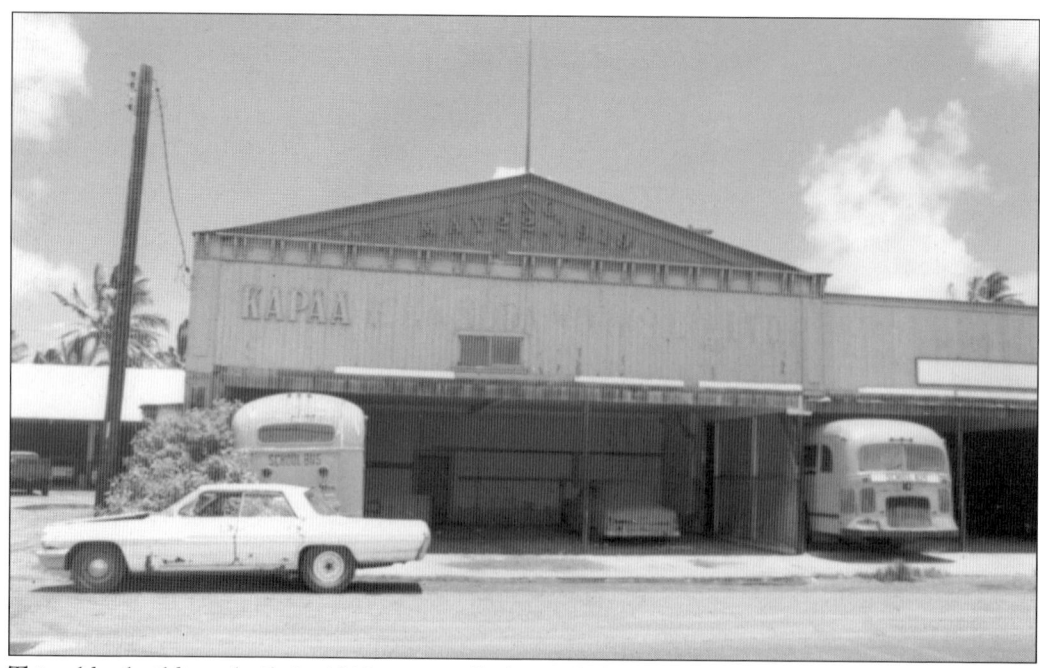

This older building, built in 1918, originally housed the Kapaʻa Ice and Soda Works and the Kapaʻa Electric Power Company, owned by John B. Fernandes. At the time, the electric company provided power to homes and businesses from Wailua to Anahola. In the 1950s, the building was purchased by Big Mice Yoshida to house his school buses, as shown above. This building was located next to Otsuka Service Station and no longer stands today. (Courtesy of KHS.)

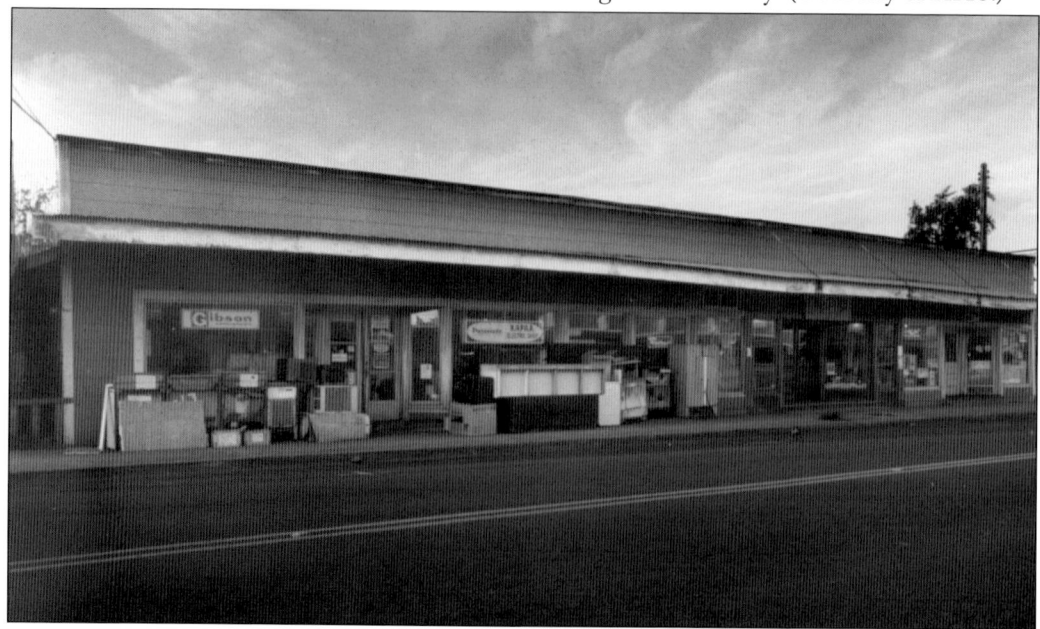

Pictured here in 1981, this building housed the Kapaʻa Electric shop and Kuhio Market. Kapaʻa Electric, owned by the Kuboyama family, sold and serviced appliances and also issued marriage licenses. Kuhio Market operated as a fish market, and today the building houses an import furniture and accessories business, as well as a beauty center. (Courtesy of KHS.)

Ichiji Matsumura was a well-respected building contractor. He and his wife, Masako, built and operated the Coral Reef Hotel in Kapaʻa in 1956 next to the Kapaʻa Fire Station. The hotel started with eight rooms and eventually expanded to 10 rooms. At the time, it was the only modern hotel in Kapaʻa. It was affordable and catered to traveling businesspeople and the occasional tourist. It has changed ownership and today has 21 rooms and offers many amenities. (Courtesy of Bonnie Matsumura.)

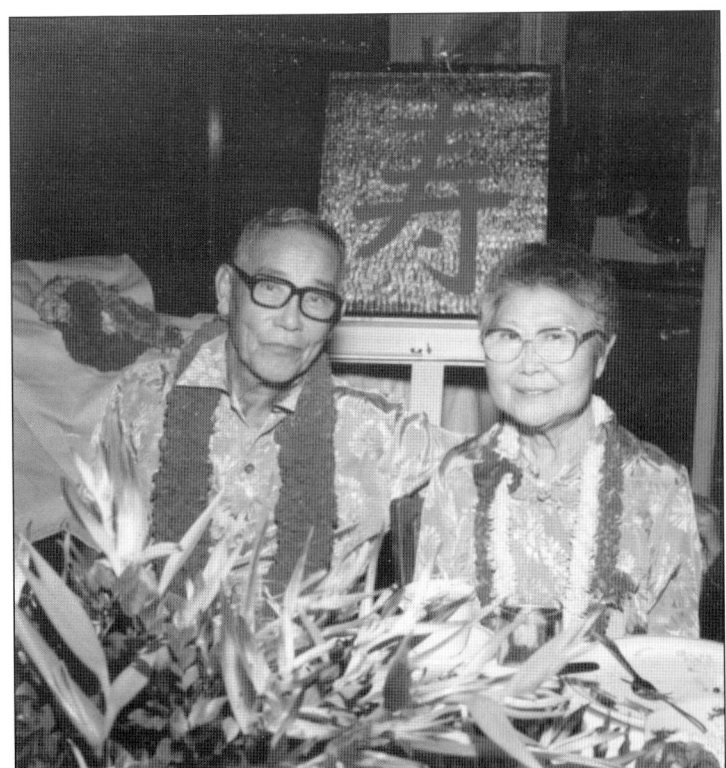

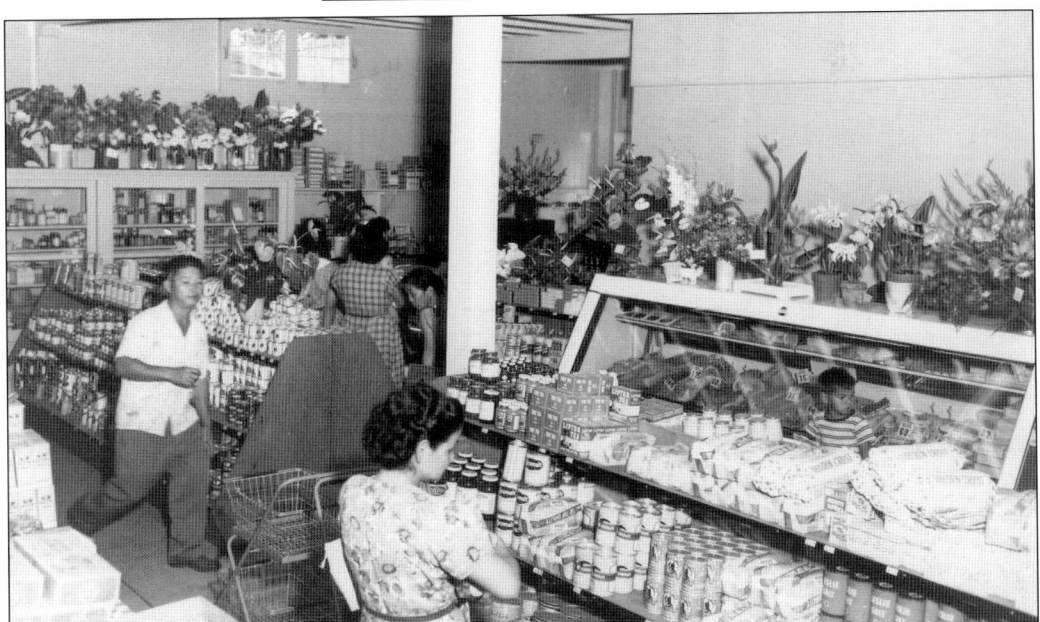

Pictured here is the reopening of Nakamura Store in the 1960s by Shigeto Nakamura (walking on the left). The store was in the AHKO Building on Kukui Street. It sold general merchandise and had a butcher shop, which bought beef and pork from local ranchers. Nakamura's extended credit to customers and delivered grocery orders made by telephone. It closed its doors one week before Hurricane Iniki hit the island on September 11, 1992. (Courtesy of Marilyn Suzuki Haugh.)

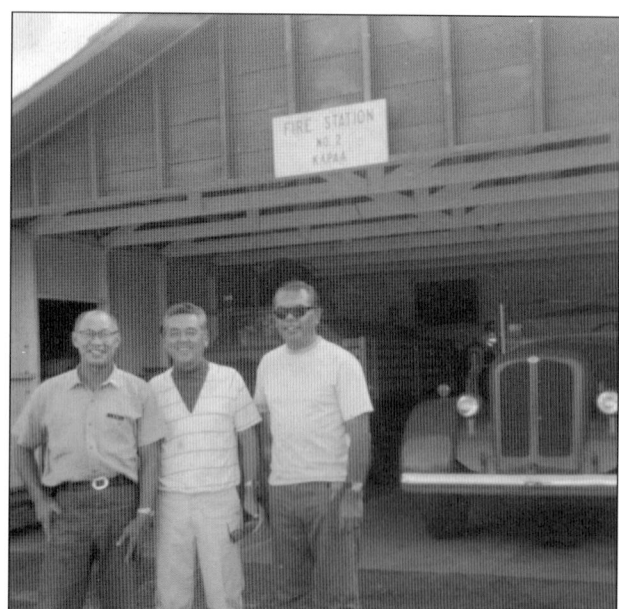

The original Kapa'a Fire Station was a wooden structure located on the north side of the Mo'ikeha Canal, adjacent to the present-day Coral Reef Hotel. Pictured in front of the two fire trucks are fireman Jack Paik (left) and two unidentified friends. The station was demolished and moved to its present location in Waipouli. (Courtesy of Linda Paik Moriarty.)

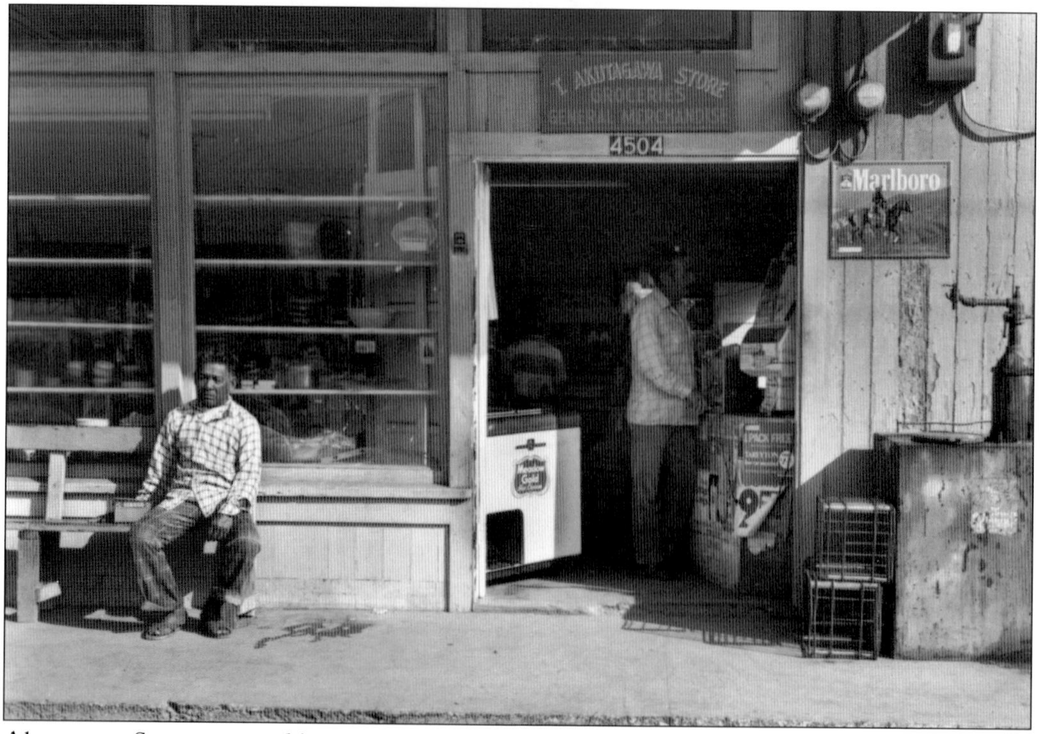

Akutagawa Store, pictured here in 1978, was housed in a building owned by the Aloiau family. Today, a new building is known as the "Dragon Building." The store sold dry goods, especially those from post-war Japan, Japanese medicine, general merchandise, and its most popular item, kerosene. The pump for the kerosene is at far right. Customers brought their own containers to pump kerosene for their stoves and lanterns. Interestingly, the original building on the site, prior to the Aloiaus, was the residence of the Hui Kawaihau and King Kalakaua when they were establishing sugar in Kapa'a. (Courtesy of Diane Ferry.)

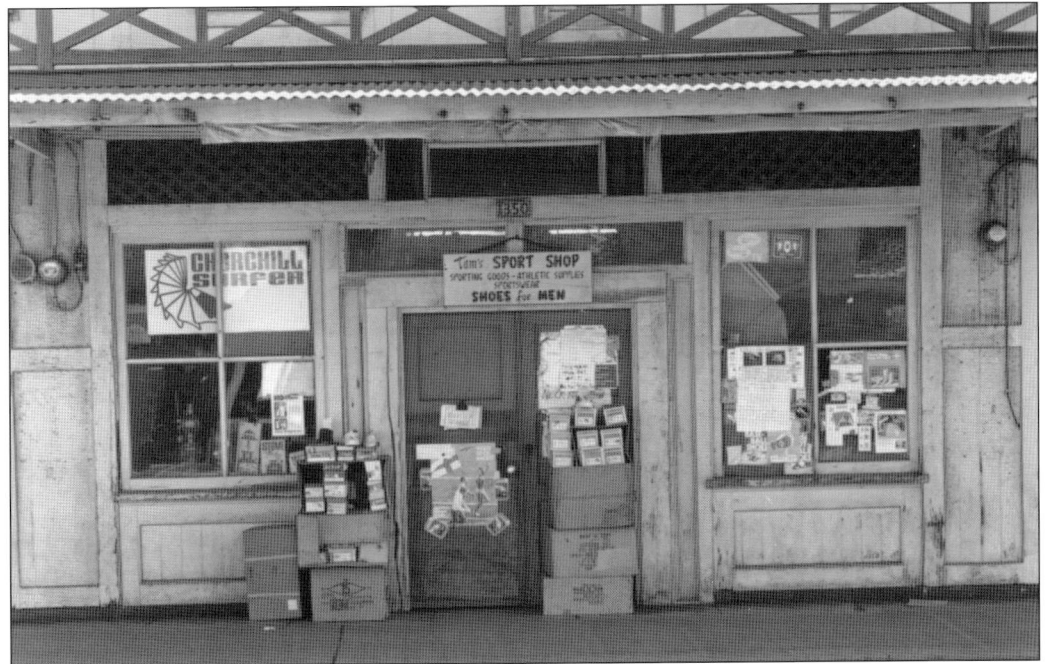

Pictured here in the 1970s, Tam's Sport Shop, located in the Hee Fat Building, was run by Gordon Tam, who took over the site from his father, early Chinese merchant Tam Kee. Tam Kee sold Chinese goods and herbs, specifically to the early Chinese community. In later years, his son sold all sorts of sporting equipment. (Courtesy of Diane Ferry.)

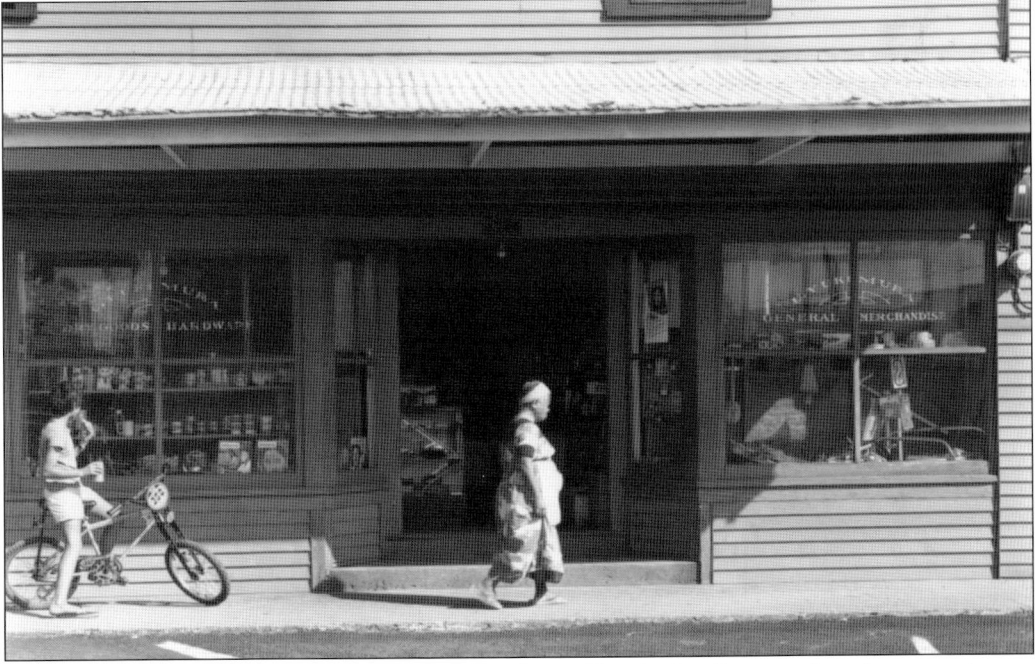

U. Yukimura Store, pictured in 1970, is the classic Kapaʻa family-owned-and-operated store that sold general merchandise, dry goods, and hardware. The Yukimuras lived in the back of the store and had their warehouse on the same property. (Courtesy of Diane Ferry.)

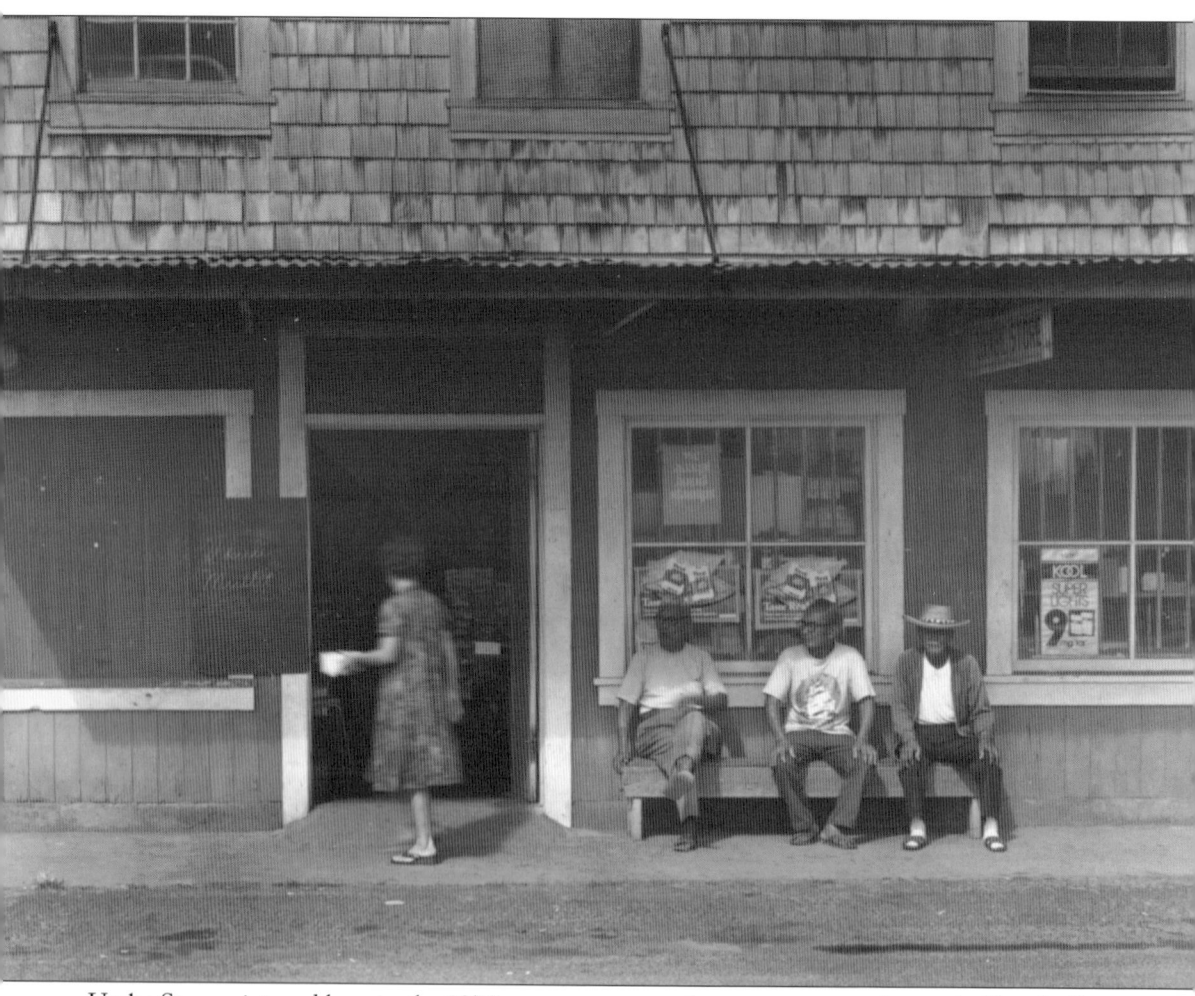

Urabe Store, pictured here in the 1970s, was a mom-and-pop store, one of many in Kapaʻa. But, each sold something unique that differed from the others. Urabe Store specialized in fishing supplies and fresh fish. Pedro Ponce Barbershop was located next door in the same building as the Urabe Store. The ubiquitous bench in front of the store with three men was a typical sidewalk scene in the town. (Courtesy of Diane Ferry.)

The present Pono Market was established in 1968, when the Kubota family bought the business from the Tamashiro family. Truly a family-run business, it specializes in local foods to go, bento lunches (small meal with rice, meat, and salad), and traditional Hawaiian dishes, plus local pastries. The coffee bar is very popular. Lines at 7:00 a.m. snake out the door. Pictured here on opening day are, from left to right, Minoru and Kiyoko Kubota, Hiroko Tamashiro, Jerry Kubota, Charles Tamashiro, and Kenneth Kubota. (Courtesy of the Kubota family.)

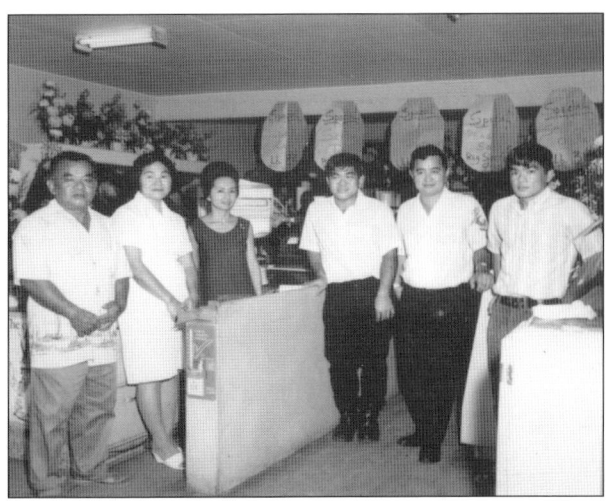

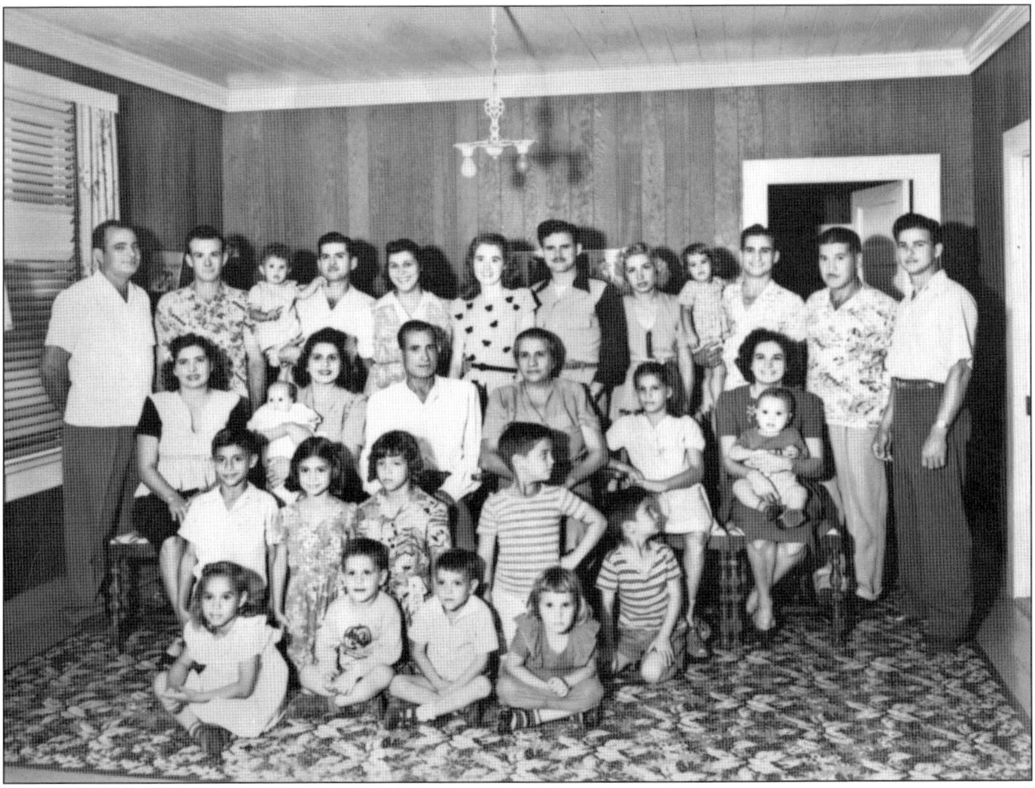

In November 1947, Manuel and Helena Bettencourt's family gather at their Kapaʻa home. This family photograph presents three generations born in Kapaʻa. Manuel was born in Kapaʻa in 1890. His parents, Joseph (Jose) Freitas Bettencourt and Maria de Jesus Gomes, emigrated from Madeira, Portugal. By 1886, Joseph was a land owner and cattle rancher living on the north end of Kapaʻa town among other immigrant families. He lived in Kapaʻa for 44 years and raised five children. He made higher education possible for his children and others in his neighborhood. His son Manuel remained in Kapaʻa, where he and Helena had 10 children. Many of their children and grandchildren continued to live in Kapaʻa. (Courtesy of Doreen Vilela Geiger.)

This c. 1940s map of Kapa'a town was hand-drawn from memory by Albert Fukushima, a lifelong Kapa'a resident. (Courtesy of Albert Fukushima.)

# Four

# THE PINEAPPLE INDUSTRY

In the late 19th and early 20th centuries, sugar was the predominant industry on Kaua'i. The economy was primarily agrarian at the time, and remained so until after World War II. Kapa'a, a bedroom community of Kealia and its Makee Sugar Company, began to take hold as a commercial hub in the area. This new opportunity was a catalyst for Kapa'a's growth—drawing Japanese and Chinese immigrants who sought independence by opening local stores. The northern region was also developed as Portuguese immigrant families also began purchasing property in Kapa'a.

In 1915, Hawaiian Canneries Ltd. was constructed in the heart of Kapa'a and began canning and export operations for the juice and fruit markets of the continental United States. As the pineapple industry continued to emerge as a central economic force in the small community, a second pineapple cannery was established in 1932 called the Growers Association Cannery (later Hawaiian Fruit Packers). It was founded and operated by independent growers, but the venture was short-lived. During the Great Depression, the demand for the fruit dwindled.

In later years, the industry invented mechanical harvesters with long conveyor arms to receive the pineapples, which were hand-picked in the fields and deposited into waiting trucks. Similar improvements were made in the planting, fertilizing, and cultivation of the crops. Side-by-side, working in harmony, pineapple and commercial activities would continue in Kapa'a until after statehood in 1959.

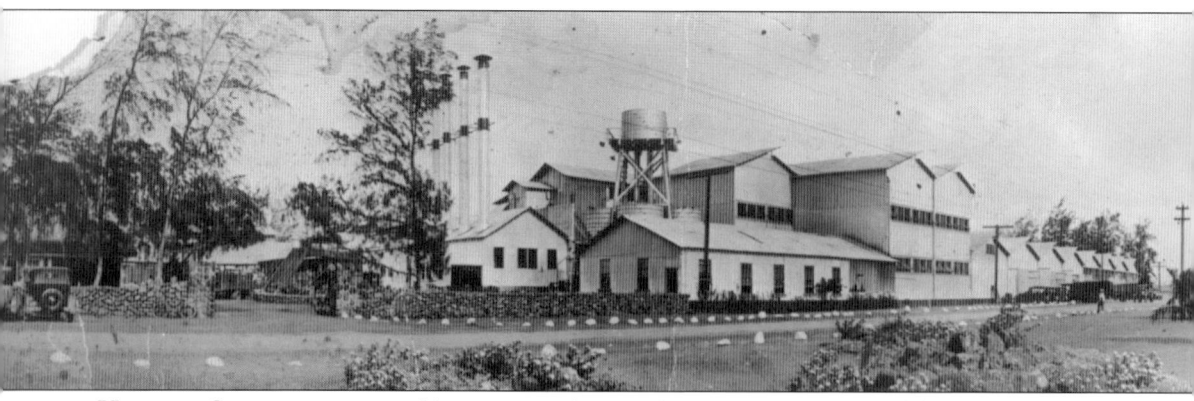
Hawaiian Canneries is pictured here in its early years, having started in 1913. This photograph was taken across from Kūhiʻō Highway at the triangle, or gateway, to Kapaʻa. (Courtesy of KHS.)

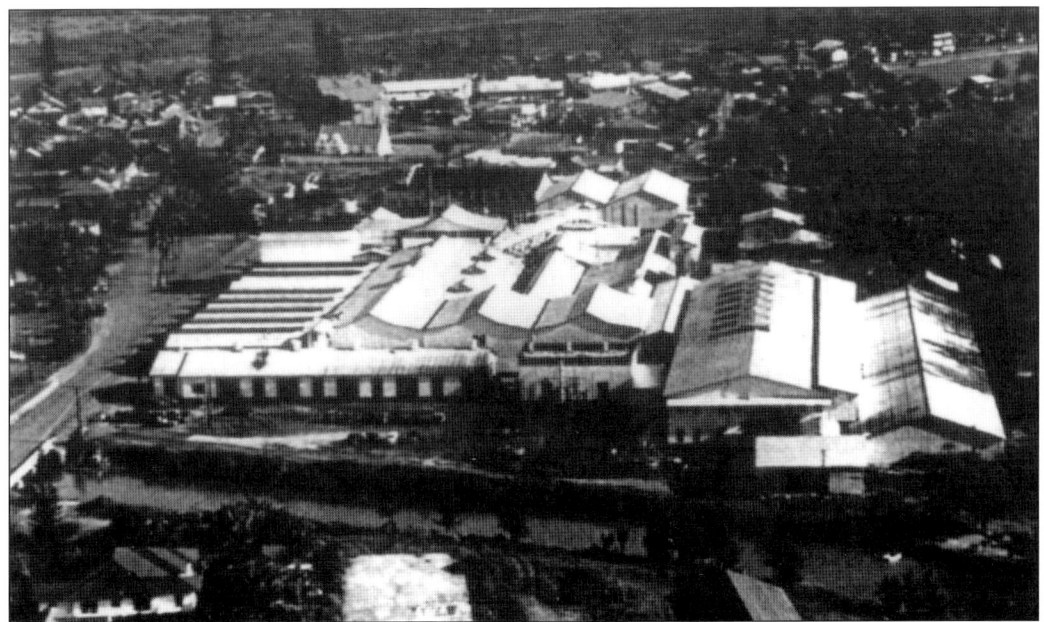

This is an aerial view from about 1950 of Hawaiian Canneries, which was situated on over 13 acres. (Courtesy of Albert Fukushima.)

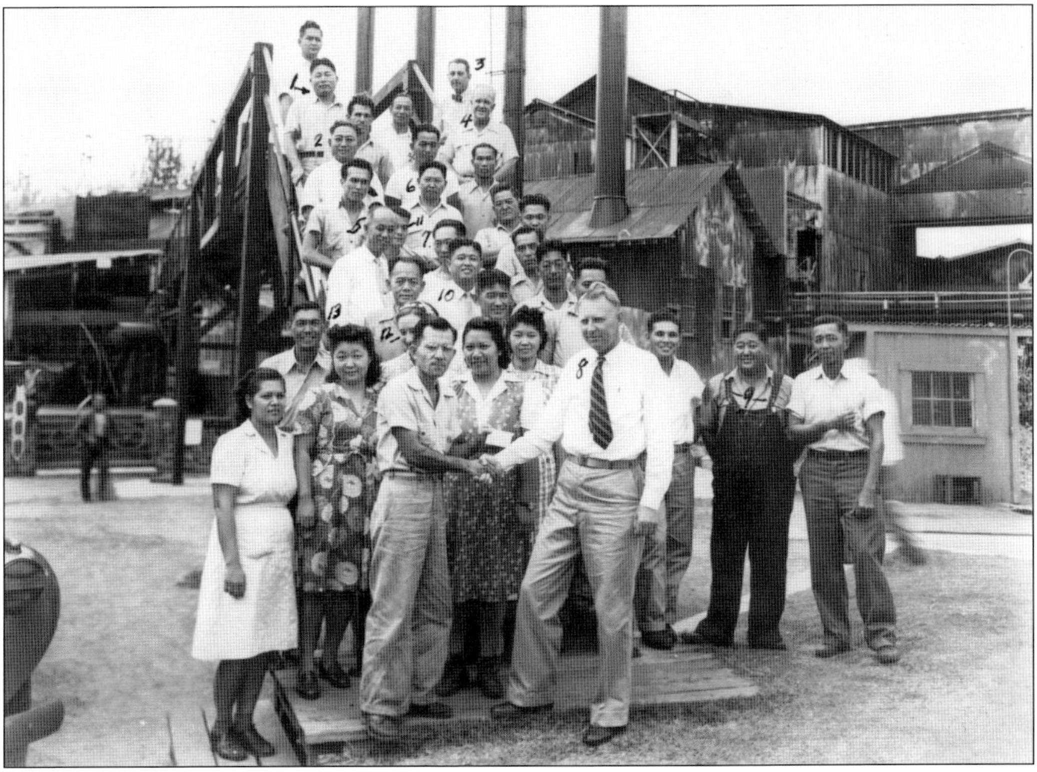

Pictured here around 1935 is the administrative staff at Hawaiian Canneries, Albert Horner, the manager; Vincent Lizama, office manager; and Mr. Shack in accounting, to name a few. (Courtesy of KHS.)

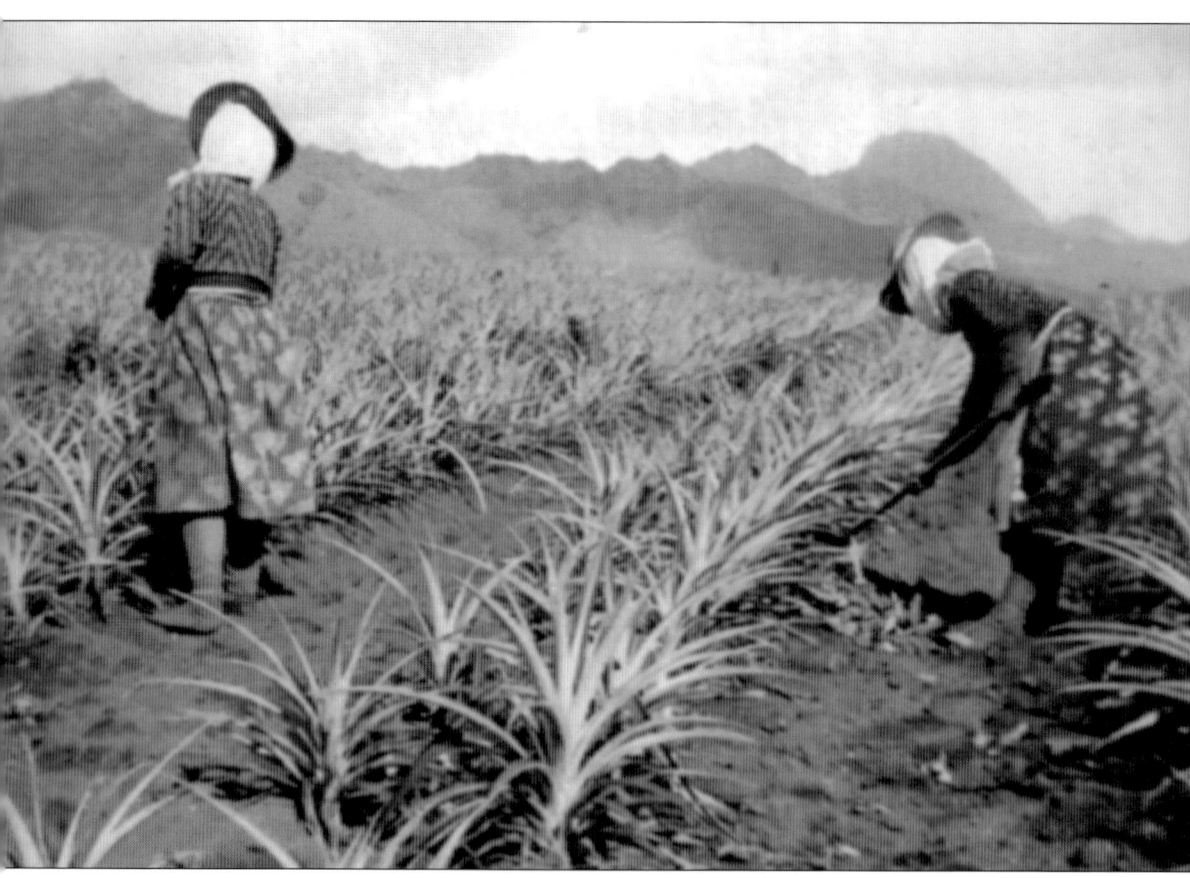

Women as well as men picked pineapple and prepared the ground for planting. Protective clothing was a necessity to protect against the thorny plants as well as the harsh sun. These women are *hoe hana* (hoeing) these young fields. Growing pineapple was labor intensive and took two years from field to table. (Courtesy of Albert Fukushima.)

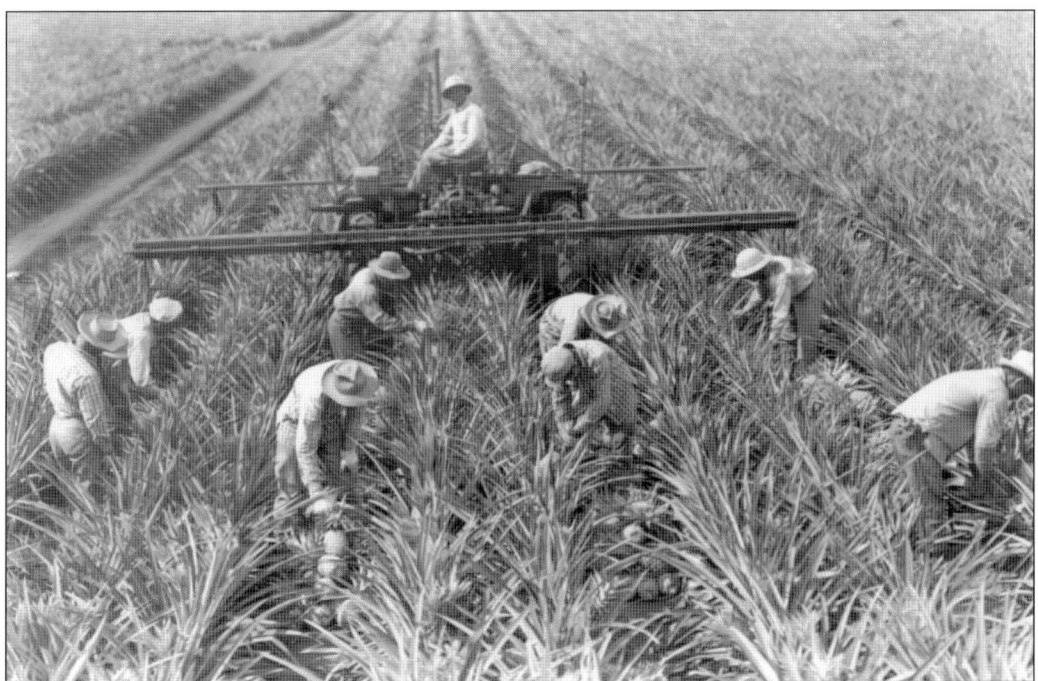

Hawaiian Canneries field hands pick pineapple and place the fruit in the rows between the plants. The pineapples were then placed on a conveyor belt and moved to waiting trucks that transported the pineapple to the cannery. (Courtesy of KHS.)

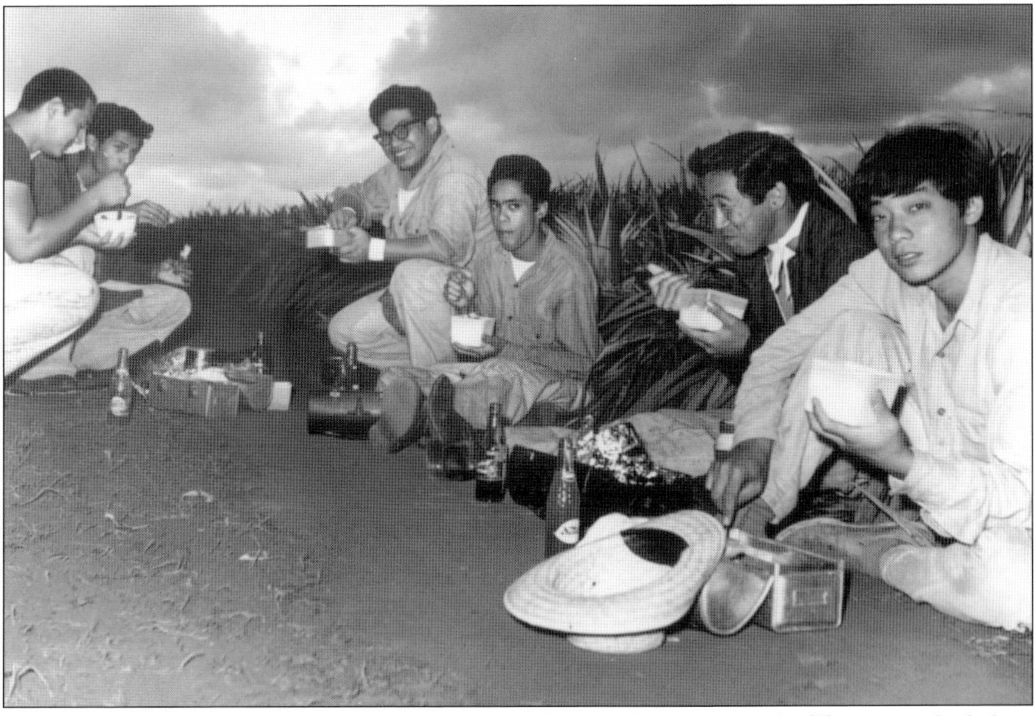

Young summer hires take a well-deserved break from picking pineapple. They unpacked their *kau kau* tins (lunchboxes) and shared their ethnic foods. (Courtesy of KHS.)

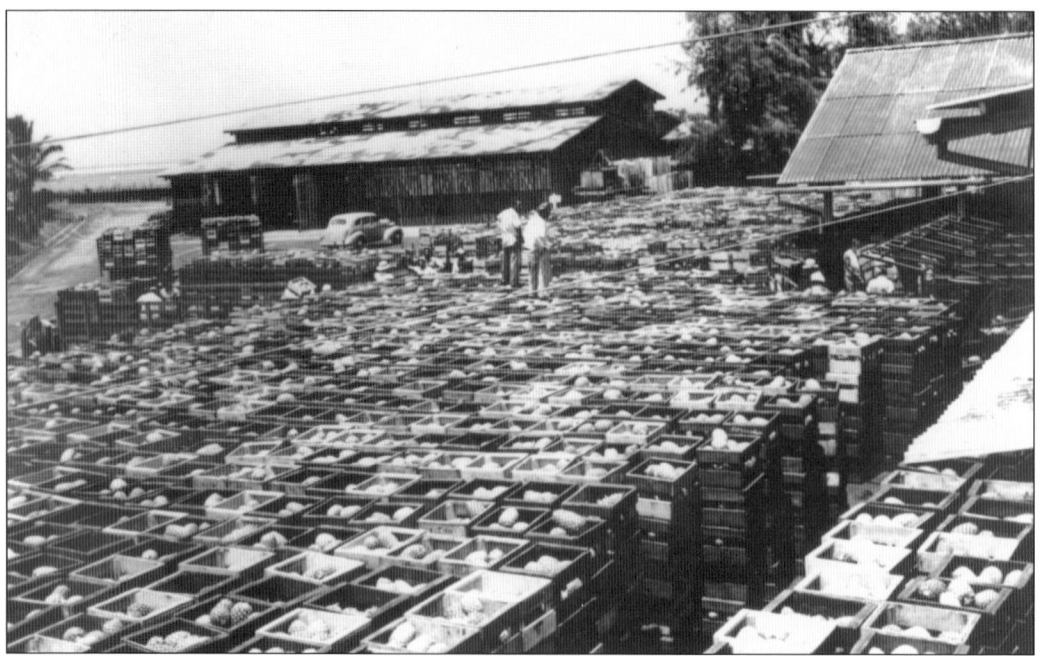

Crates of pineapples, fresh from the field, were trucked to the cannery. Here they await transfer to Ginaca machines for processing. (Courtesy of KHS.)

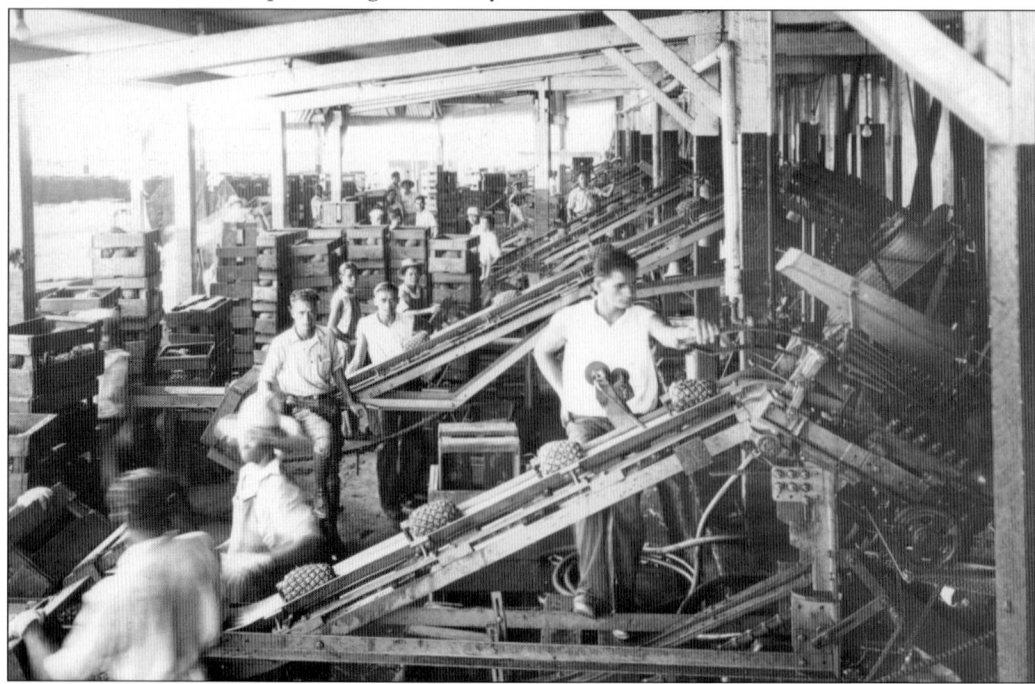

Young local summer hires place the pineapples in the slots of the Ginaca machine, which moved the freshly harvested pineapples to the conveyor belt. The Ginaca machine was invented by Henry Ginaca in the early 1900s. It sized the fruit, cut off the ends, peeled them, removed the fibrous cores, and retained crushed pineapple and juice from the skins. The machine increased production to about 50 pineapples per minute. (Courtesy of KHS.)

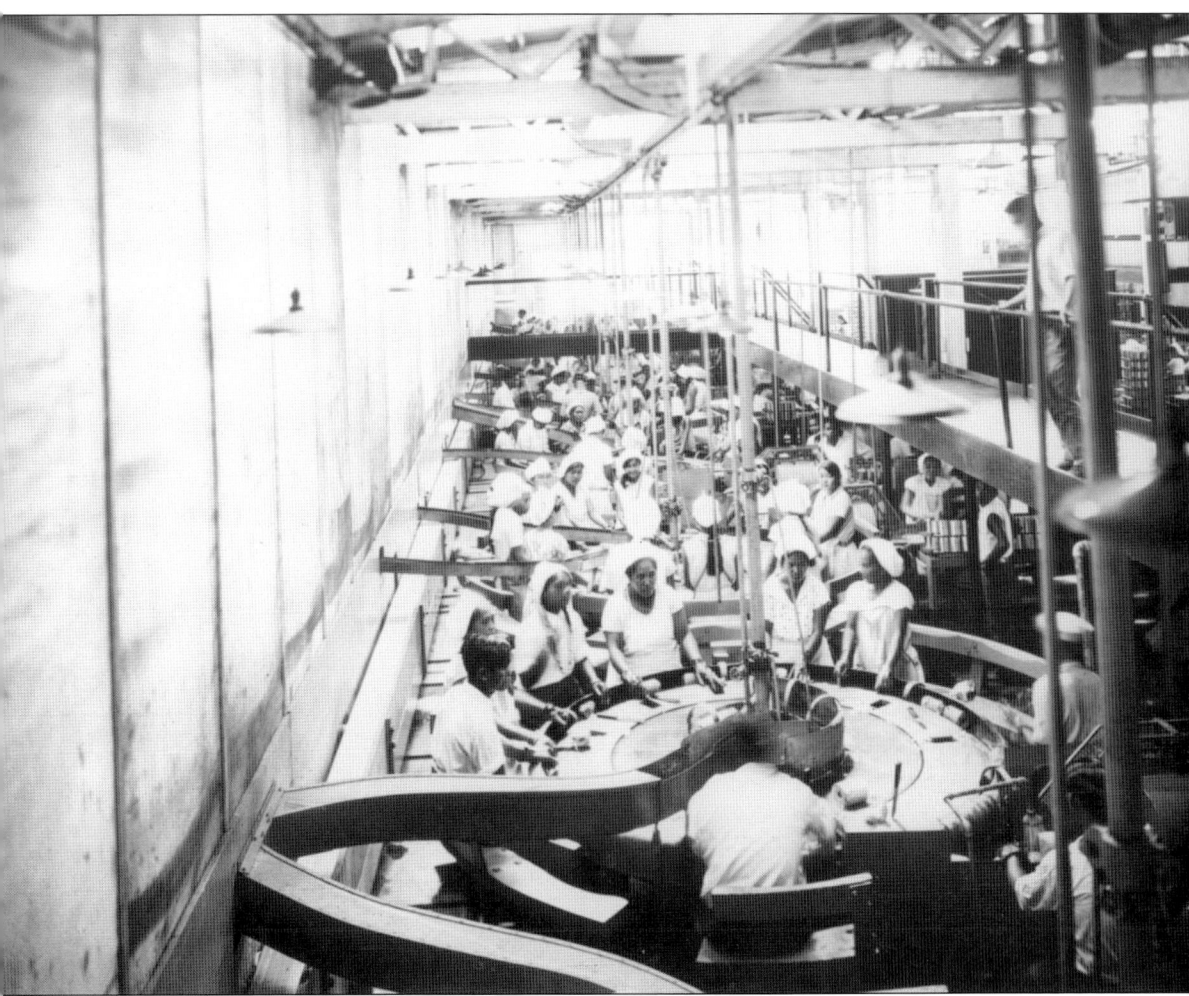
These young women are trimming the eyes and skin from pineapples that were missed by the Ginaca machine. They wear long gloves to protect their hands from the high acidity of the fruit. (Courtesy of KHS.)

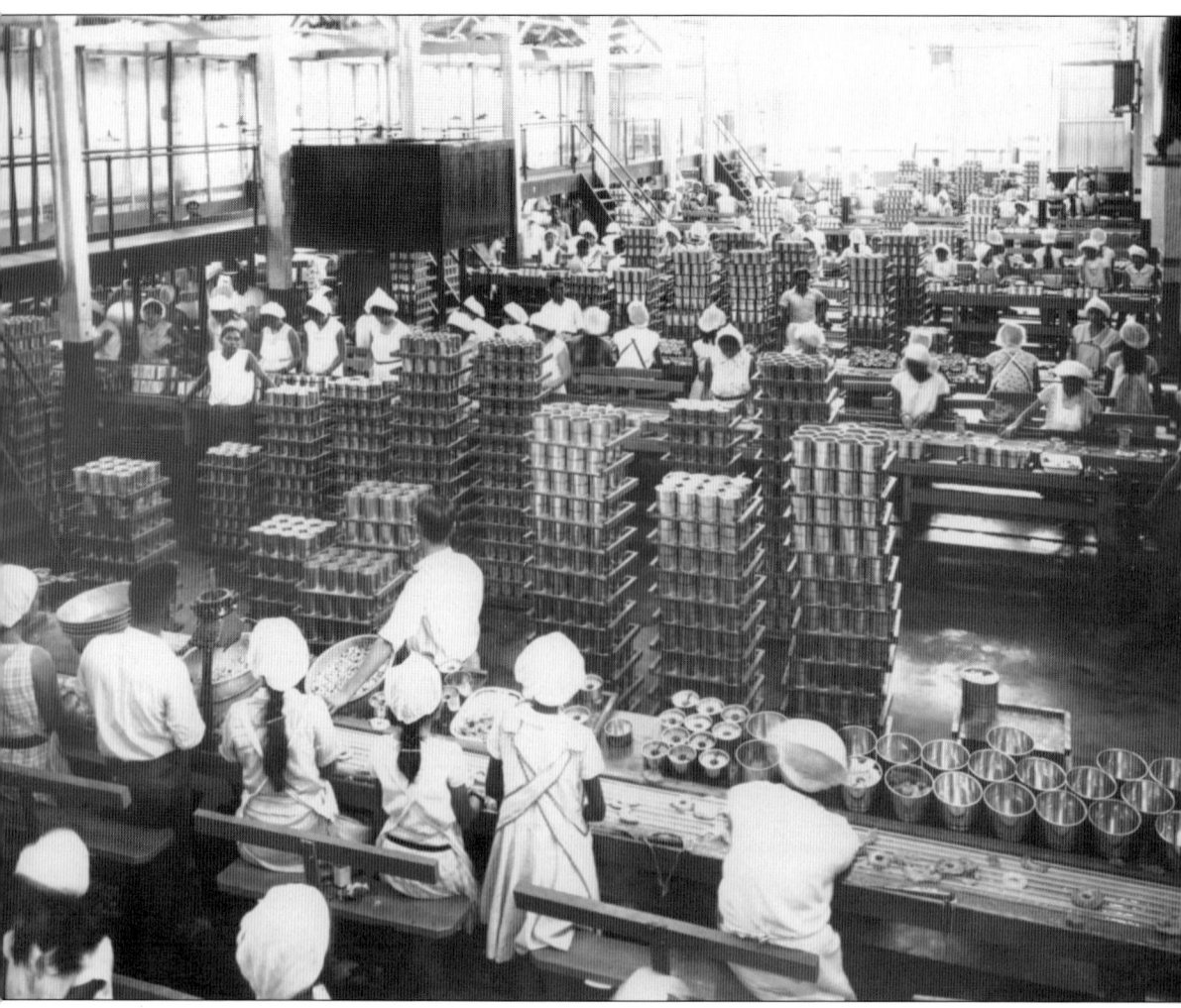

Shown here are workers at the packing tables, one of the steps in canning pineapple. The can sizes varied and came in sizes named flats, No. 2.5, and gallon. The canned pineapple varieties included slices, chunks, crushed, and tidbits. This photograph was taken around 1950. (Courtesy of Albert Fukushima.)

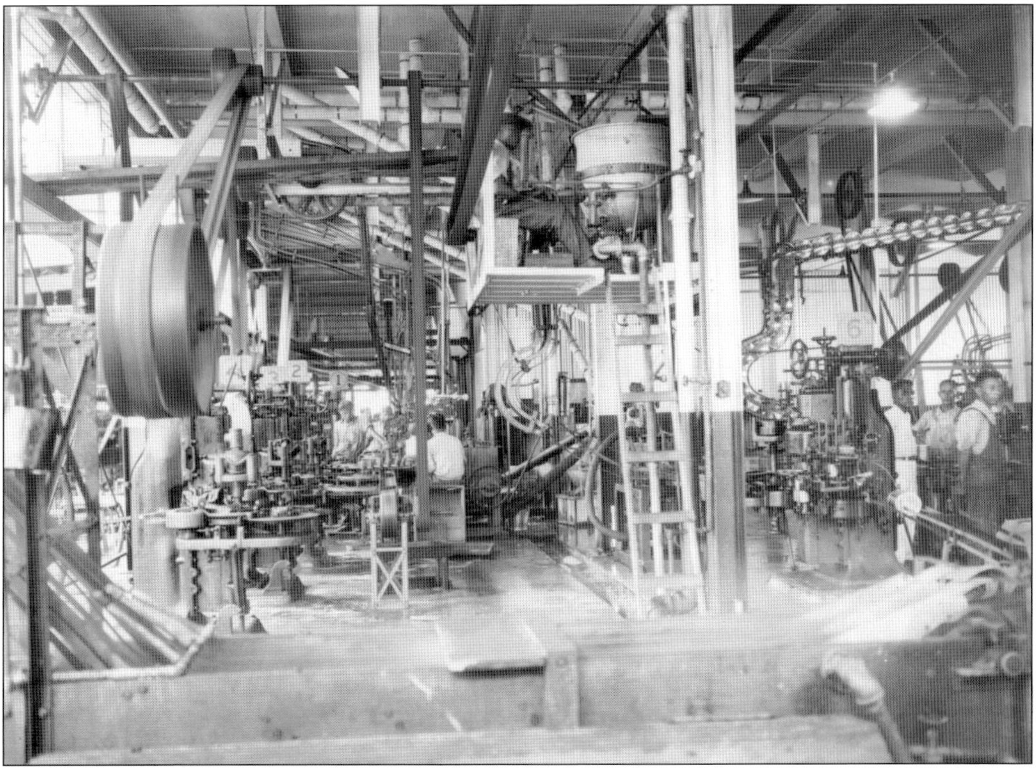

These machines sealed and labeled the pineapple cans and put them on the conveyor belt, where they were sent to the packing department. American Can Company, located in a building adjacent to the cannery, made the cans for both canneries. (Courtesy of KHS.)

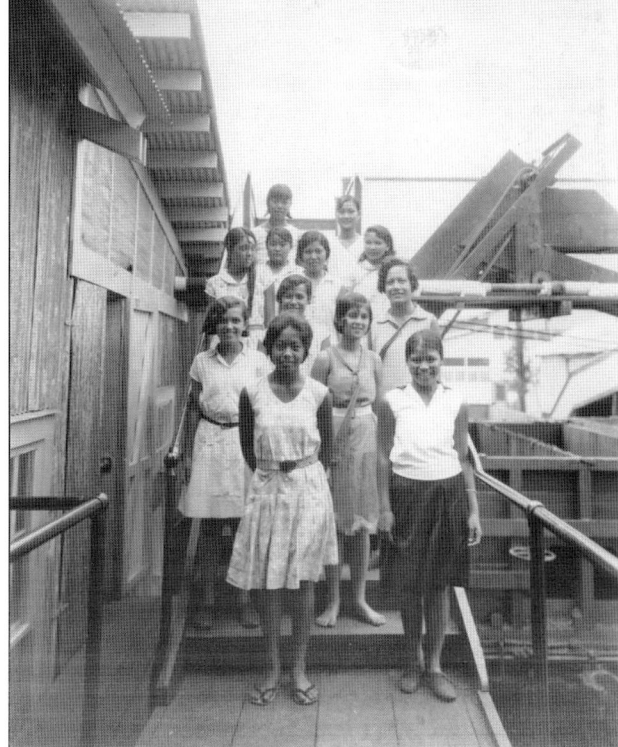

This is a photograph of high school–aged seasonal employees who worked during the summer at the cannery. (Courtesy of KHS.)

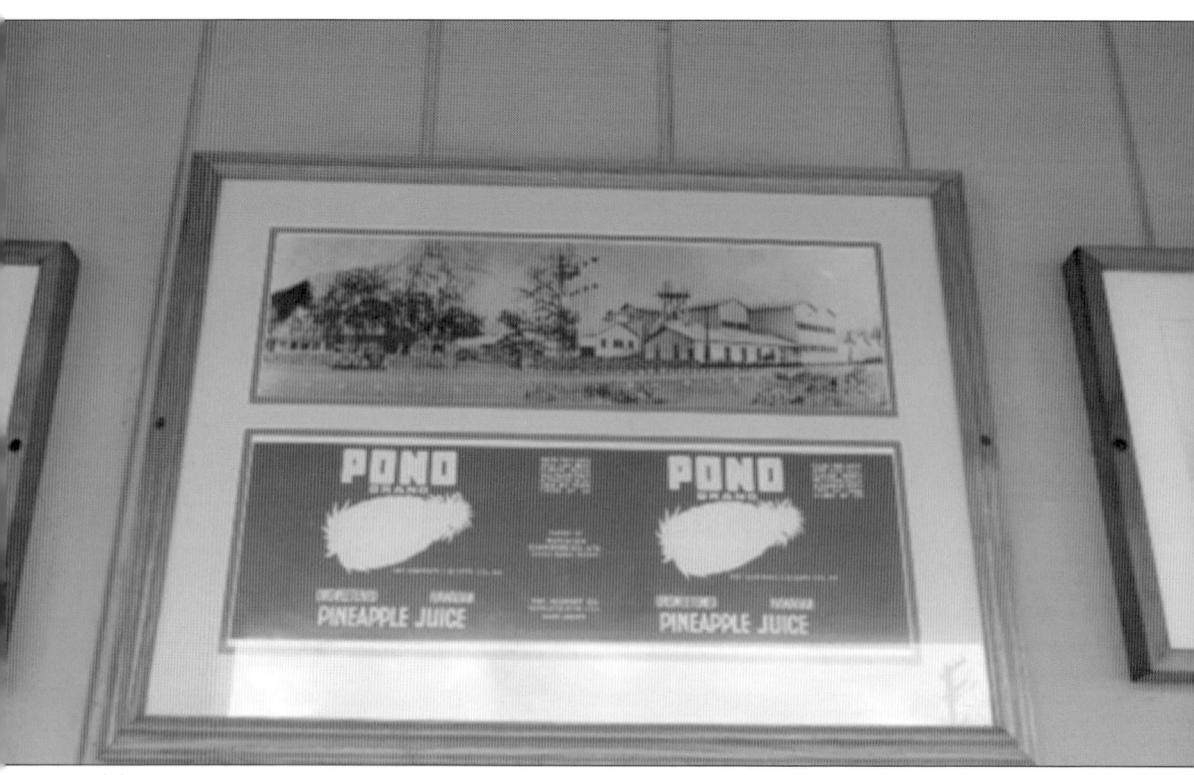

This plaque with a photograph of Hawaiian Canneries (around 1918) and a Pono label is displayed at the entrance to the Pono Kai Resort, which sits at the site of the former cannery. (Courtesy of Marta Miller Hulsman.)

# Five

# WAR YEARS 1941–1945

A giant thunderclap of war roused the people of Kapaʻa from their simple life. With the attack on Pearl Harbor in Oʻahu, fear of invasion and disloyalty replaced complacency. Kauaʻi was 40 percent Japanese. Island-wide, the military imposed the first martial law since the Civil War, three and a half years of personal and material limits, curfews, blackouts, rationing of gas, tires, and food, restricted sea access, bomb shelters, and internment. Gas masks and evacuation plans were in place if the enemy landed on undefended shores. The new (and only) Kauaʻi radio station KTOH (Kauaʻi Territory of Hawaiʻi) went off air by 1:30 p.m. on December 7, 1941.

That miserable winter brightened when thousands of men in khaki from New York arrived on Kauaʻi in April 1942, doubling the island's population. A war camp grew behind Sleeping Giant Mountain, and these men needed entertainment and came to Kapaʻa for rest and relaxation at the two movie theaters, the United Service Organization (USO), and bars. As the war receded to the west, the town rocked with sounds broadcast from the movies plus music and dancing at the USO.

The impact on Kapaʻa business was huge. Young entrepreneurs became shoeshine boys and gofers. Grocery stores and bars thrived. Restaurants opened. Local people gave back to the servicemen, as Kapaʻa families opened homes with traditional aloha hospitality.

Submarine warfare meant slower importation of goods. Kapaʻa people planted victory gardens and provided other essentials for residents. All ethnic groups shared and took care of each other, creating a sense of unity.

Despite thousands of Japanese Americans being interned in America, scores of Japanese Americans (*nisei*) from Kapaʻa volunteered to fight. Soon, Anzio, Salerno, and Monte Casino would become household words as nisei soldiers died there, proving their loyalty to America. Japanese American units became the most decorated for their size in American military history.

War woke a slumbering town from isolation. People glimpsed the great world beyond its shores. An easy-living rural community changed into a world-wise town. Its people continued to support America in future wars.

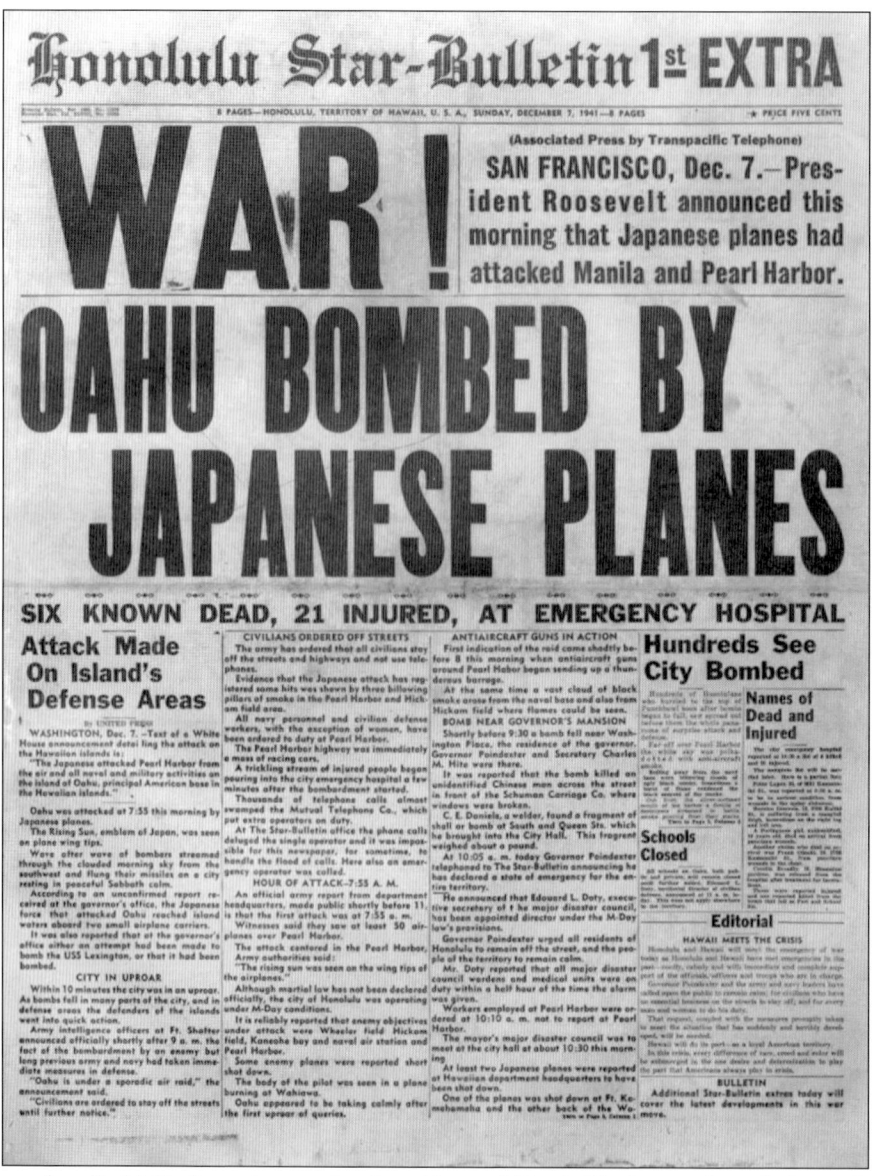

On December 7, 1941, Japan's surprise bombing of Pearl Harbor pulsated throughout the islands. KTOH announced it, describing the activation of plans made for two years by the military and Civil Defense, then went off the air. Martial law began (and lasted for three and a half years): blackouts, curfews, rationing, orders to plantations to plant food crops, weapons confiscation, monetary controls, gas masks, Red Cross activities, frozen wages, telephone calls traced, and mail censored. Men in black suits rang doorbells. People disappeared. Would Japan invade? Everyone knew what to do, went into action, and responded with determination to "work to win" despite the shock. Civil-defense director Charlie Fern praised people in *The Garden Island* for their lack of hysteria and confusion. Before the attack, he had urged people to continue their island ways—working together and not being suspicious. He repeated the advice to ignore rumors and remember island respect for all religions and cultures. Some Japanese were interned, but the overwhelming majority was not. The 1945 armistice was far away. (Courtesy of *Star Bulletin*.)

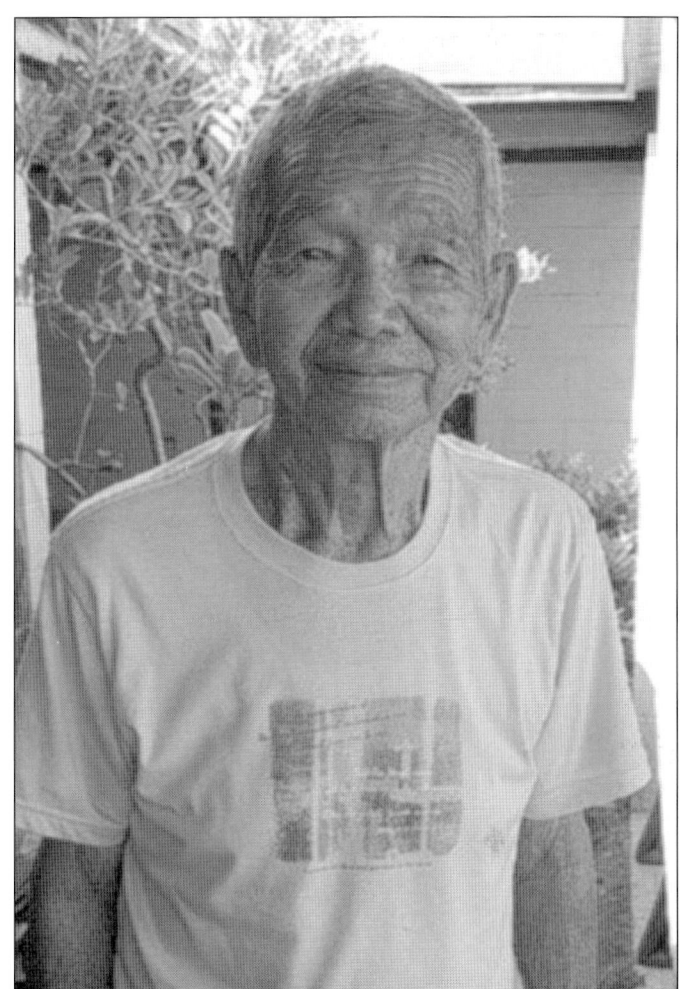

Albert Fukushima, at age 10, was fingerprinted like all other children and adults and required to carry an identity card (pictured below) at all times. Albert and friends played war right behind a real machine-gun nest. They dug their own nest, covered it with palm branches, and threw small coconuts for grenades. (Courtesy of Albert Fukushima.)

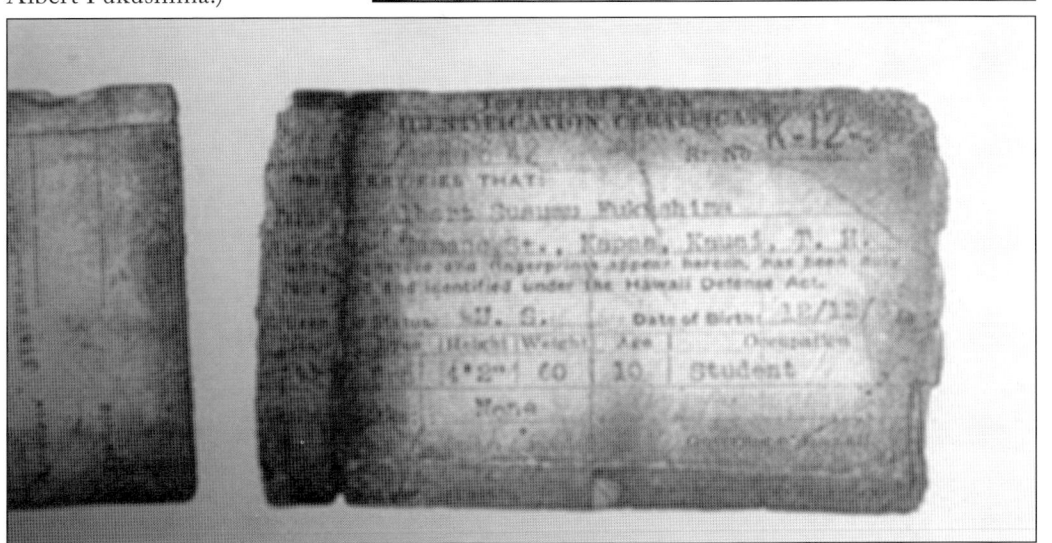

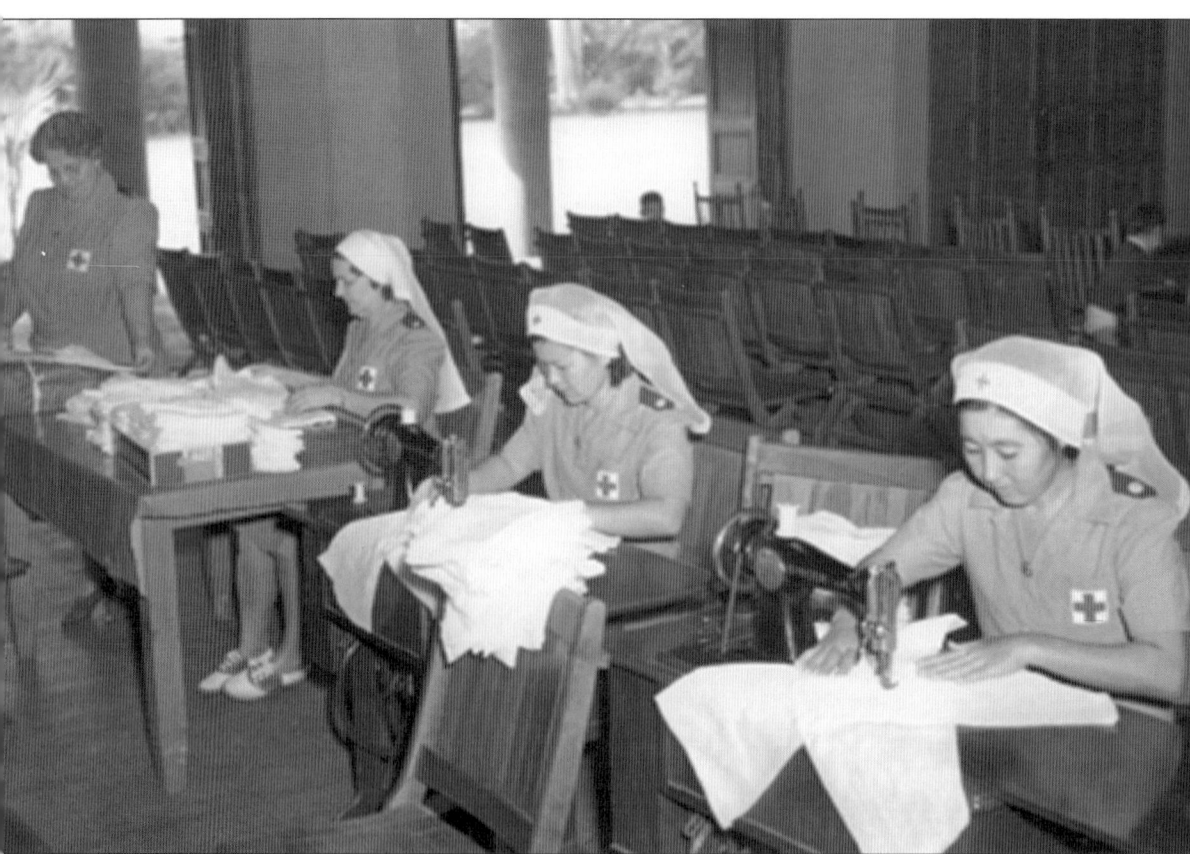

People eagerly volunteered and bought US war bonds. Red Cross volunteers swung into action after training for months making bandages and other preparations. The civil defense "just in case" course of preparations, should war occur, had practiced air-raid drills and blackouts. People collected metal and tires for military-machine manufacturing. Tire ownership was limited to five. The war unified people working for a purpose. (Courtesy of KHS.)

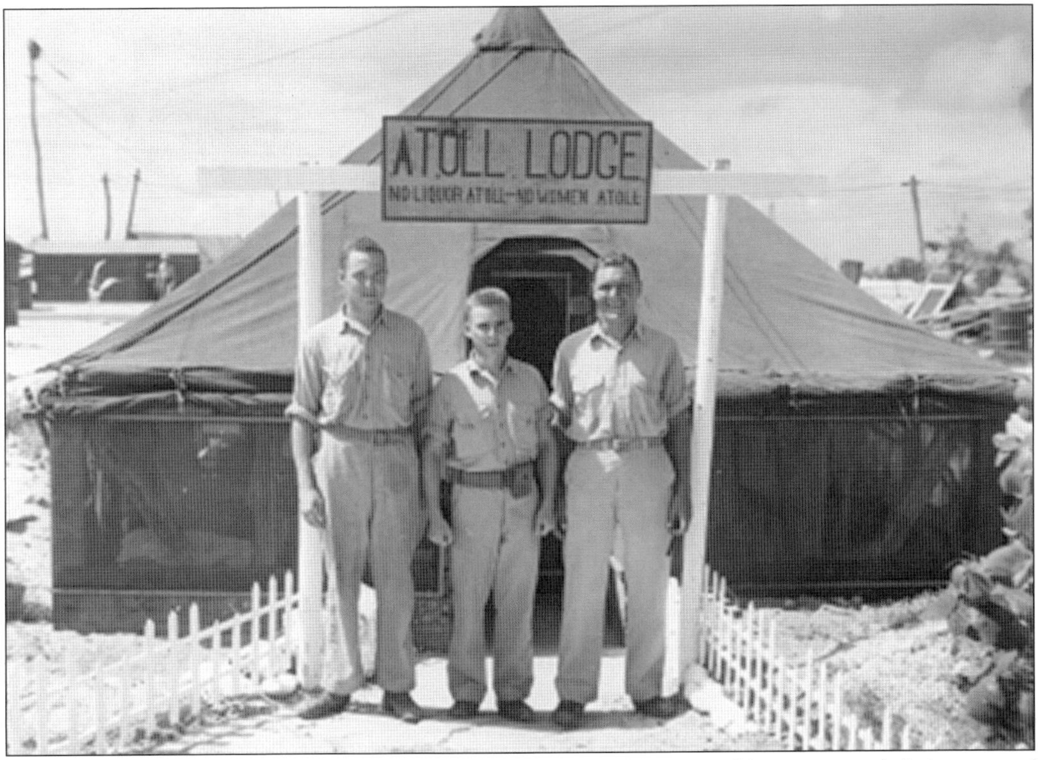

Although war is grim, and military life in the field is unpleasant, soldiers retained their sense of humor. Most were young, barely 18 years old. Many seemed surprised that Kaua'i people were US citizens. At first, they treated the local Asian people harshly but later showed a modicum of respect to the Chinese and Filipino because they were allies. Below is a photograph of the Roxy, the location of many soldiers' entertainment. The Army brought in busloads of soldiers to enjoy the Roxy and Pono Theaters, the USO, and bars like the Blue Lei—good food, beer, and dancing with local young ladies. This photograph depicts the Roxy with soldiers and shoeshine boys on the far left. (Above, courtesy of KHS; below, courtesy of Bill Fernandez.)

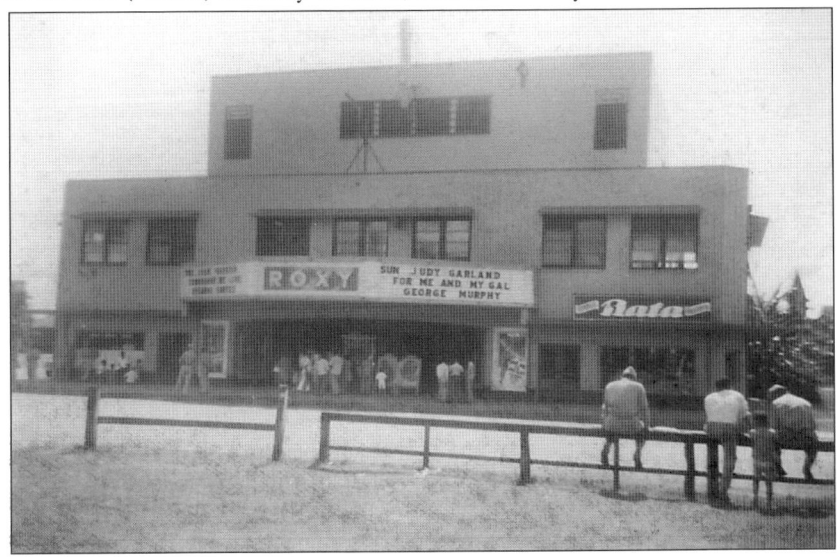

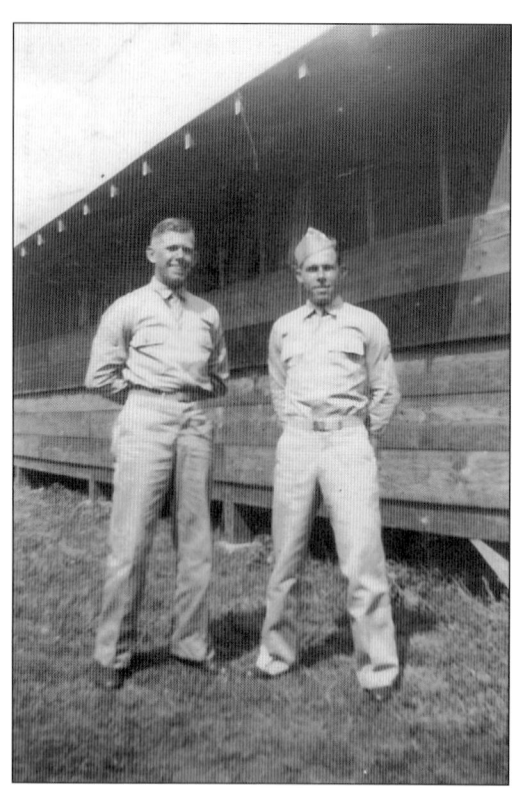

In April 1942, New York's Fighting 69th soldiers arrived for defense and training. Kapaʻa people, mostly Asian and Hawaiian, had little experience with *haʻoles*. One recalled it was the first time a white man treated him nicely. Soldiers created beach defenses: bunkers, machine-gun nests, and barbed wire. Locals extended aloha with food and friendship. Children shined shoes, became gofers, imitated soldiers, and learned about American life. (Both, courtesy of William Fernandez.)

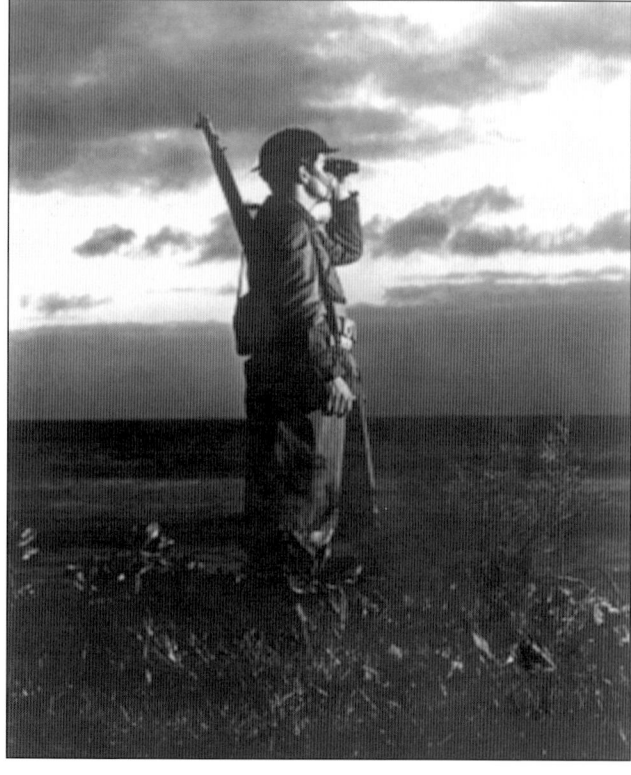

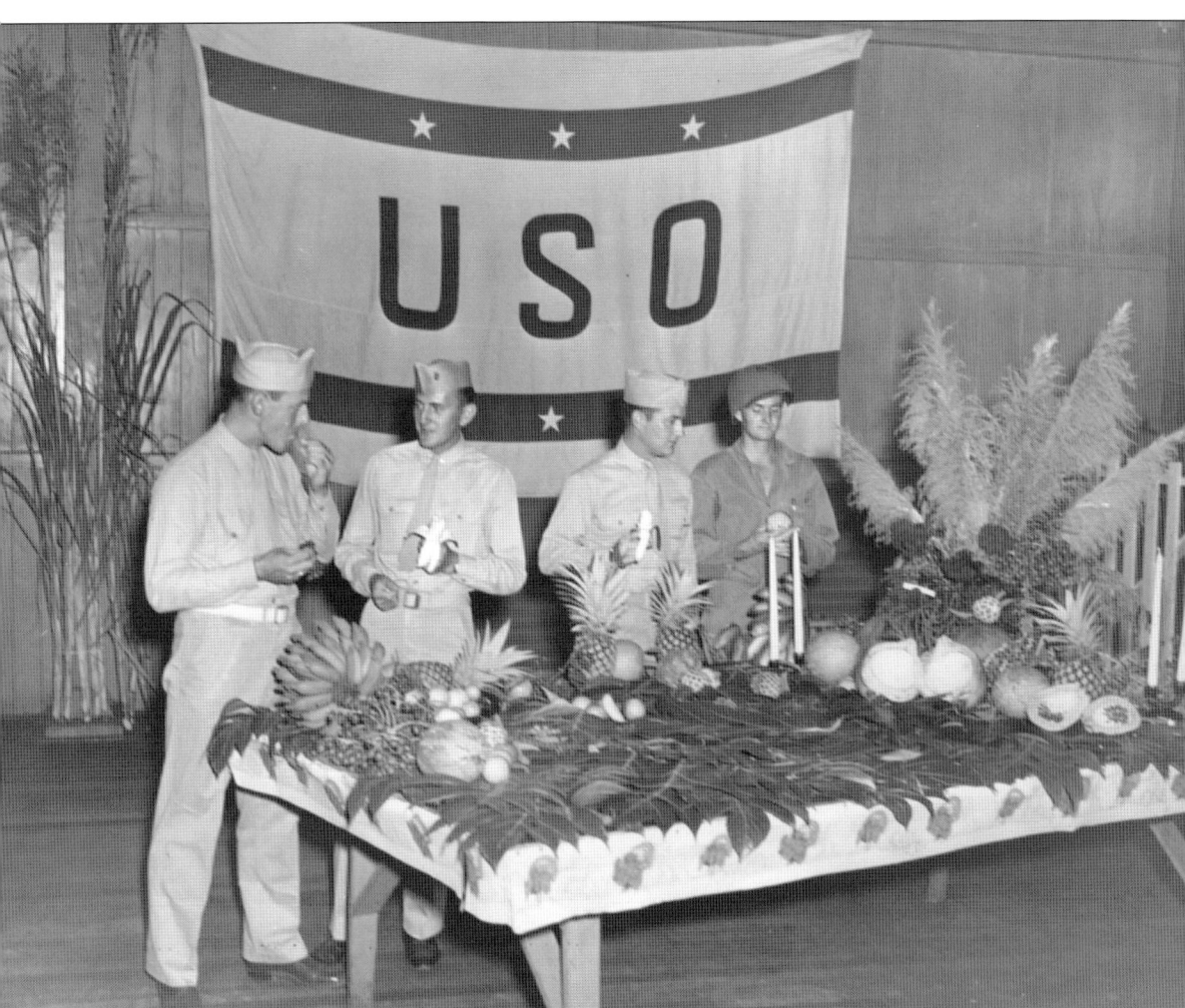

The USO mission "to lift the spirits of our troops and their families" was led by its director, Elsie Wilcox, from a prominent family. The lounges, food, entertainment, social events, organized sports teams, and contests raised morale. World-class performers like Bob Hope came to entertain soldiers. Townspeople saw movie stars they could only dream of seeing in person. The USO continues this proud tradition of helping members of the services and their families. They can be found in most major airports. (Courtesy of *The Garden Island*.)

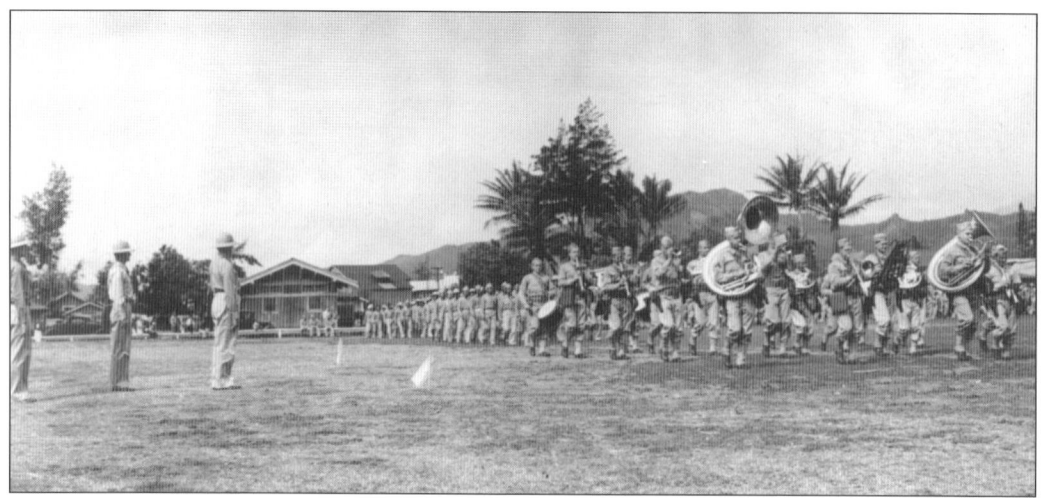

Local men, draftees and volunteers, parade in Kapaʻa Park led by the Army band. Scores of local men fought for America around the world. Many nisei served in the Military Intelligence Service as interpreters, interrogators, and translators. The language skills of the Japanese American men were described as cutting the war short by two years. Nisei women served in the women's military branches in clerical and nursing work. (Courtesy of KHS.)

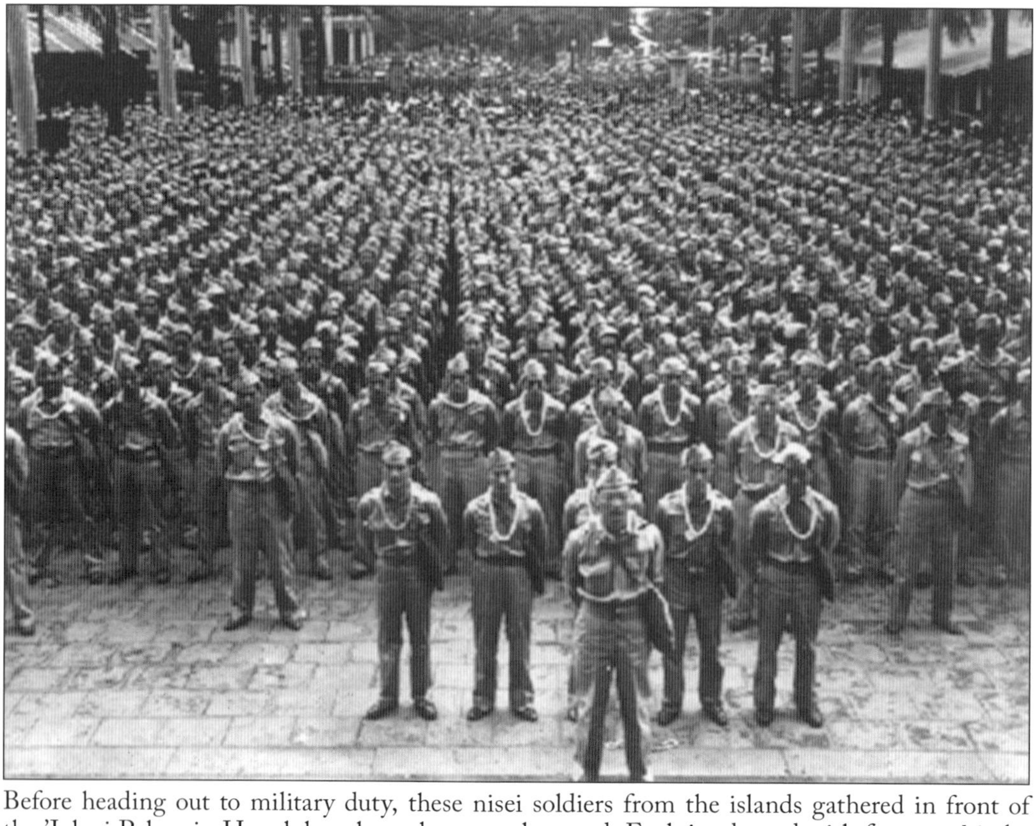

Before heading out to military duty, these nisei soldiers from the islands gathered in front of the ʻIolani Palace in Honolulu, where they were honored. Each is adorned with fragrant *lei*, the Hawaiian custom when greeting or saying goodbye. The palace was the site of the American overthrow of the Hawaiian monarch Queen Liliʻuokalani in 1893. (Courtesy of Go For Broke.)

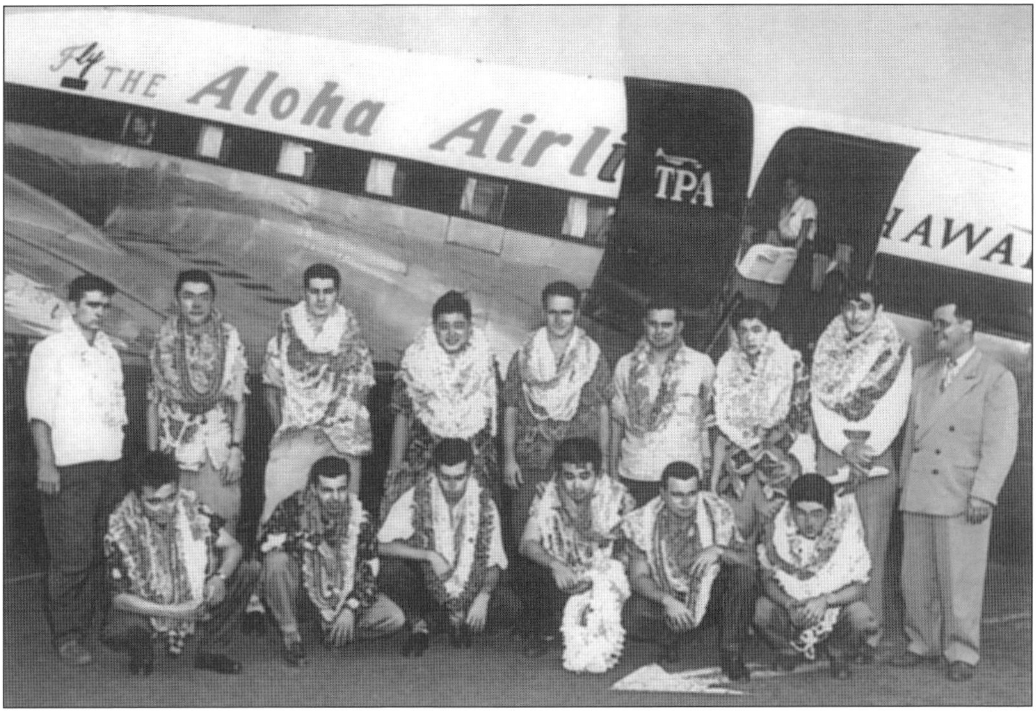

War did not end with the surrender of the Axis powers. Five years later, Kapa'a men were drafted for the Korean War. Pictured here in the first row are Abraham Machado (second from left), Joe Arruda (third from left), Albert Tokigawa (second from right), and Kaua'i mayor Antone Baptiste. George Kojima is fourth from left in the second row. The others are unidentified. In typical island fashion, they are covered with leis. Fortunately, no other wars brought martial law or military occupation to the island. By the 1960s, Kapa'a men were drafted for the Vietnam War. The US Army, 4th Platoon, All Kaua'i completed basic training in Fort Ord, California. Kapa'a draftees pictured below include Brian Atendido, Hughes Ebinger, Michael Hama, James Kaui, Joseph Kauanui, David Mawae, Robert Paik, Felix Primero, Richard Ramones, William Sanchez, and Duane Souza. All survived. Tours of duty were usually one year. (Above, courtesy of Ernest Palmeira; below, courtesy of Robert Paik.)

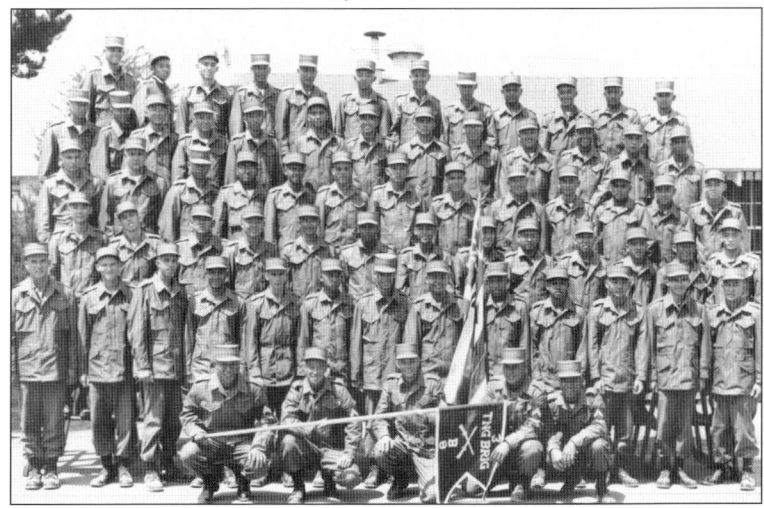

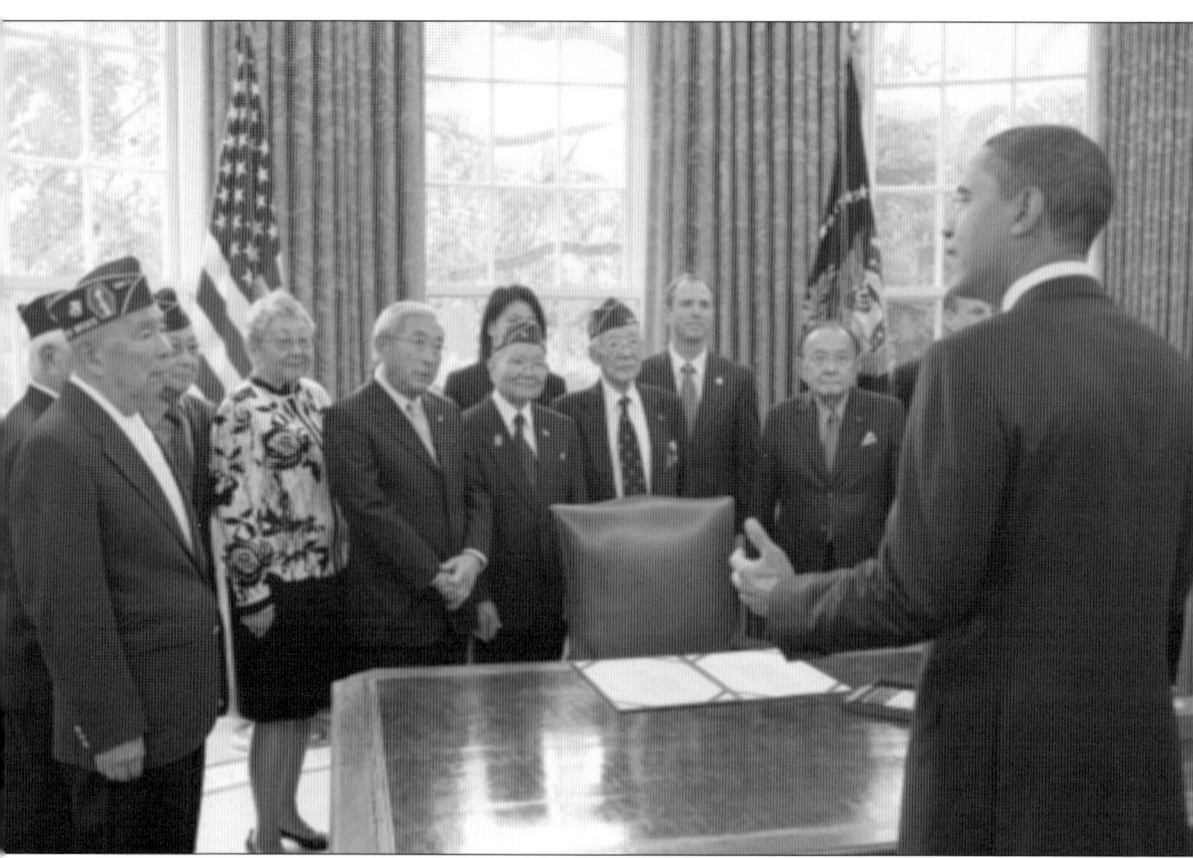

The US Congressional Gold Medal recognizes and honors those who perform an outstanding deed or act of service for the United States, the highest civilian award in America. In 2010, President Obama signed a bill awarding it to the US Army's volunteer nisei, the 100th Infantry Battalion, the 442nd Regimental Combat Team, and the Military Intelligence Service, for their extraordinary accomplishments. The approximately 18,000 soldiers of Japanese ancestry came from the Territory of Hawai'i and the continent, serving in both Europe and Asia despite America's internment of over 120,000 of their community and family in guarded camps. Their slogan "Go For Broke" meant they would take great risks to prove their loyalty and intended to fight to their deaths. Kapa'a men served with uncommon bravery and loyalty in these units. The medals and their stories toured American museums, honoring these brave men. Congressman Adam Schiff introduced the House bill with the following words: "Man for man they were the most highly decorated combat units of the war. I can't imagine a group more deserving of Congress' highest honor." (Courtesy of whitehouse.gov.)

# Six

# CHURCHES

Traditional Hawaiian religious practices were supplanted by the introduction of Christianity to Kaua'i in the 1820s by Congregational missionaries from New England and the conversion of the Hawaiian monarchs. On Kaua'i, Queen Deborah Kapule was an early convert and established the first Christian church in Kapa'a in 1836.

Other Christian denominations followed, including Catholics, Methodists, Episcopalians, and the Church of Jesus Christ of Latter-day Saints. All of these religious communities initially held services and study in people's homes. As the town grew and prospered, so did these religions. By the early 1900s, most of the major Christian churches had consolidated their followers, procured land, and raised the necessary funds to build permanent churches in town.

With the arrival of the immigrants came a diversity of religious practices. The Portuguese and Filipino brought Catholicism. The Chinese, Koreans, and Japanese introduced Buddhism and Taoism. Like the early Christians, early services were held in camps and in the houses of the faithful, until the congregation could afford more permanent sites. The Japanese, especially the Buddhist community, raised funds to send ministers from Japan to perform the all-important rituals surrounding the deceased. They also functioned as language teachers to ensure that the children would understand the Buddhist teachings and help preserve the culture.

Today, Kapa'a is host to many religious institutions, a reflection of the ethnic and religious diversity that has evolved over the years. Churches today not only serve the spiritual needs of the congregation, but many provide much-needed social services.

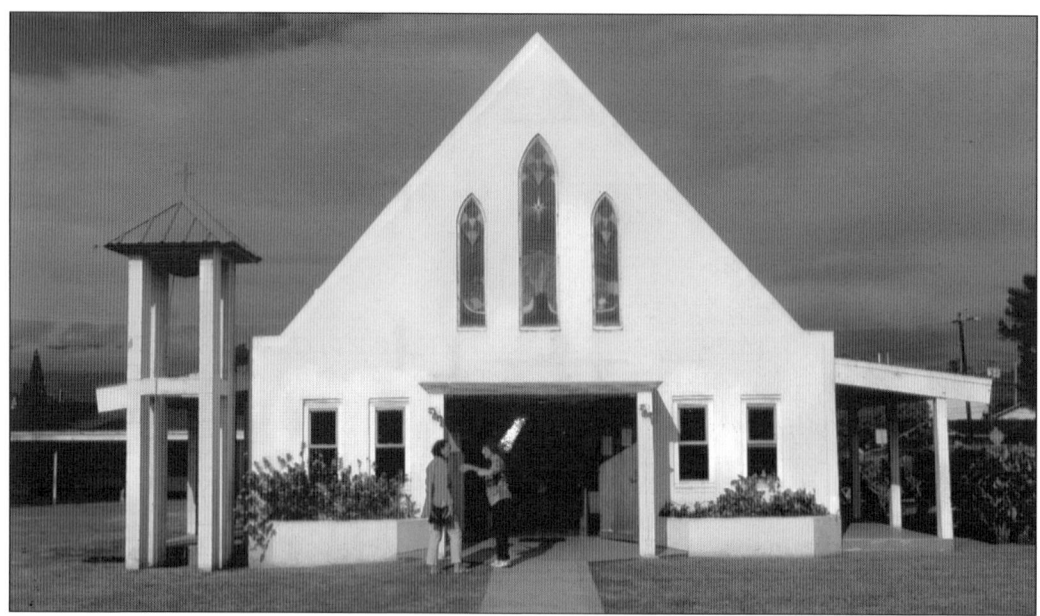

Kauai's Queen Deborah Kapule, wife of Kaumuali'i, King of Kaua'i, established the Kapa'a First Hawaiian Church in 1836 on the grounds of the former Coco Palms Hotel in Wailua. Known as Luakini O Mo'ikeha after a chief, the church was initially built for the ali'i, with the commoners not allowed inside. This was the first Christian church in the area. The original grass-hut church was replaced with a wooden building, and in 1880 it was dismantled and moved two and a half miles to its present site in the middle of Kapa'a town. In 1948, a new building was dedicated and a multipurpose center completed in 1967. Queen Kapule, knowing her people's love of singing, permitted the commoners to stand along the side of the church to sing and chant with the ali'i. (Above, courtesy of Clyde Furumoto; below, courtesy of Kapa'a First Hawaiian Church.)

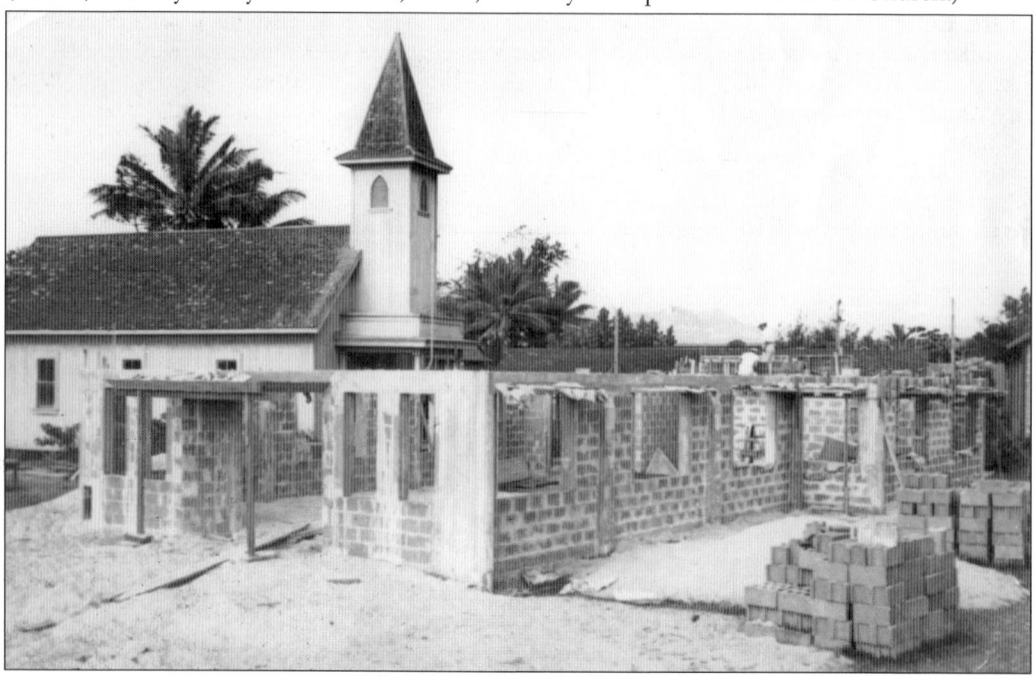

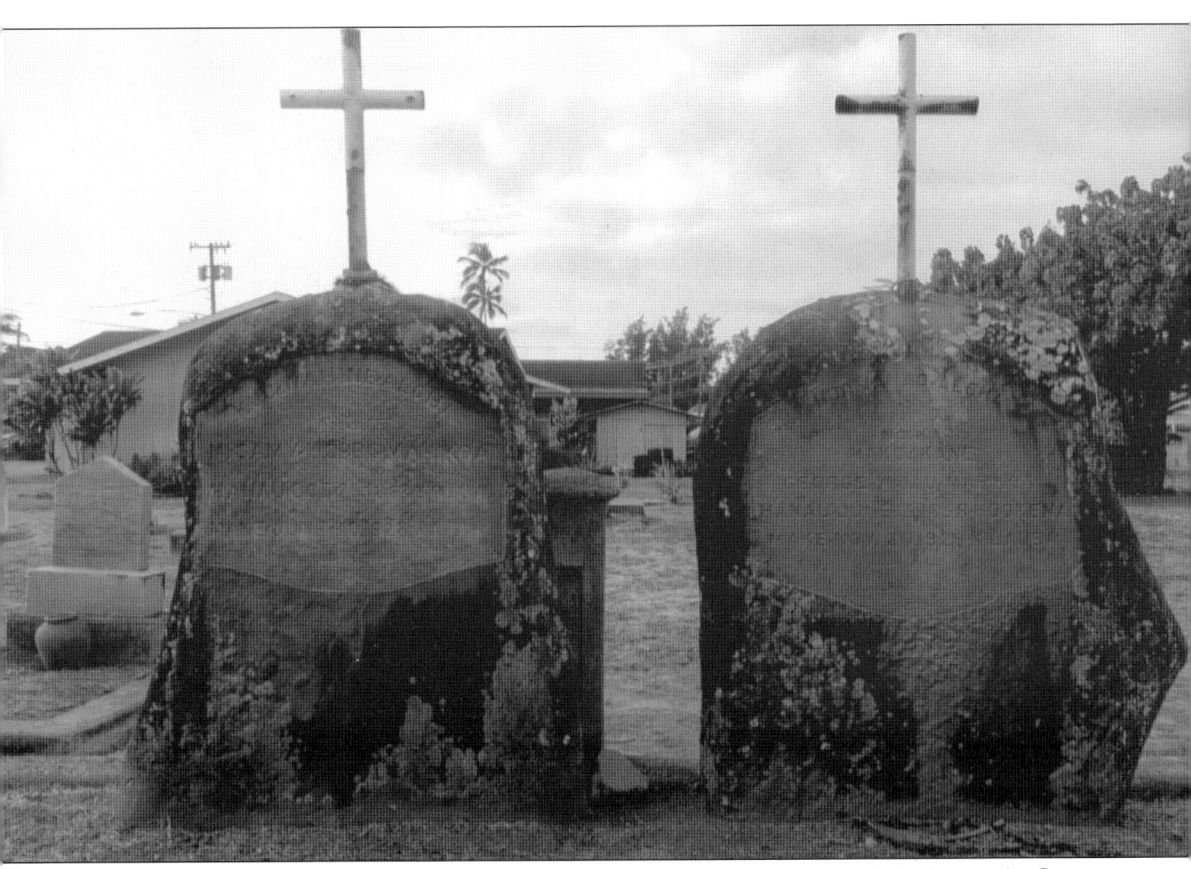

The Kapaʻa First Hawaiian Church and its adjoining graveyard were established in 1853. Some of the earliest marked gravestones date to the 1890s. The left headstone is for Amy Hobbs Mahikoa, *Kuu Wahine Aloha* (beloved wife), who was *hanau* (born) on October 25, 1888, in Koloa and *make* (died) June 30, 1928, in Kapaʻa. The right headstone is for George Waiau Mohikoa, *Hoomanao Aloha Na Ka makua Kane* (fond memories of our father), who was hanau on June 5, 1858, in Hookena and make on November 20, 1929, in Kilauea. Some of the other early church family members were Opio, Puailihau Mahikoa, Kauai, Kaiu, Kon, Kodama, Cummings, Kane, Ah Chong, Kaleiohi, Haʻae, Mundon Kaʻauwai, Hepa, Kiʻilau, Keahi, and Kealoha. (Courtesy of Clyde Furumoto.)

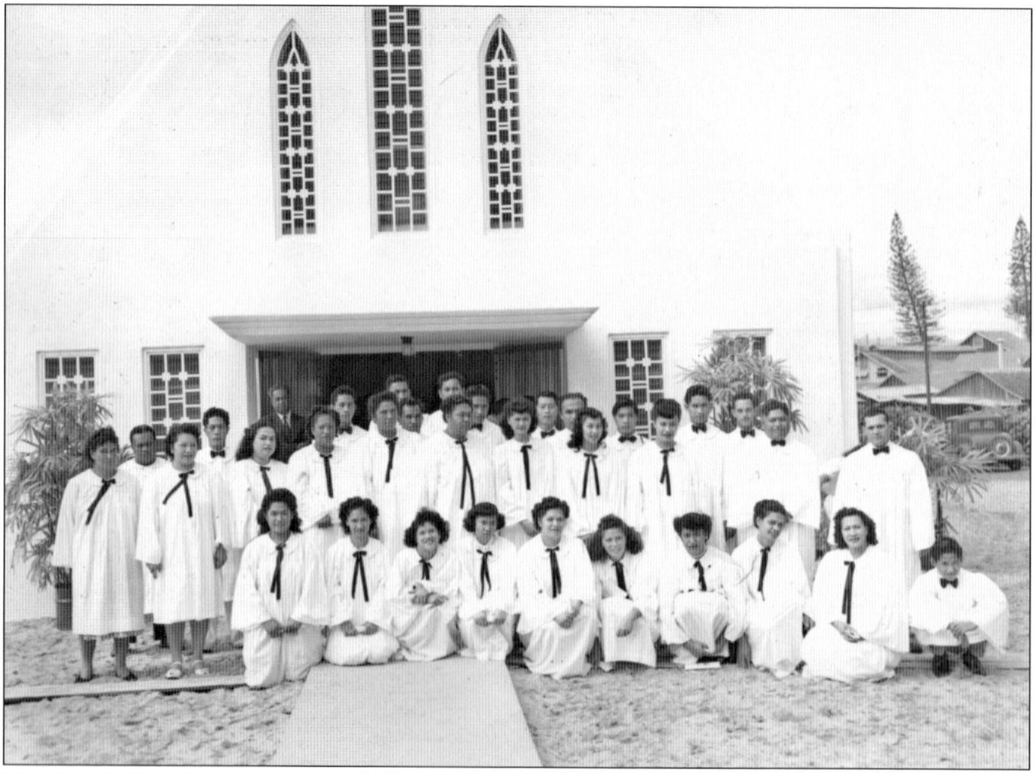

The Kapa'a First Hawaiian Church choir is pictured at the dedication of the new church building in 1948. The church has a rich history of conducting services in both Hawaiian and English. It is open to people of all ethnic backgrounds. (Courtesy of Kapa'a First Hawaiian Church.)

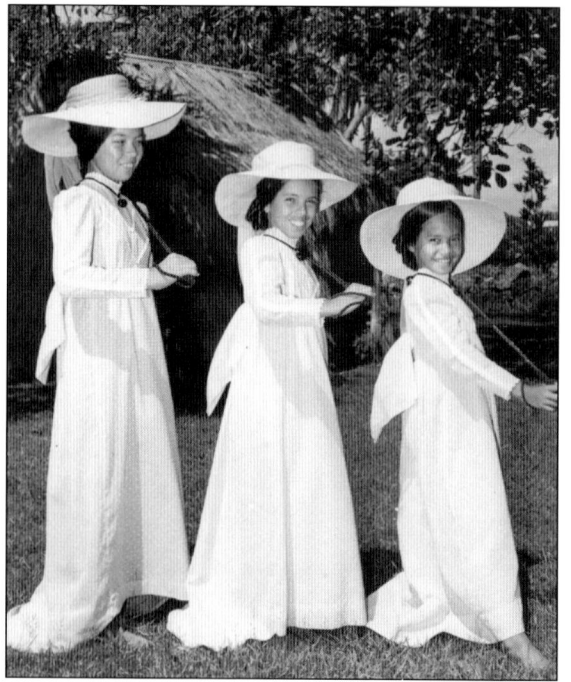

The church served the community in many ways beyond its religious obligations. It provided space for community meetings, classes, and recreation, and continues to do so to this day. Uncle Joseph Kamoka'i Kahoulelio, Kumu Hula, taught at the Kapa'a First Hawaiian Church and later at St. Catherine's Church for many years. His students, pictured here in traditional *holoku*, are, from left to right, Tammy Miner, Ginger Kaneakua, and Helene Kahaunaele. The *halau* (school) performed at various community events, including May Day celebrations. (Courtesy of Helene Kahaunaele-Akiona.)

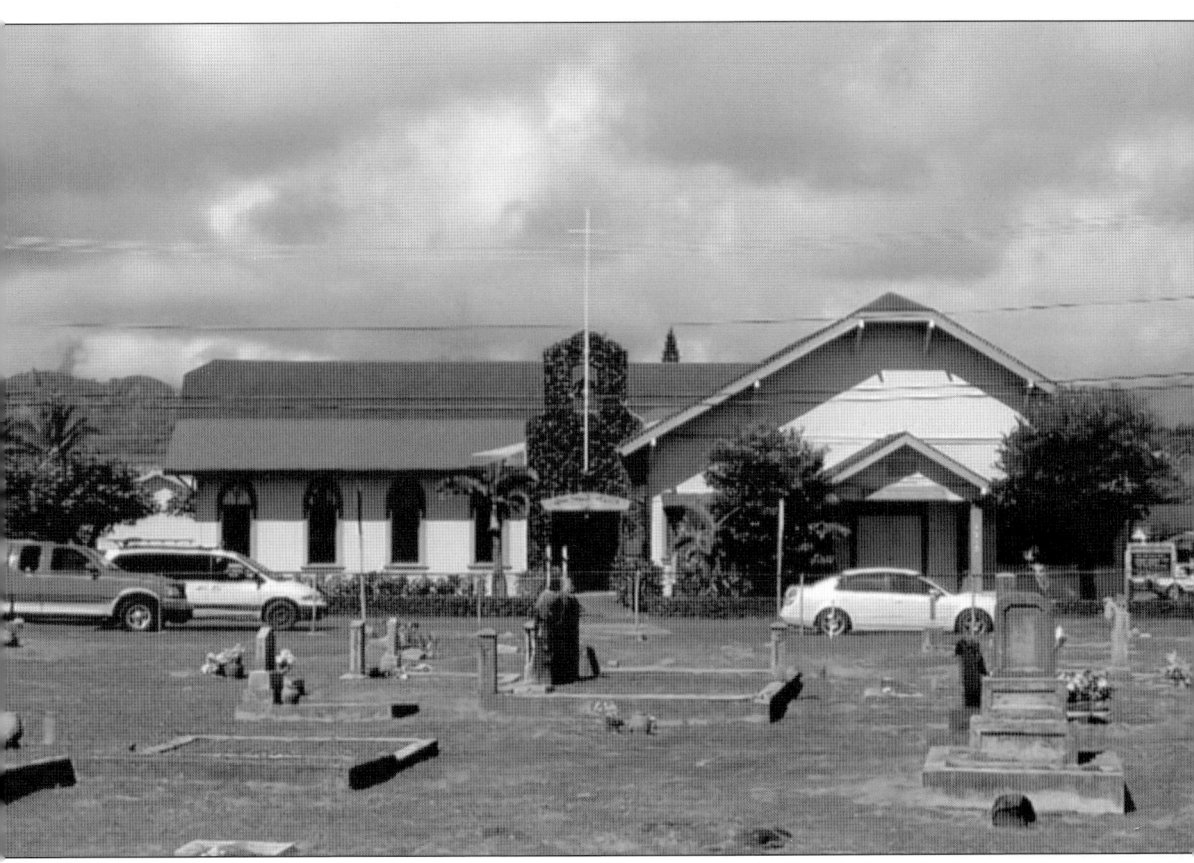

The Rev. Henry Gengo Wakai pioneered the Christian ministry to the Japanese people of Kapaʻa. He and his wife, Ryu, arrived in Hawaii from Hiroshima in 1921. Since there was no church building, services were held in the parsonage and at Kealia, Anahola, Koʻolau, and Kilauea. Reverend Wakai taught at Japanese-language schools on Kauaʻi and established the Japanese Congregational Church in Kapaʻa. He and his family were interned at a relocation center in the mainland for the duration of World War II. He returned to Hawaiʻi as minister, missionary, and teacher. He worked to build the congregation of the Kapaʻa Japanese Christian Church. In 1927, the church was officially organized and consolidated and the present-day building dedicated in 1929. Today it is known as the Kapaʻa United Church of Christ. The church works in conjunction with the Kapaʻa First Hawaiian Church, across the street, in providing community-outreach social-service programs. (Courtesy of Marta Miller Hulsman.)

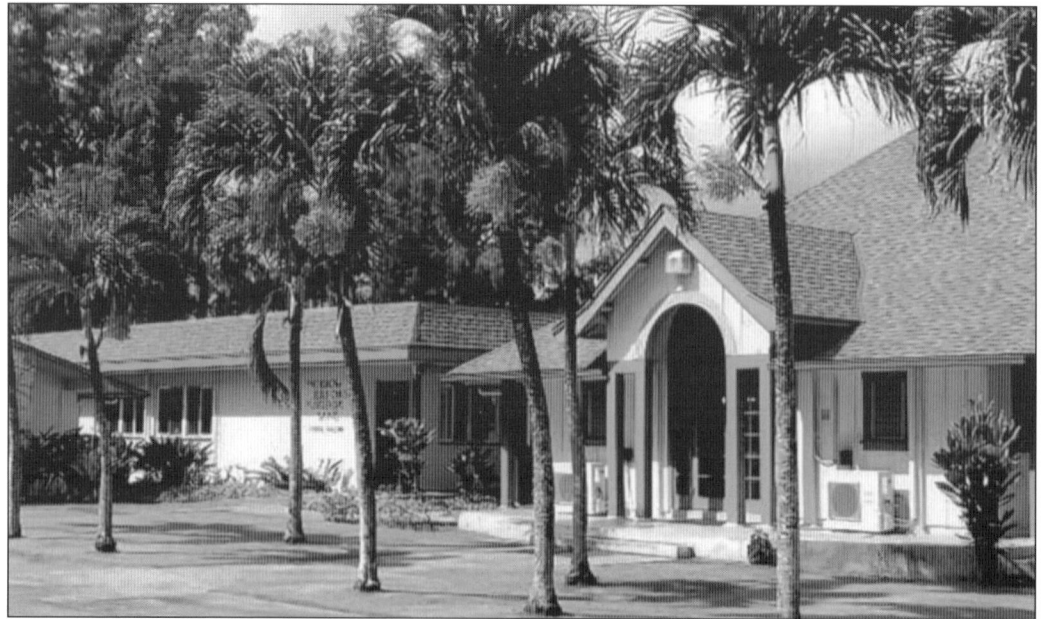

The land for the first Church of Jesus Christ of Latter-day Saints chapel, located across from the present-day Pono Kai Resort, was acquired in the early 1900s. The first chapel was completed in 1912. In 1932, a replacement chapel, as pictured here, was built. It was designed by Robert Brooks Taylor, who was the engineer at the Hawaiian Canneries. He also designed the Seto Store building in town. (Courtesy of Albert Fukushima.)

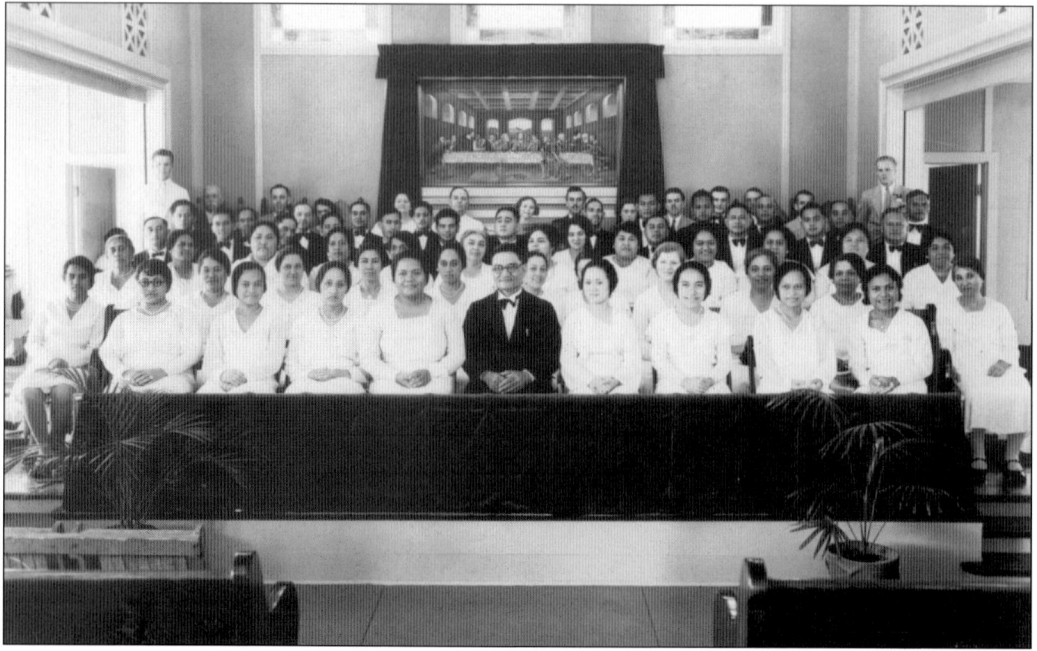

The Kapaʻa Church of Jesus Christ of Latter-day Saints celebrated the opening of their new building in 1932. At that service, these choir members participated in the musical celebration. The choir served the church and, with the growth of tourism, the community, by performing regularly at Coco Palms Hotel. (Courtesy of KHS.)

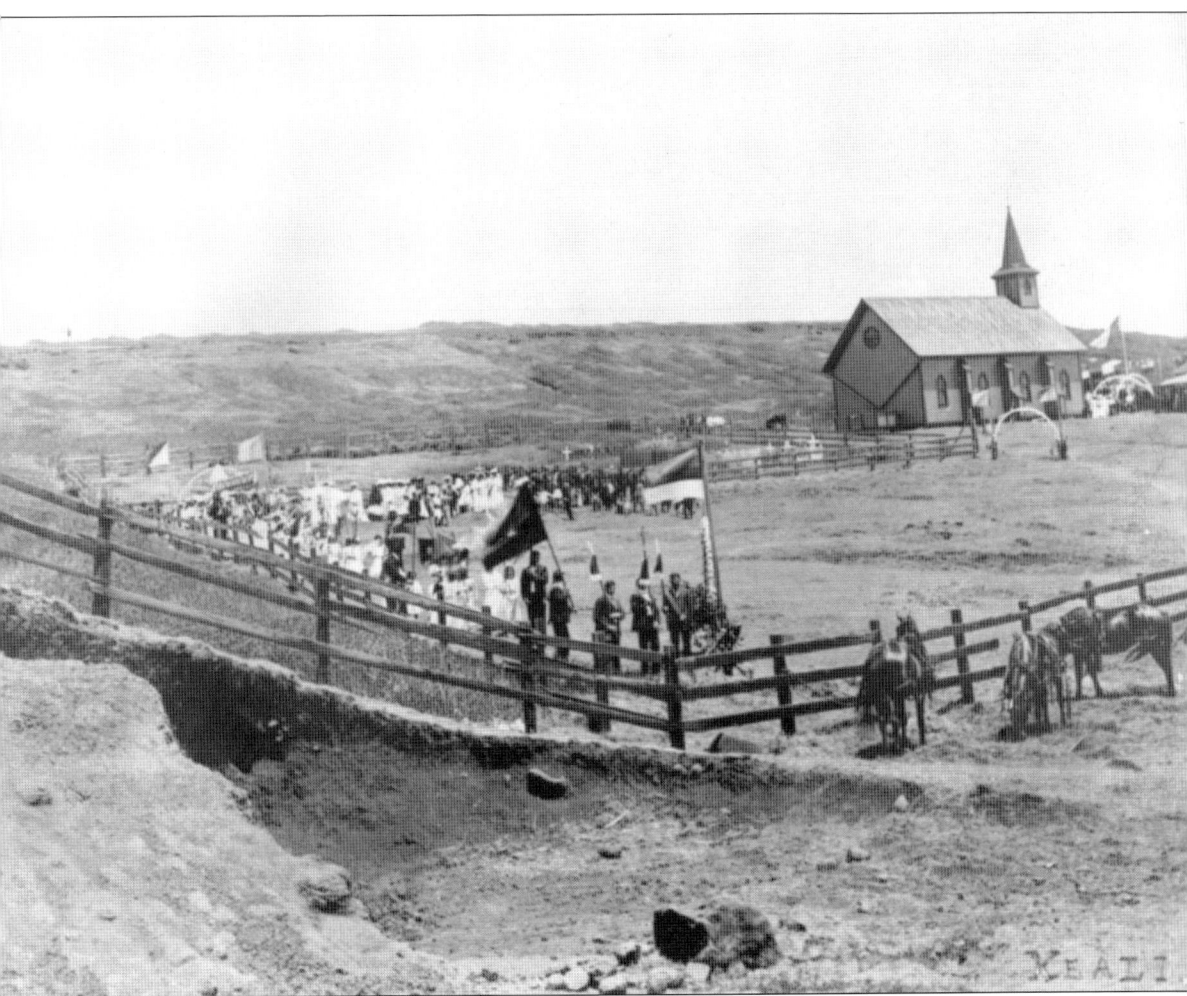

This Holy Ghost Feast procession was celebrated by Portuguese immigrants at St. Catherine's Catholic Church in Kealia in the late 1800s. The church was built and dedicated in 1887 on scenic property overlooking Kealia Bay. The land and materials were donated by the Makee Sugar Company, with plantation workers providing the labor. Father Emmeran Schulte designed the Gothic wooden structure with three abutments on each side supporting the high-vaulted interior. In the foreground is the beginning of the cemetery. The landscape lacked vegetation, a result of cutting trees for firewood, overgrazing, and the limited amount of plant life at the time. The original church has undergone major changes in its 71-year history. In 1932 and 1938, side wings were added to increase the seating capacity of the church. Church growth was affected by the Hawai'i Sugar Planters' Association recruiting workers in large numbers from the Philippines. Many Filipino were devout Catholics, and worshipped at St. Catherine's and the two mission churches, St. Sylvester's at Kilauea and St. William's at Hanalei. (Courtesy of St. Catherine's Church.)

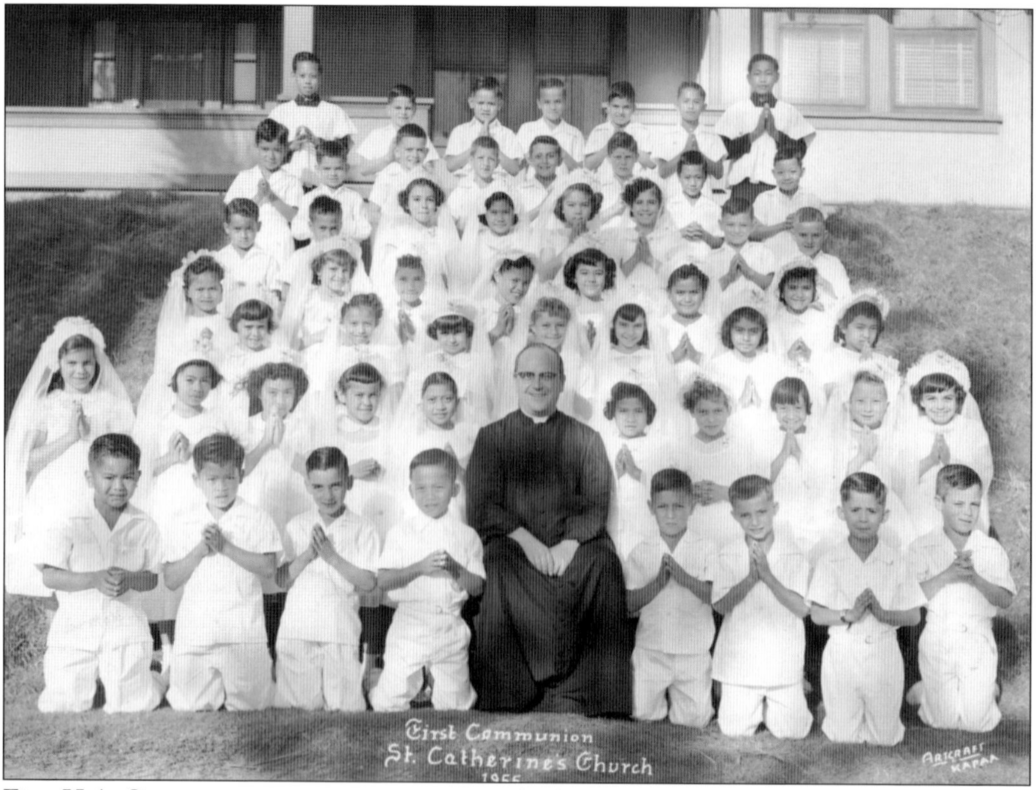

First Holy Communion was a joyous occasion for St. Catherine's families. This photograph of the First Communion class of 1955 was taken in May on the steps above the original church leading to the rectory. Today, the old church site is part of the cemetery. The students were second graders from St. Catherine's School and third graders from Kapaʻa Elementary. Father Thomas J. Hughes served the parish for many years and was well respected and loved by the community. (Courtesy of Linda Ornellas Kaialoa.)

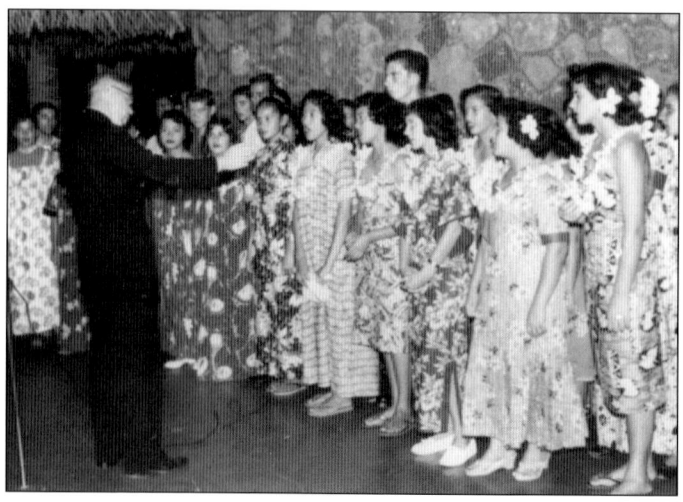

In the fall of 1955, with the help of the famous von Trapp Family Singers of the movie *The Sound of Music*, Father John McDonald organized a choir to fulfill the duties of a parish. Composed primarily of high school students, this choir also performed weekly concerts at the Coco Palms Hotel. They recorded several albums, made concert trips to Honolulu, and appeared on national television. (Courtesy of St. Catherine's Church.)

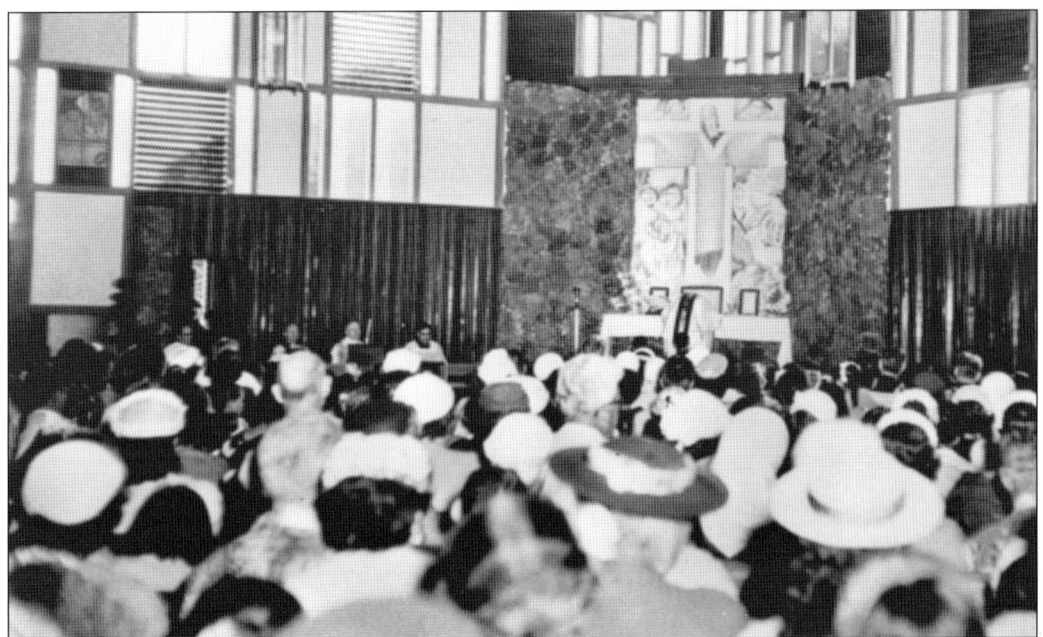

In 1958, a new church was built on the corner of Kawaihau Road, next to St. Catherine's School Convent. Father John McDonald directed the fundraising and building project, and the church was designed by Edwin Bauer and Federick Liang. The design is diamond shaped, with no interior columns, and includes seating for 600 people. It was a modern design, with an open-air island feel. The pews were constructed by Kauai Technical School students. The cost of construction was greatly reduced because the contractor, Kaoru Kato, allowed parish volunteers to work on the project. An outstanding feature of the interior is the artwork featuring three renowned Hawai'i artists—Jean Charlot, Juliette May Fraser, and Tseng Yo Ho. The first mass in the new church was celebrated by Father McDonald on April 20, 1958. It was blessed and dedicated by Bishop James Sweeney. St. Catherine's Parish remains the primary Catholic church, which includes two mission churches. (Courtesy of St. Catherine's Church.)

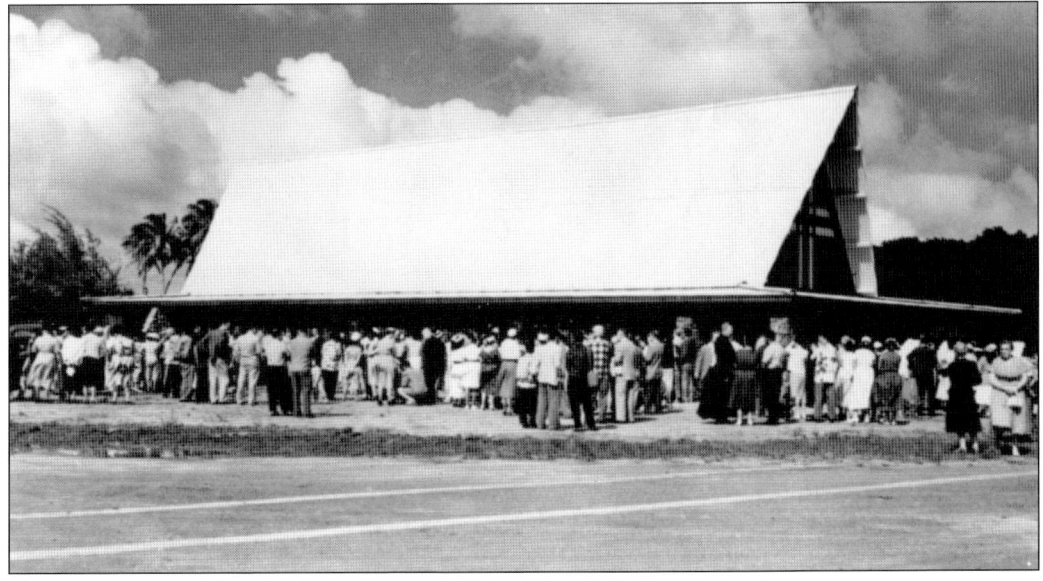

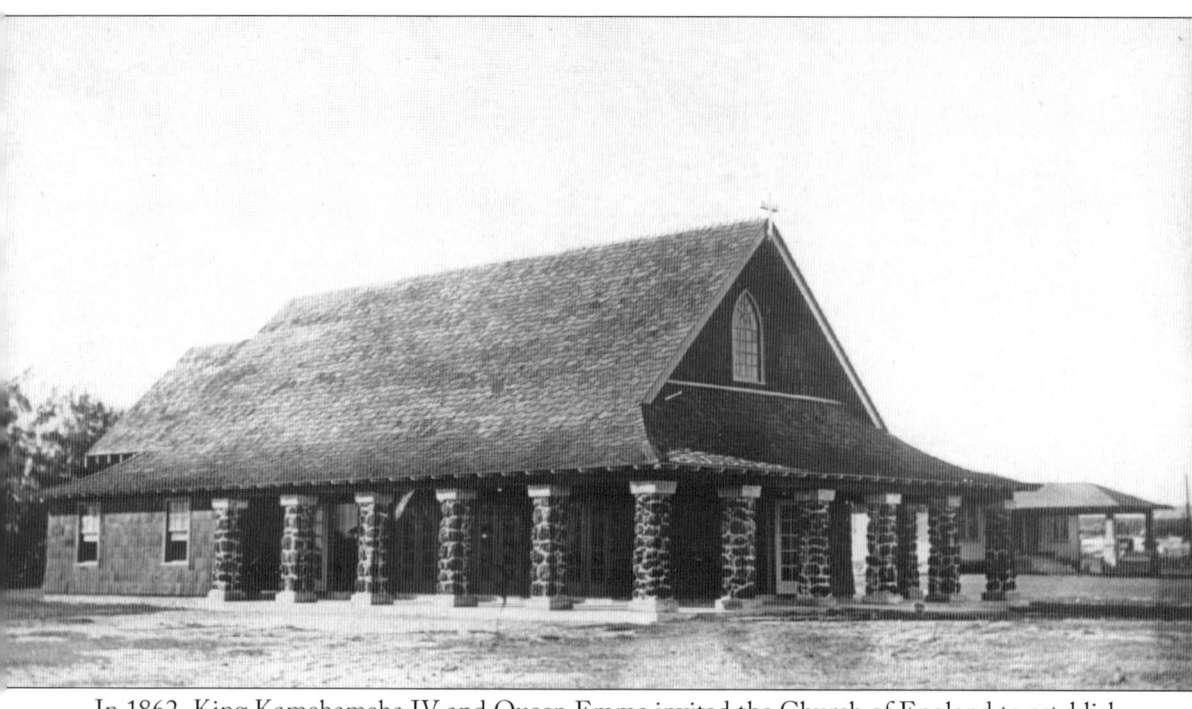

In 1862, King Kamehameha IV and Queen Emma invited the Church of England to establish missions in Hawai'i. The monarchy provided gifts of land for the missions throughout the islands. The first Anglican church on Kaua'i was established in Kealia by Rev. Henry Alpheus and Juelle J. Willey in 1924. It was an interracial church, whose congregation voted on the name All Saints. The church struggled for months to find a location until Reverend Willey accepted a gift of approximately five acres in Kapa'a town from Mr. and Mrs. Henry Digby Sloggett. All Saints Episcopal Church and the adjacent Memorial Church School building were designed by architect Guy N. Rothwell and built in December 1925. The building incorporated native lava-rock construction. The interior features lovely stained glass. The gymnasium was built in 1929 and has served the church and community over the years with performances, sports games, and dinners. During World War II, servicemen were encamped on the large church property. In 1980, the Sloggett Center and preschool were built. (Courtesy of KHS.)

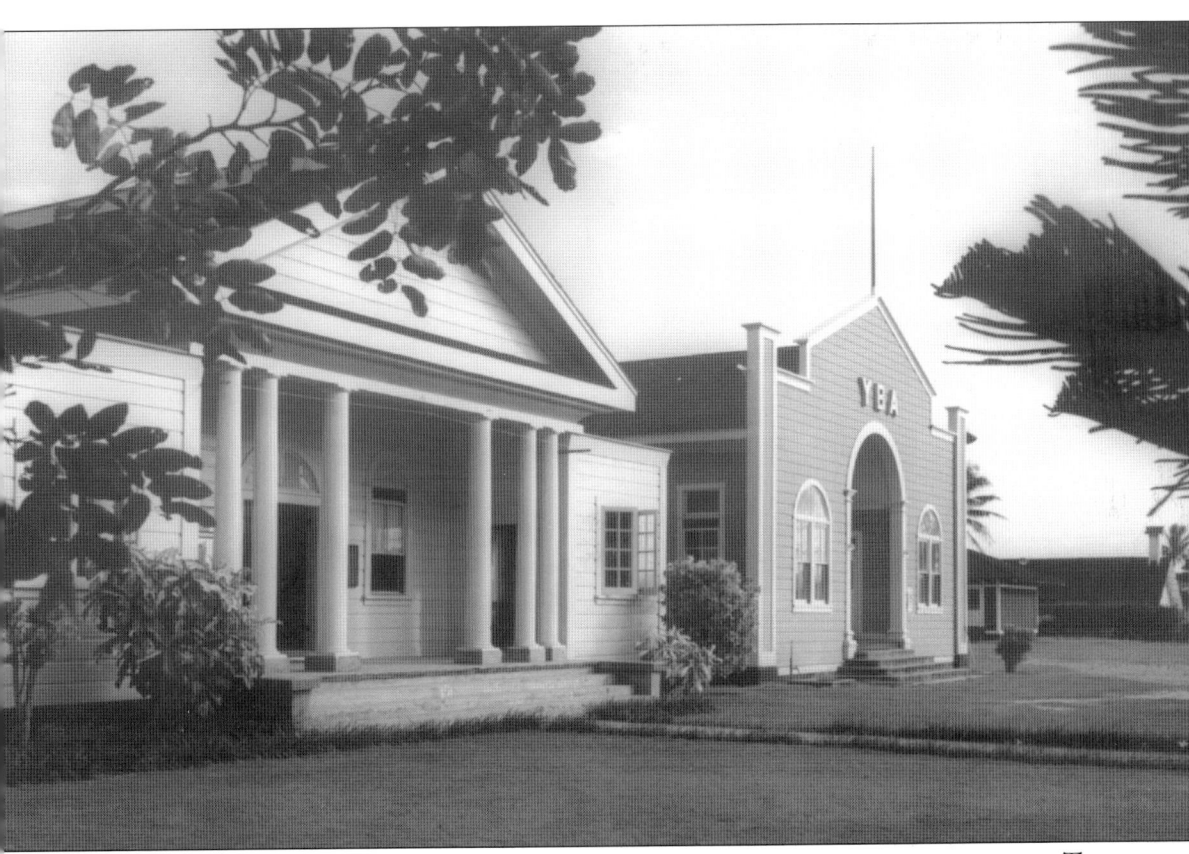

In 1910, Hongwanji Buddhist Temple was established in Kealia for Japanese immigrants. The minister initially held services in various homes in the Kealia/Kapaʻa area. By 1922, a temple was built in Kapaʻa on land leased from the County of Kauaʻi. The temple was destroyed by fire in 1929. In 1938, three parcels of land were purchased from the Territory of Hawaiʻi. The buildings pictured here were built on that purchased land. All Buddhist ministers in Hawaiʻi experienced very difficult times during World War II. Kapaʻa minister Reverend Nishie and his family were sent to a relocation camp on the United States mainland. Jihei Miura was elected to take care of the *butsudan* (shrine). The temple facilities became the US Army officers' headquarters. During this time, all properties belonging to Kapaʻa Hongwanji were deeded to Honpa Hongwanji Mission of Hawaiʻi. In 1972, celebrating the 50th anniversary, a new temple was built by local contractors Kaori Kano, Ichiji Matsumura, and Hideo Tanaka. Later, a social hall and kitchen were added. During the annual O bon season for commemorating the deceased, the temple hosts traditional dances. The Bon dance draws members of the church and the community for two festive evenings in the summer. (Courtesy of KHS.)

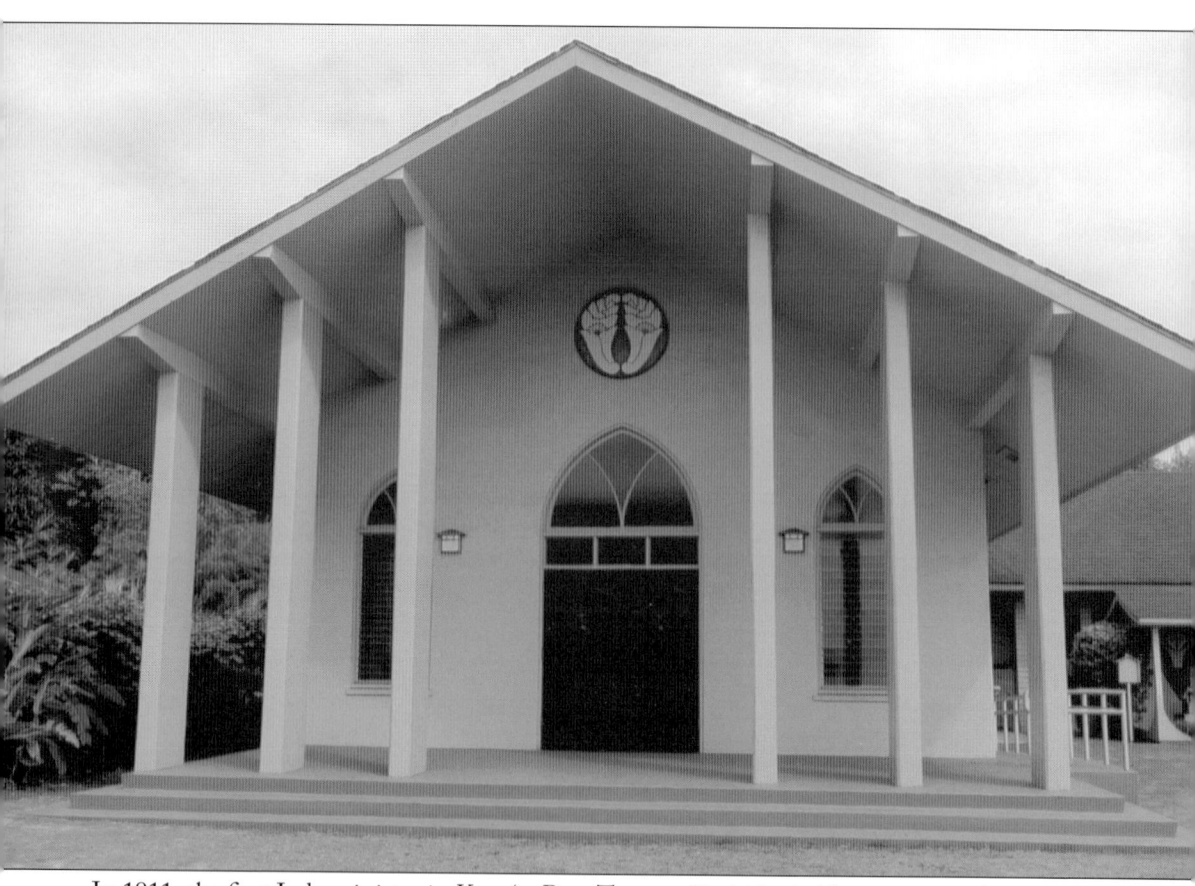

In 1911, the first Jodo minister in Kapaʻa, Rev. Tatsuyu Yoshida, held services in a house rented from a Chinese owner in Kapaʻa. He was followed by Rev. Gentetsu Harada, who secured land and money to build a temple, parsonage, and elementary school in 1912. The temple officially became Jodo-Shu Kyokaido (Kapaʻa Jodo-Shu Temple) and Kapaʻa Nisshin Jinjo Shogakko (Japanese-language school). The new mission supported the spiritual and cultural needs of the large Japanese immigrant community. Reverend Kitajima and his family were interned for the duration of World War II and returned to open the temple in 1945. In 1952, a remodeled temple was built, and a social hall and columbarium were added in 1982. The exterior of the temple architecturally resembles a Christian church except for the crest at the top front, which identifies it with the Jodo sect of Buddhism. (Courtesy of Clyde Furumoto.)

# Seven

# SCHOOLS

Along the seashore in North Kapaʻa in a place called Kaiakea by the Hawaiians, Kapaʻa English School, a one-room schoolhouse, opened in June 1883. Colonel Spalding, owner of Makee Sugar Company, built the school for the children of his plantation workers. The immigration contract between the Hawaiian Kingdom and Portugal stated that the plantation was responsible for providing housing, medical services, and a school for the immigrant children. After 25 years, the school was moved to its present location, called Mailehune. The new school site was Makee Sugar Company's Field No. 26. The new school was constructed by a Mr. Evanson of Honolulu and opened in January 1908. Subsequently, additional land was acquired with the last purchase of 16.4 acres in 1968 for a sports complex. Today, Kapaʻa Elementary and High School is situated on 47.57 acres, and Kapaʻa Middle School is on Olohena Road.

Several Japanese-language schools were also established on plantation land. They provided language and cultural education for their children.

St. Catherine's Catholic School opened in September 1946 on 9.41 acres on the corner of Kawaihau and Huaala Road. Additional acres were bought, and today the 11.76-acre site has the original school, additional classrooms, a cafeteria/church hall, and rectory.

In the 1950s, the demand for preschools encouraged many Kapaʻa churches and private citizens to provide this service to the public.

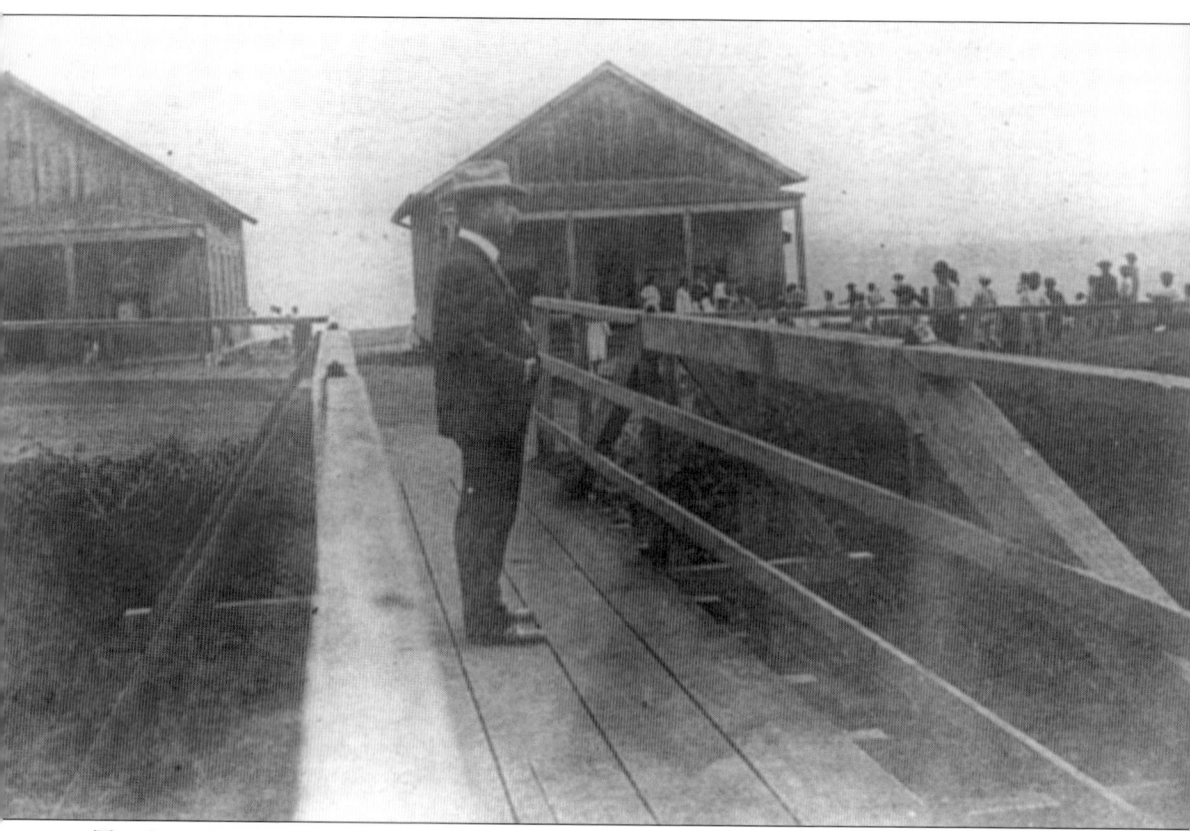

The first school in Kapa'a, the Kapa'a English School, opened in 1883. This photograph from the early 1900s shows two classroom buildings. Pictured here is P. Tople, the principal from 1899 to 1907. He is standing on a footbridge over the railroad tracks, which is today's coastal bike path. The school was built by the Makee Sugar Company, and students came from the Kealia/Kapa'a area. (Courtesy of KHS.)

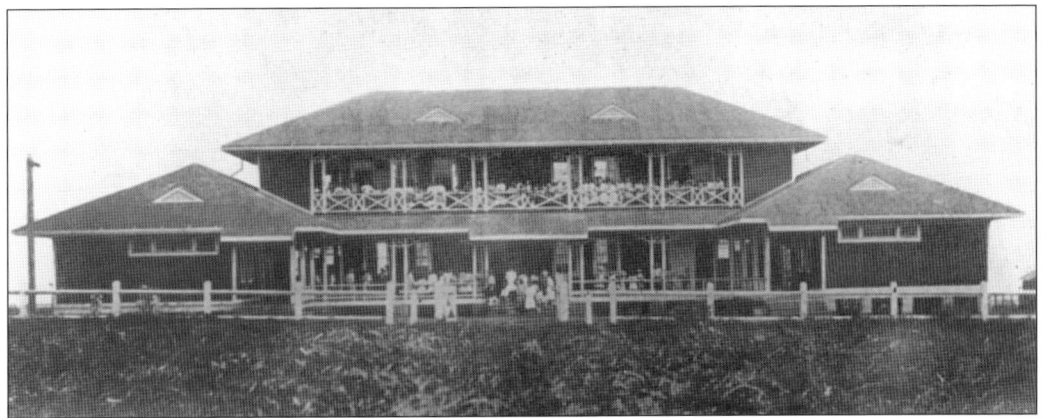

In 1908, a new school was constructed on a four-acre site at Mailehune, located on the hill above the original school. The land, Field No. 26, was donated by Makee Sugar Company. Kapaʻa School was built at a cost of $10,000. Prior to the opening, students came for weeks to plant grass. This building was demolished in 1941 for an expanded student body. (Courtesy of KHS.)

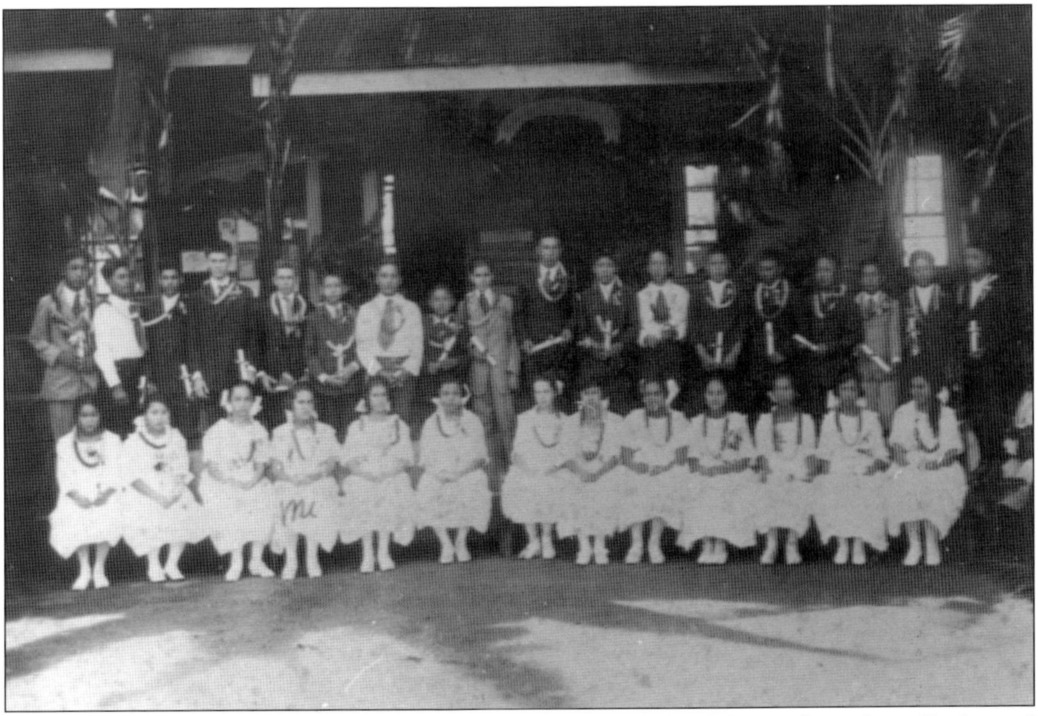

This 1921 photograph of the eighth grade class of Kapaʻa School shows them formally dressed and holding their diplomas at the graduation ceremony. They are standing in front of the original Kapaʻa School building at Mailehune. The faces of the students reflect the multicultural population of the Kapaʻa area. (Courtesy of Linda Paik Moriarty.)

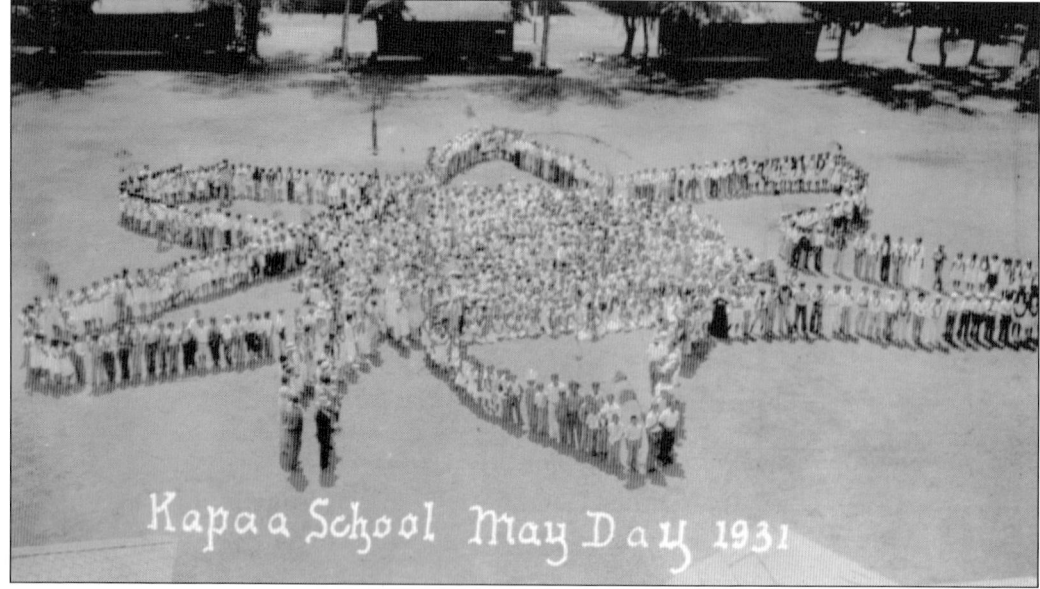

"May Day is Lei Day" was a popular island song, sung at the festivals on May 1. This 1931 photograph shows the entire student body of Kapaʻa School arranged in a floral design. The students dressed in aloha attire and wore leis. May Day celebrations featured a royal court with a king, queen, and princesses representing each of the islands. Hawaiian songs and dances and other ethnic performances highlighted the day. (Courtesy of KHS.)

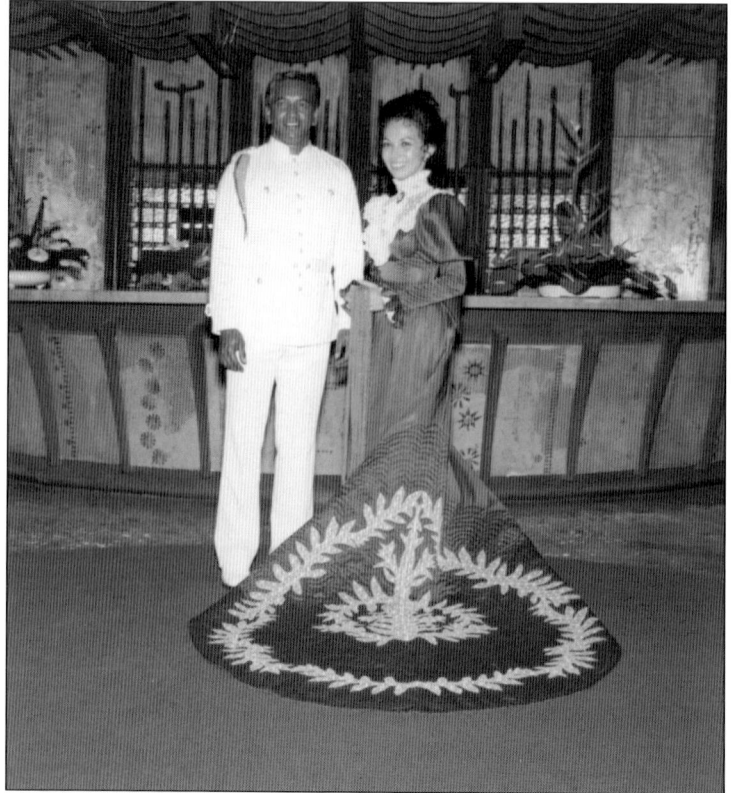

Dressed as a royal couple, Larry and Alma Kahaunaele of Kapaʻa celebrate their Hawaiian heritage. Alma Kahaunaele's holoku features a unique quilted train whose pattern, Na Kauʻi o Hilo, was designed by her great-grandmother Adeline Kamanuwai. The stylized design is floral, depicting *lauaʻe* fern and mixed flowers. Holokus were typically worn at formal Hawaiian celebrations, May Day programs, and weddings. (Courtesy of Alma Kahaunaele.)

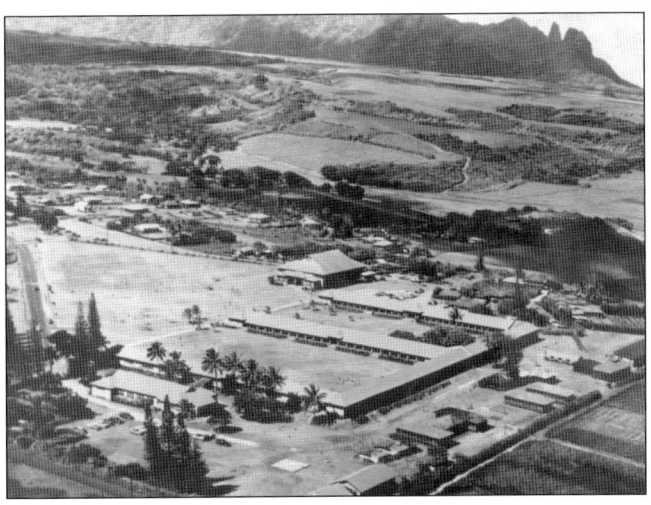

This 1955 aerial photograph of the Kapaʻa School campus shows the old bungalow-style classrooms at the bottom and the new E-shaped classrooms. In 1908, the school occupied four acres of land. Over the years, the school grew incrementally, with additional land and buildings. In 1997, the new Kapaʻa Middle School was built on property on Olohena Road. (Courtesy of KHS.)

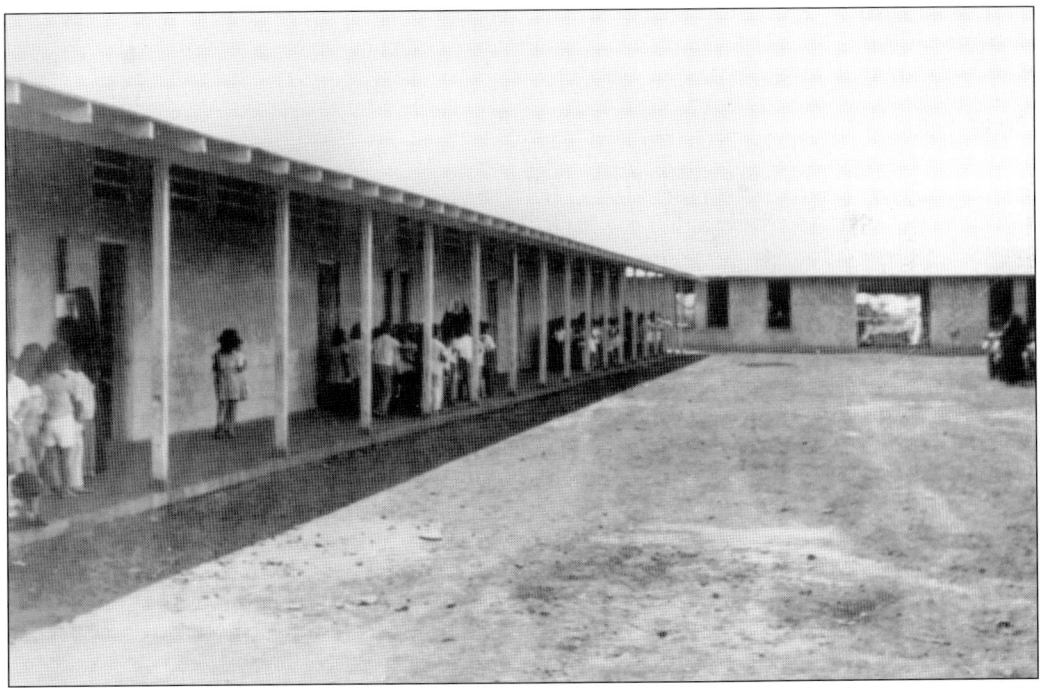

In 1945, the Catholic diocese of Honolulu made building parochial schools throughout the territory a top priority. The parishioners of St. Catherine's Church were delighted. Sen. J.B. Fernandes, a church member, helped with the acquisition of three parcels of land adjacent to Kapaʻa School in 1946. Architect Van Oort of Honolulu designed the U-shaped school complex, which consisted of parallel wings of four classrooms. The bottom of the U held the administrative office and music and health rooms. The contractor was Mr. Maeda, who used hollow-tile building blocks provided by E. Aguiar. The school opened on September 3, 1946, after the many challenges involved in acquiring materials during the war years. (Courtesy of St. Catherine's Church.)

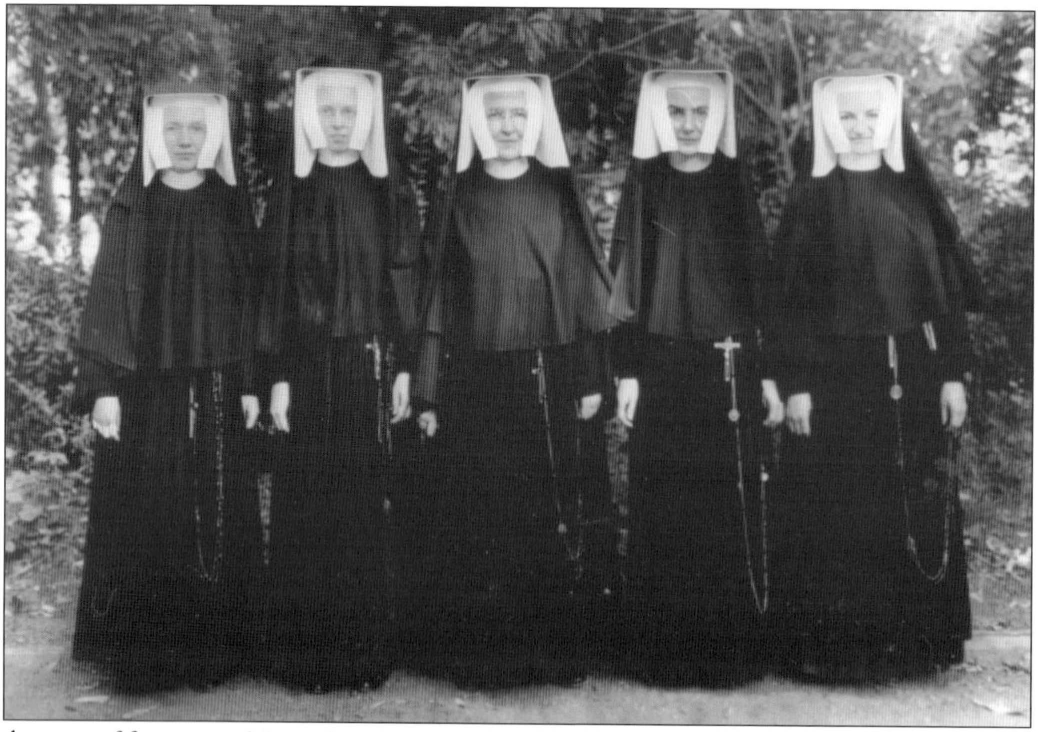

A group of five nuns of the order of the Sisters of Charity of the Blessed Virgin Mary arrived in August 1946 to staff the newly opened school. Pictured from left to right are the original five nuns, Sister Mary Raymunda (kindergarten), Sister Mary Ann Elizabeth (music and second grade), Sister Mary Annette (fourth grade), principal Sister Mary Presentice (first grade), and Sister Mary Dorita (third grade). Each subsequent year, an additional grade was established until the eighth grade in 1951. The first graduation class was in 1952. The Sisters of Charity staffed the school for 23 years, followed by the Dominican Sisters in 1969. Today, the school is staffed by lay teachers. St. Catherine's School today looks much like the 1953 photograph below. A multipurpose building that houses the cafeteria, stage, and the rectory were constructed over time. (Both, courtesy of St. Catherine's Church.)

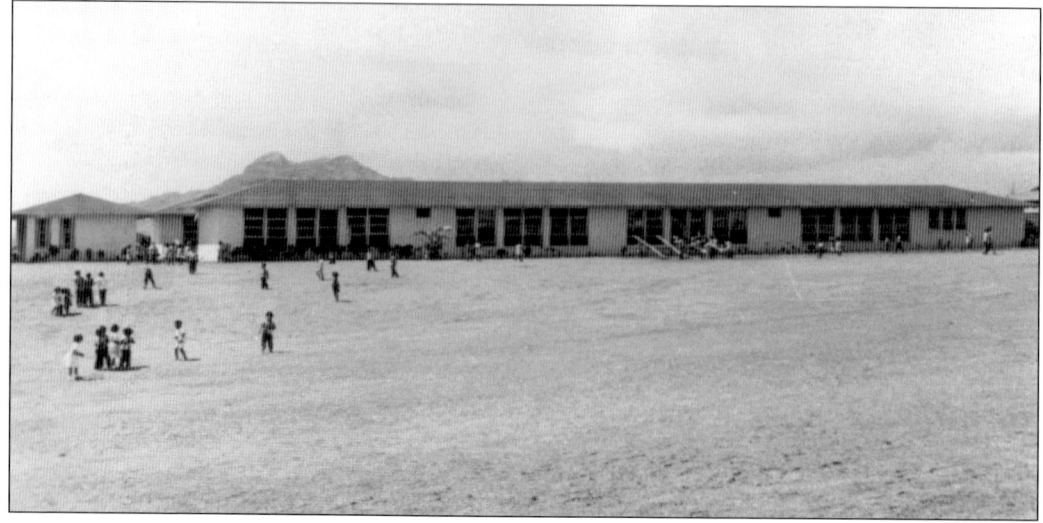

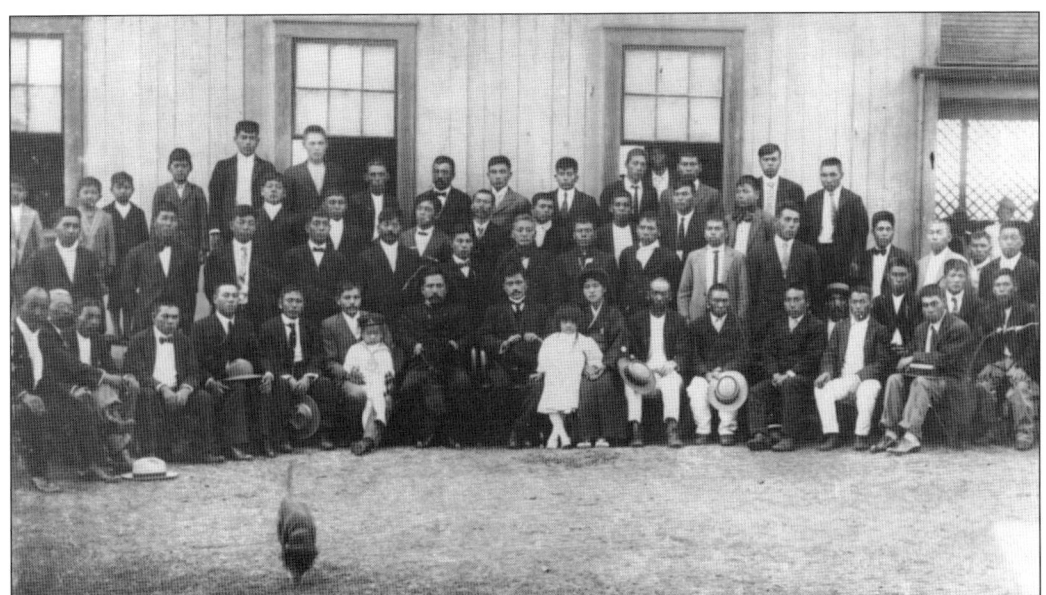

A Japanese school was established in Kealia camp by the large Japanese immigrant population in order to preserve their language and culture. The building was purchased from the Kapa'a English School at Kaiakea Point in 1908 and moved to the school site on the banks of the Kealia River. This photograph shows students in front of the school in 1913 or 1914. (Courtesy of KHS.)

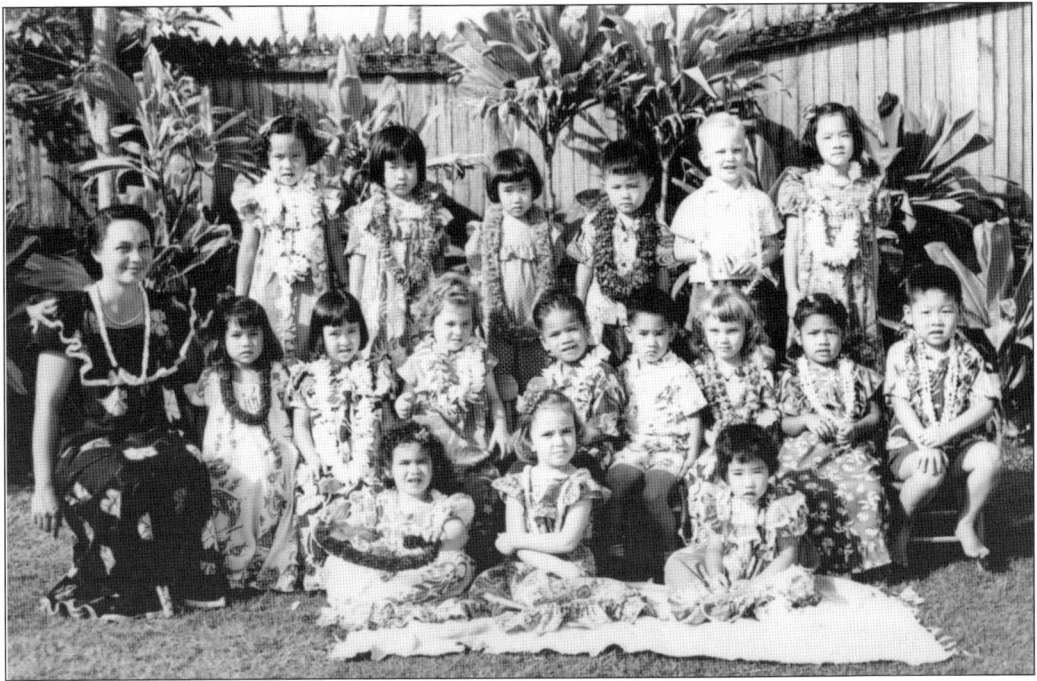

As the community grew, there was a demand for preschool education in Kapa'a. Sarah Sheldon ran a preschool at her house, next to the Kapa'a Courthouse, present-day Kapa'a Neighborhood Center. The occasion for the island dress of *muumuus*, aloha shirts, and lei is May Day 1951. (Courtesy of Linda Paik Moriarty.)

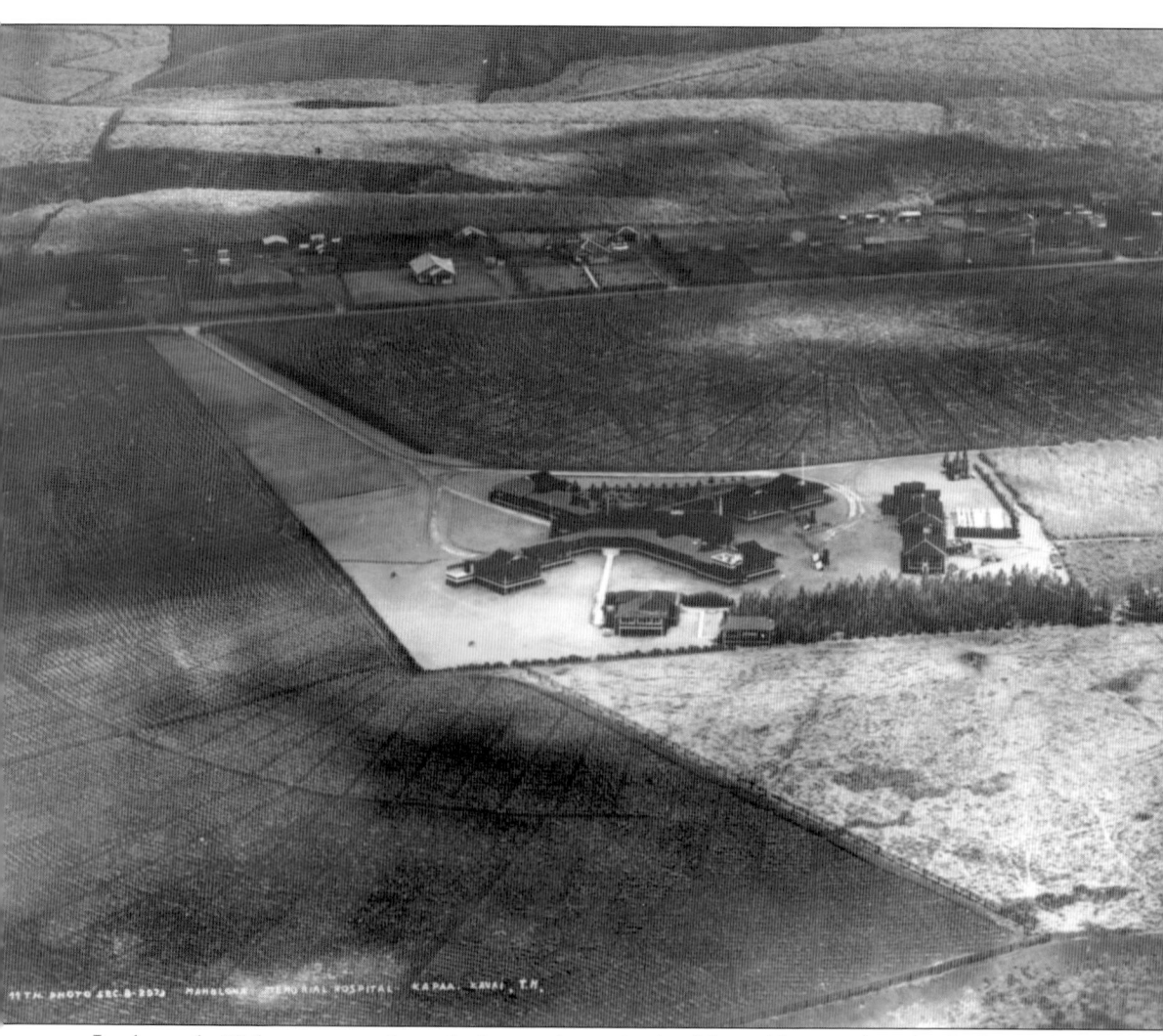

In the early 20th century, tuberculosis was the major health problem in the islands for students and their families. In 1915, Hawaii had a tuberculosis death rate greater than the mainland, and Kaua'i had an infant mortality rate from tuberculosis three times greater than O'ahu. As there was no foreseeable cure for tuberculosis, there was a need for a facility to isolate the infected and provide rest and a proper diet. The territorial legislature set aside 120 acres on a bluff above Kapa'a, and the Kaua'i Sugar Planter's Association, Albert and Emma Kauikeolani Wilcox, and the County of Kaua'i provided funds for its construction. Clinton B. Ripley, a Honolulu architect, designed the building. (He also designed the Kauai County Building.) Samuel Mahelona Memorial Hospital was built in 1917 as a memorial to Samuel Mahelona, son of Emma Mahelona Wilcox, who died of tuberculosis as a young man. Once a cure for tuberculosis was established in the 1950s and 1960s, the hospital's focus turned to long-term care and mental health. (Courtesy of KHS.)

# *Eight*

# COMMUNITY LIFE

Kapaʻa is comprised of people whose ancestors migrated from the far reaches of the world to work for the sugar plantations. Economic and historical forces of the time brought workers primarily from Germany, China, Portugal, Korea, Japan, and the Philippines. Some came as single men, others with their families. They transported their religious and cultural traditions and forged an identity for themselves in a community of native Hawaiians and other immigrants.

Men and women worked side-by-side, and their children went to school and played together. They planted gardens, fished, and hunted in the fields and mountains behind the town. Neighbors and friends were kind and shared vegetables, fruits, fish, meat, and fowl. They traded plants and recipes and learned skills from each other. They shared in the ups and downs of life. Kokua is the Hawaiian word that was commonly used and best describes people's relationships with each other. It means to help, share, and comfort.

The newcomers adopted many Hawaiian cultural traditions of food, hospitality, and music. However, they brought with them traditions surrounding birth, marriage, death, and other life milestones, duplicating as closely as possible what they practiced in their home countries. Ceremonies and celebrations surrounding the honoring of ancestors were widely practiced, including Chinese Ching Ming, Filipino All Souls Day, Portuguese Shrove Tuesday, and the Japanese O Bon.

The Portuguese introduced Catholicism and built one of the earliest churches in Kapaʻa. The Chinese transported their ancestral shrines, and the Japanese established two Buddhist missions in the town. Graveyards throughout the town with tombstones in various traditional script attest to this religious diversity.

Recreation was a big part of community life. For children, there was swimming, fishing, surfing, hiking, and foraging for wild guavas, mangos, and mountain apples. The empty fields were prime areas for sham battles and cowboy shootouts. In town, there were two movie theaters, pool halls, a baseball and football field, and a skating rink. Organized sports teams such as the barefoot football league were popular activities, as were choral groups and scouting for girls and boys.

Kapaʻa today is a multiethnic community that continues to celebrate and honor the diversity of its origins and embrace the challenges of modern life.

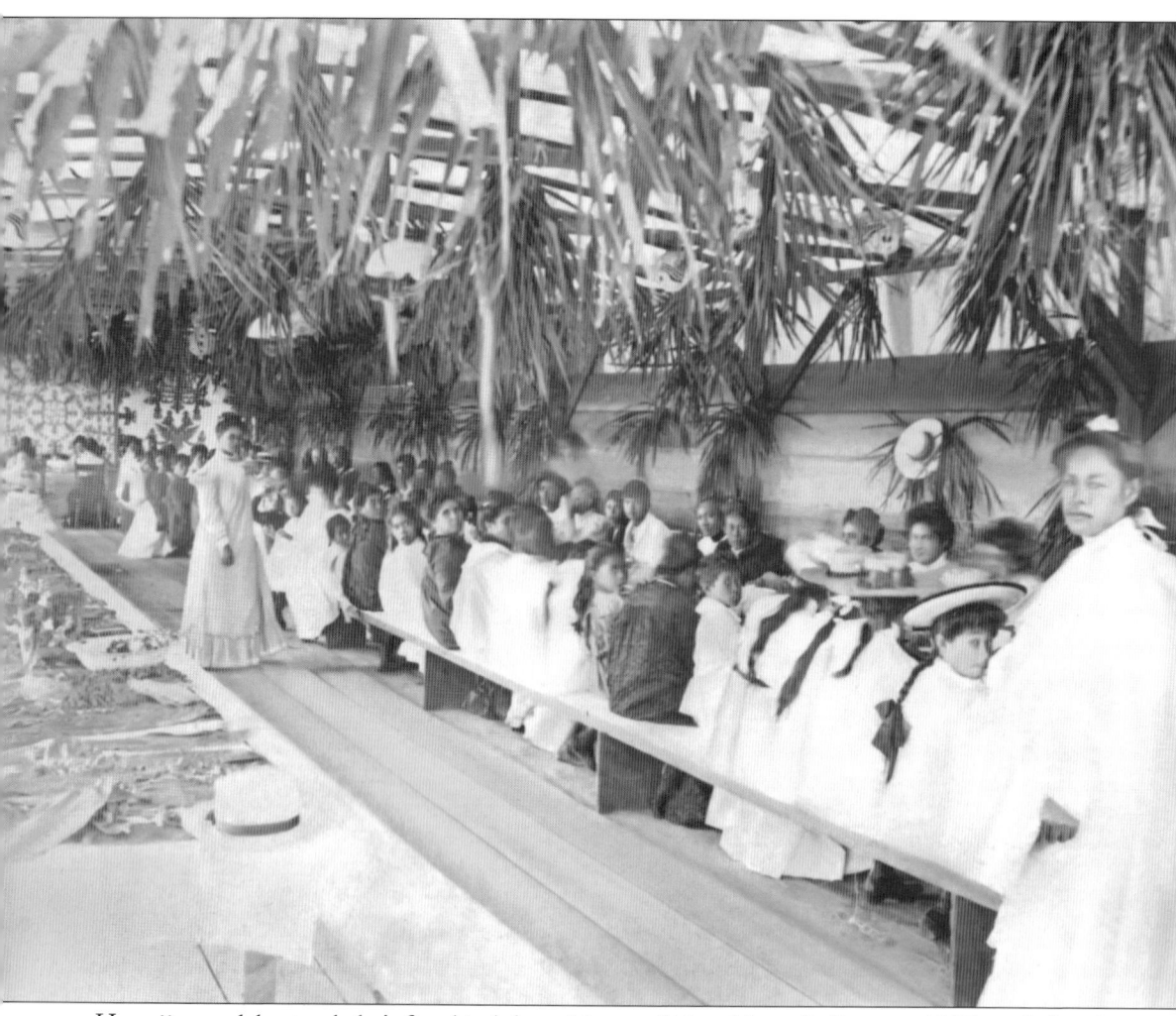

Hawaiians celebrate a baby's first birthday with a traditional luau. In January 1905, with family and friends in attendance, Helen Leimomi Morgan celebrated her first birthday in Kapaʻa. Tables are set for the luau. In the extreme rear of the hall hangs a Hawaiian-style quilt sewn by her mother, Catherine Morgan, as was tradition for a newborn child. (Courtesy of Linda Paik Moriarty.)

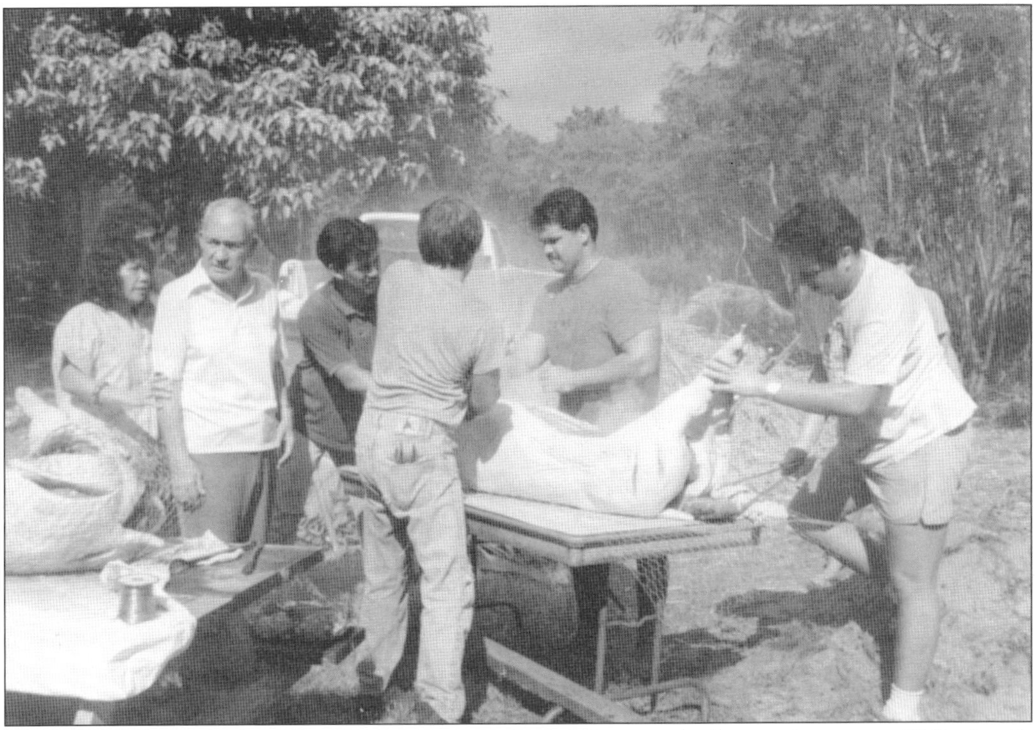

To celebrate the housewarming of Dr. Patrick and Danita Aiu's new home in 1973, family members are preparing the pig for the imu. Hot rocks are being placed in the belly of the pig to enhance cooking. Patrick Aiu was the first Kapaʻa native to practice obstetrics/gynecology on Kauaʻi. (Courtesy of Danita Aiu.)

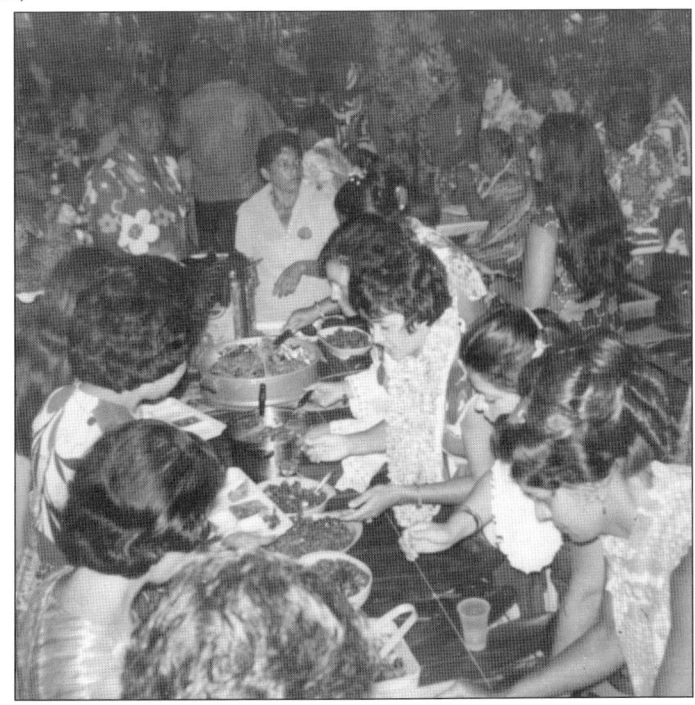

The table is laden with food, the music is playing, and the luau has begun. Guests join Danita Aiu (third from right with lei) in selecting from a table laden with traditional Hawaiian food, including *kalua* pig, raw fish, *laulau* (taro-wrapped pork), and other delicacies. (Courtesy of Danita Aiu.)

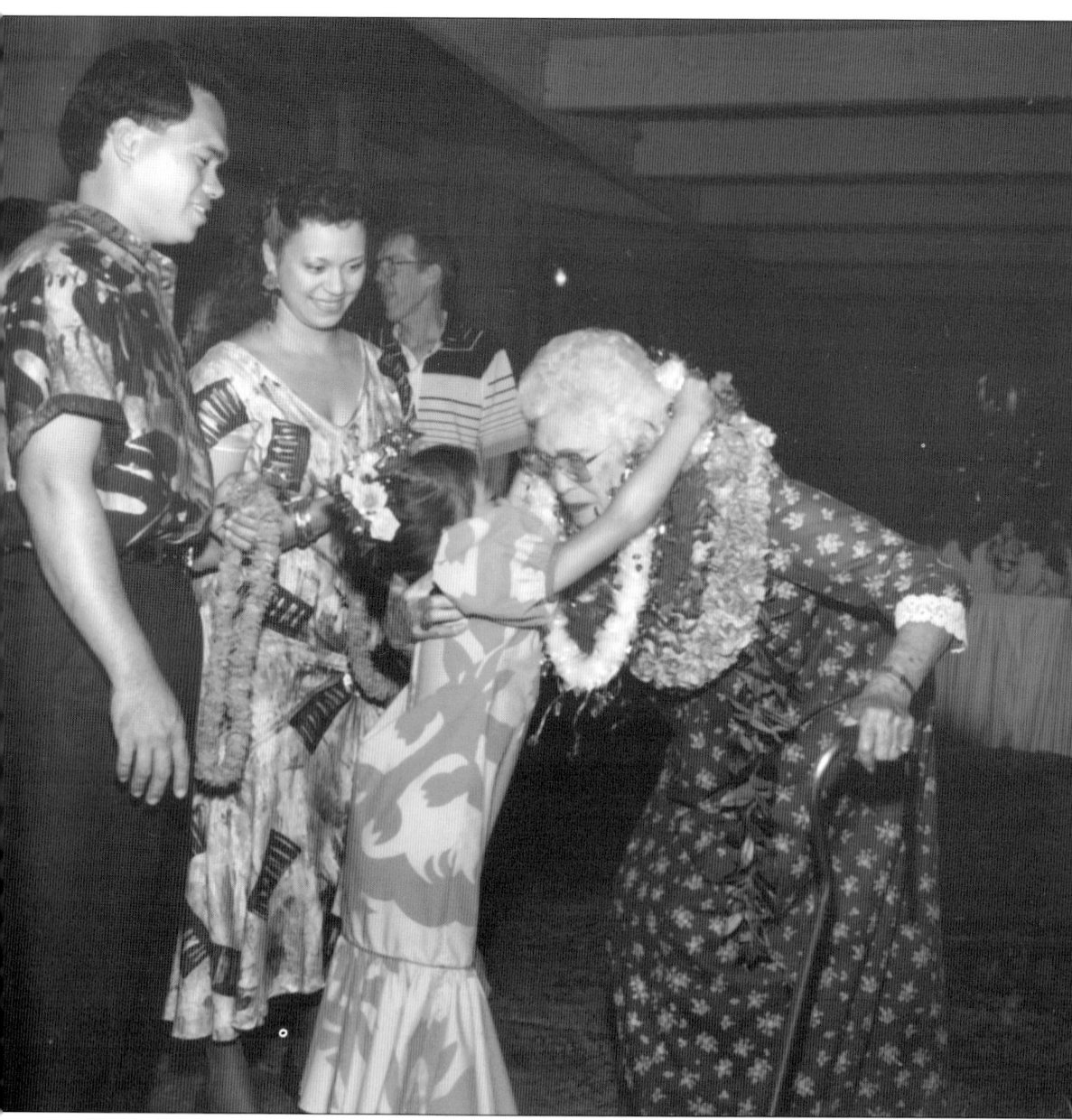

Emily Smith, matriarch of the Smith family, is given a lei by her great-granddaughter Tiffany Kaui while her grandson John Kaui and his wife, Margaret, look on. She is bedecked with lei and honored with a traditional luau on her 85th birthday, celebrated at Smith's Tropical Paradise. (Courtesy of the Smith family.)

A blessing by the Buddhist priest opens the Bon dance at the Kapa'a Hongwanji Mission. O Bon is the season, from June through August, that honors the dead with ceremony and dance at each of the Buddhist temples on the island. It is a tradition that the Japanese immigrants brought with them. (Courtesy of Kalei Arinaga.)

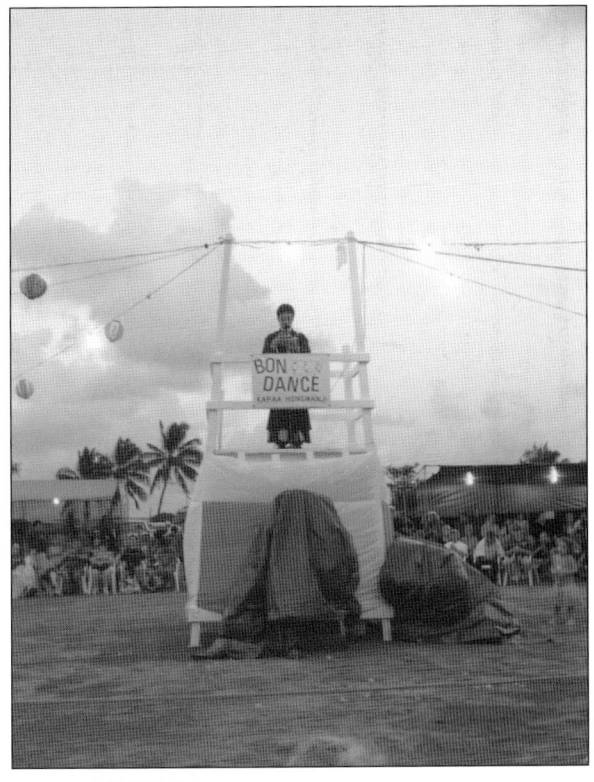

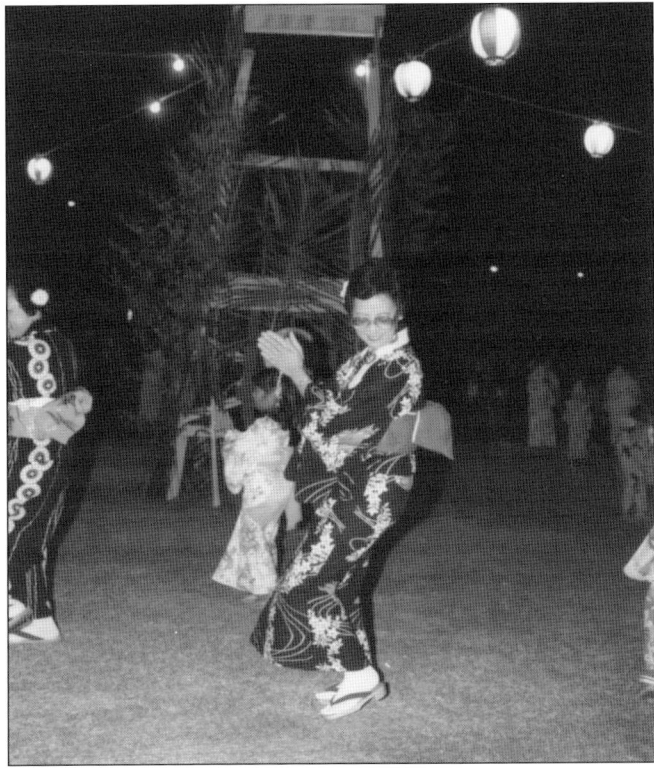

Julia Haruki Suzuki, in kimono, dances around the *yaguro*, the central tower holding the drums and singers at the Bon dance at the Kapa'a Hongwanji Mission in the summer of 1994. Bon dances have a festive, carnival-like atmosphere, popular with the entire community. (Courtesy of Marilyn Suzuki Haugh.)

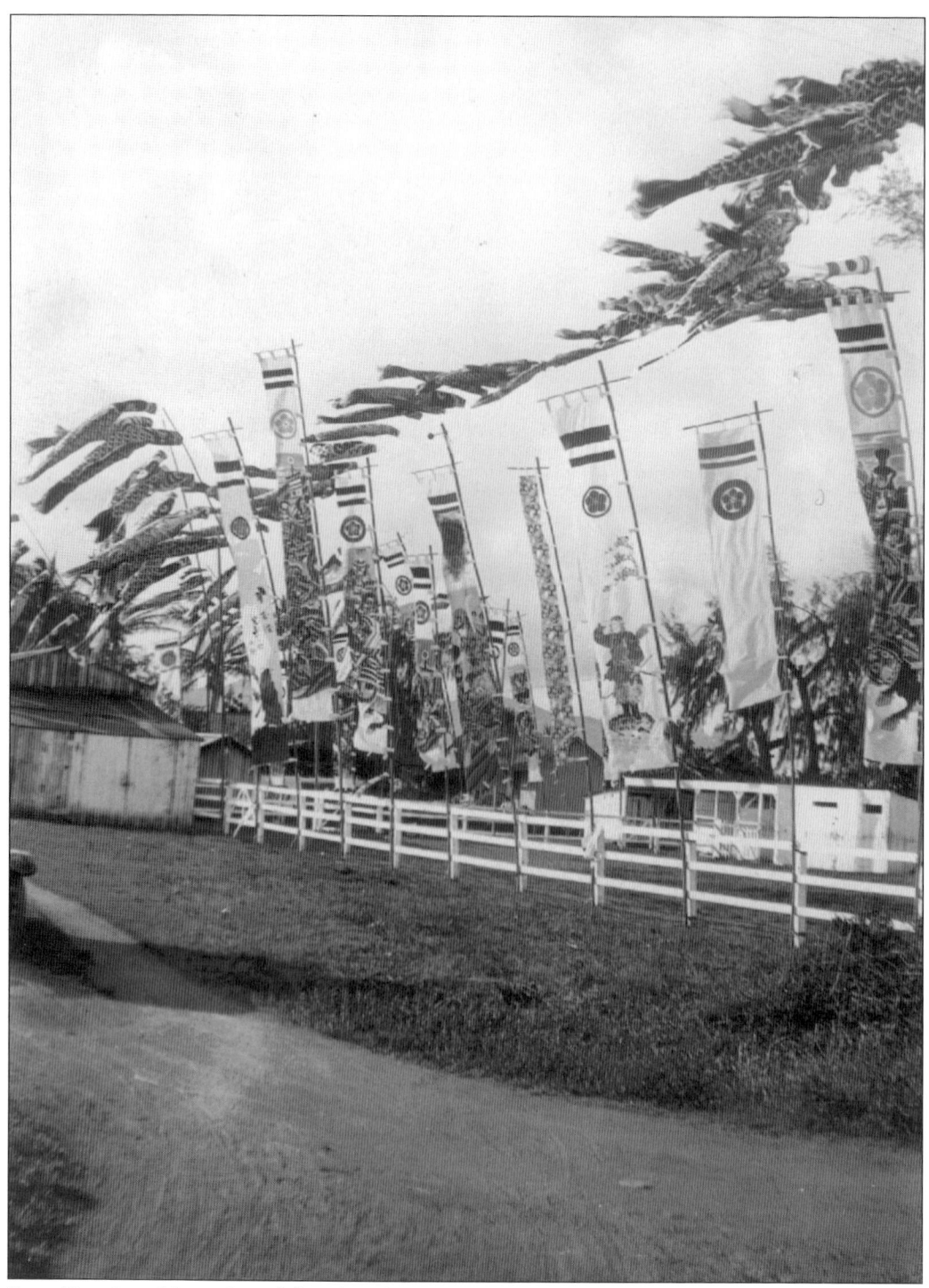

Boys Day is celebrated on May 5 each year, with the flying of colored-carp streamers and banners. This tradition came to Hawai'i in the late 1800s from Japan. A carp is flown for each boy in the family, as shown in this photograph from the 1940s. This image is part of the Robert Taylor Collection. (Courtesy of KHS.)

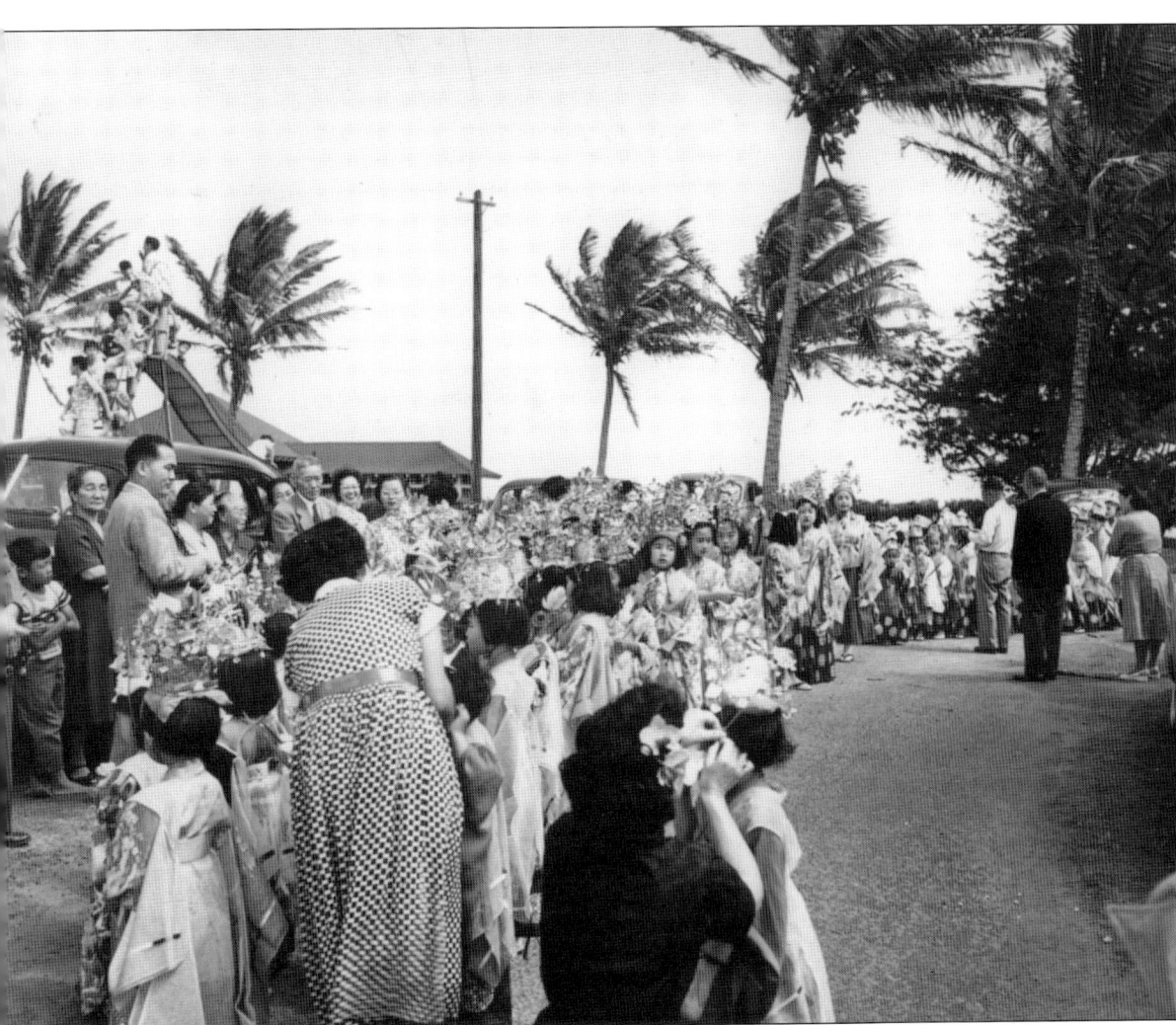
Youngsters from the Kapa'a Hongwanji Mission participate in the Chigo ceremony in May 1952, celebrating the 30th anniversary of the establishment of the mission. Dressed in traditional Japanese attire, they held a procession through the town. (Courtesy of the Kuboyama family.)

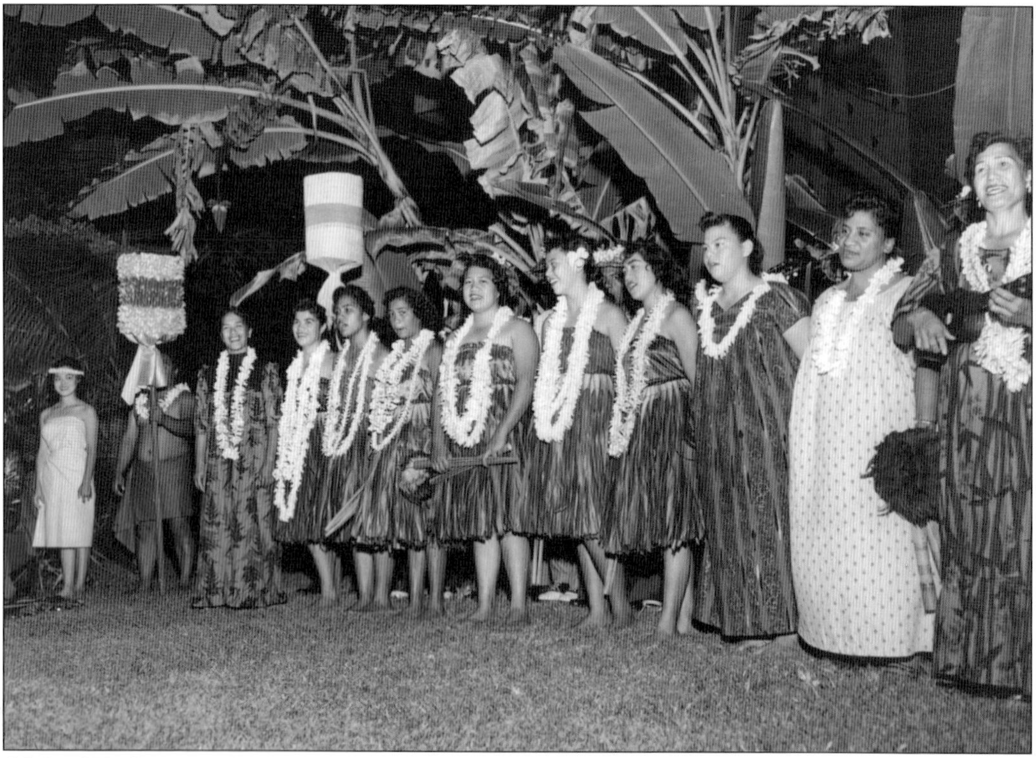

Aloha Week, a weeklong celebration of Hawaiian culture and pageantry, is celebrated in October 1960 with island song and dance performed by the Kapaʻa Mormon Church Choir. (Courtesy of Linda Paik Moriarty.)

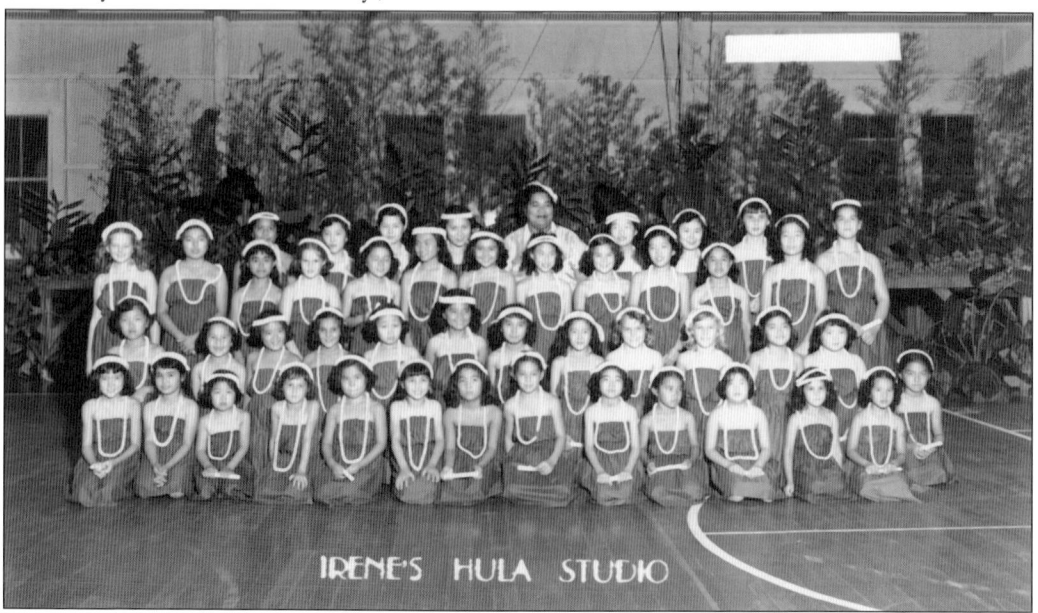

Many young girls in Kapaʻa enrolled in hula classes, a popular cultural activity. This photograph from the early 1950s documents the completion of classes at Irene McDonald's Hula Studio. (Courtesy of Linda Paik Moriarty.)

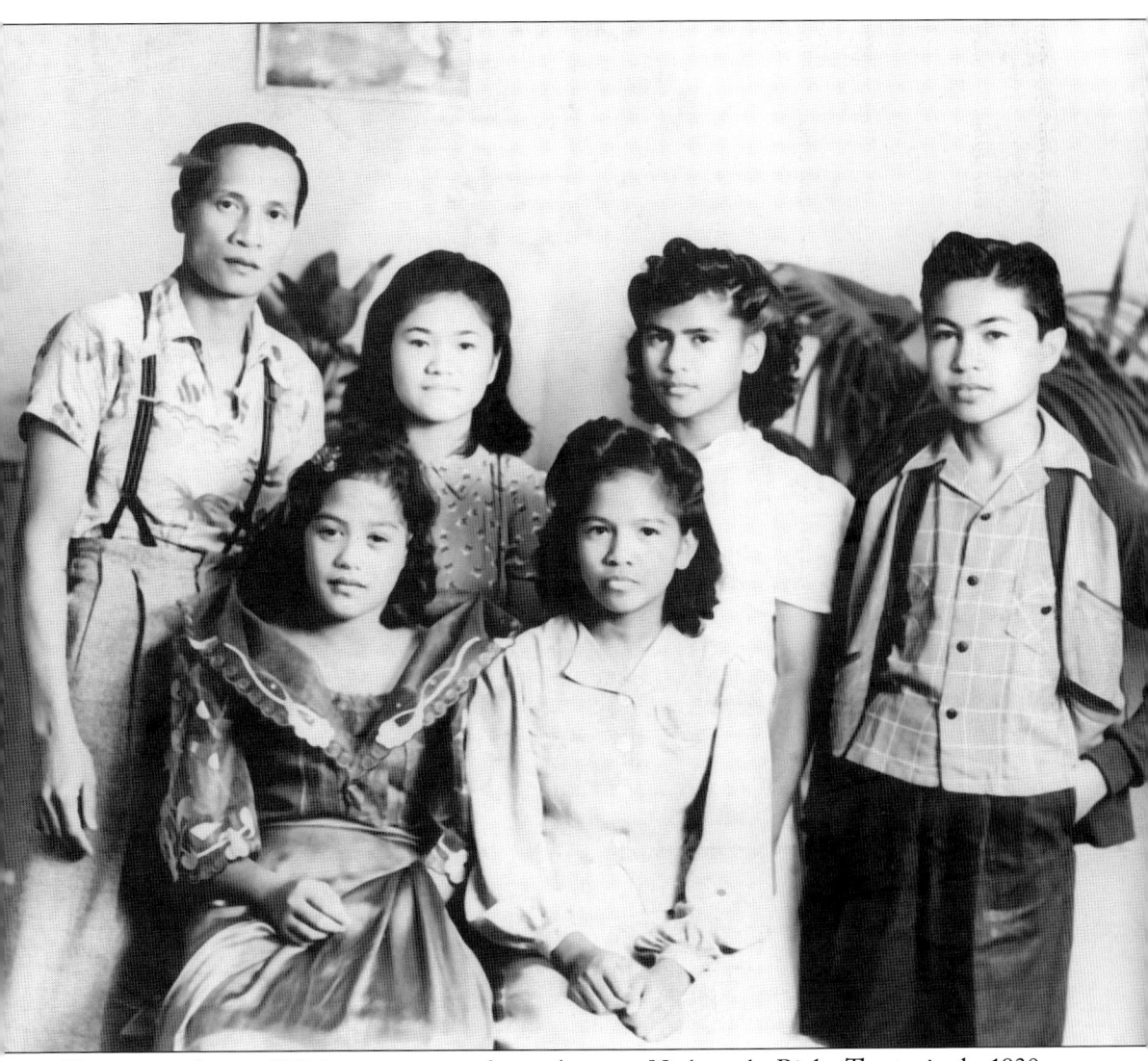

This group of young Filipino were contenders at Amateur Night at the Rialto Theatre in the 1930s. Contestants would sing and dance, competing for a prize. (Courtesy of Linda Paik Moriarty.)

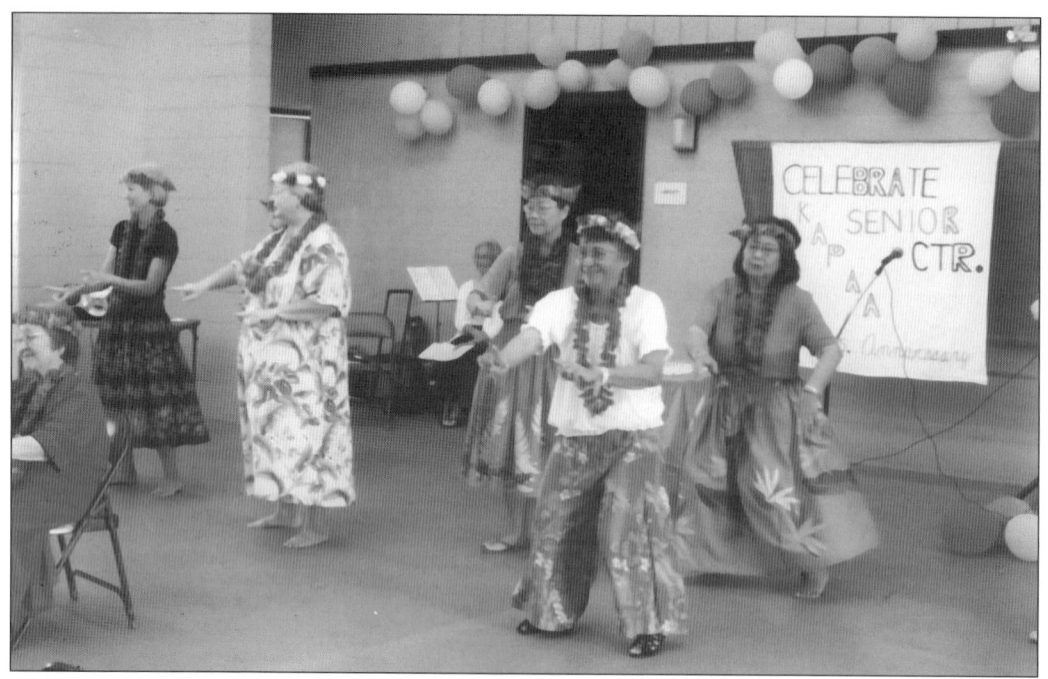

Members of the Kapa'a Senior Center celebrate their 45th anniversary in 2013 with a lively hula. (Courtesy of Marta Miller Hulsman.)

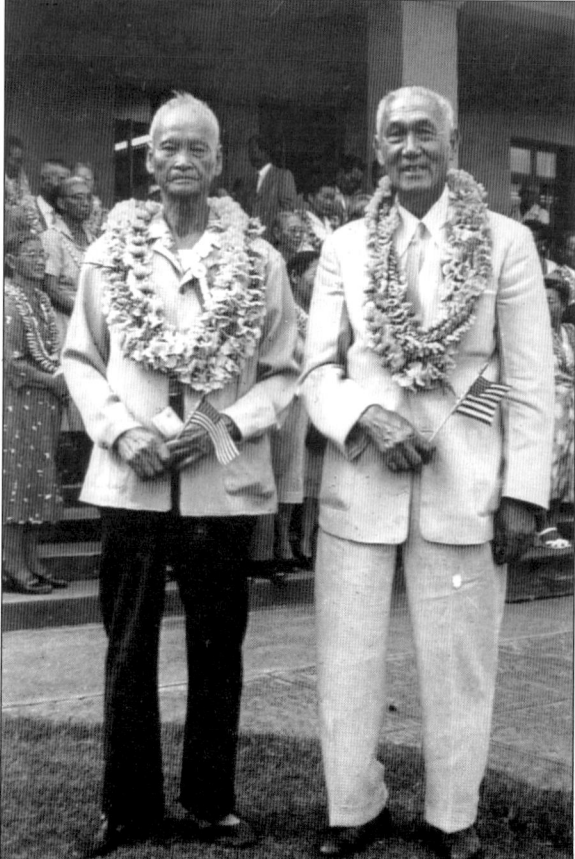

After Hawai'i received its statehood in 1959, many early immigrants became naturalized citizens. Chu Wai was in the United States for over 50 years before it was possible for him to become a citizen. Laden with lei, Chu Wai (right) and a friend are shown celebrating this happy day. (Courtesy of Janice Lee Santos.)

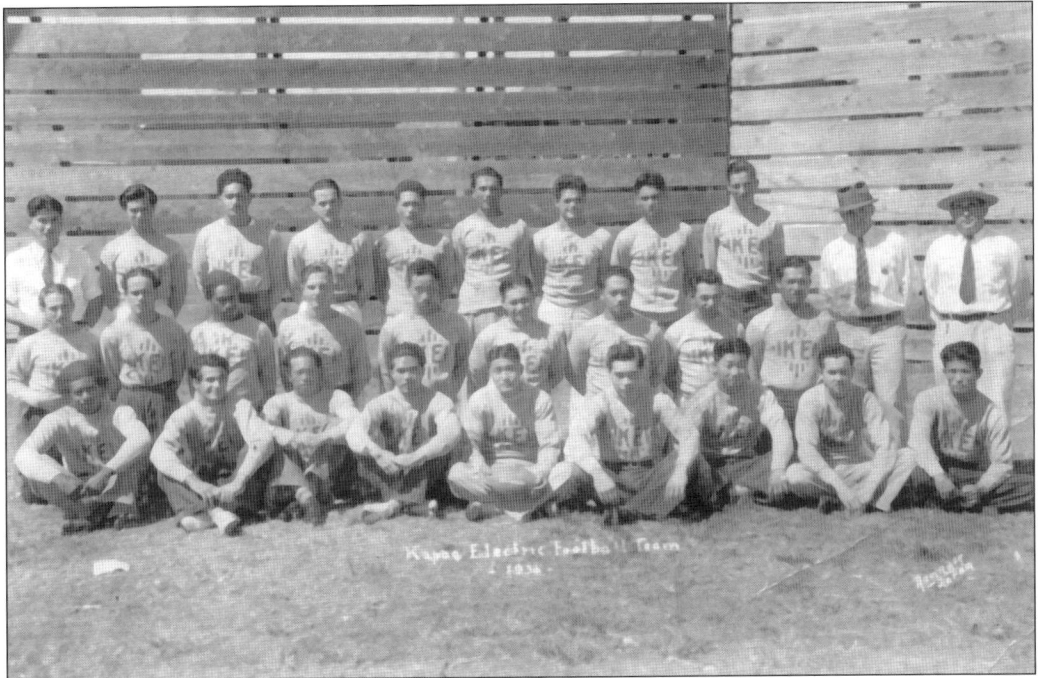

The Kapaʻa Electric football team of 1936 reflects the multiracial composition of the community. Some of the football leagues of the time were known as barefoot leagues, as they played without shoes. (Courtesy of Linda Paik Moriarty.)

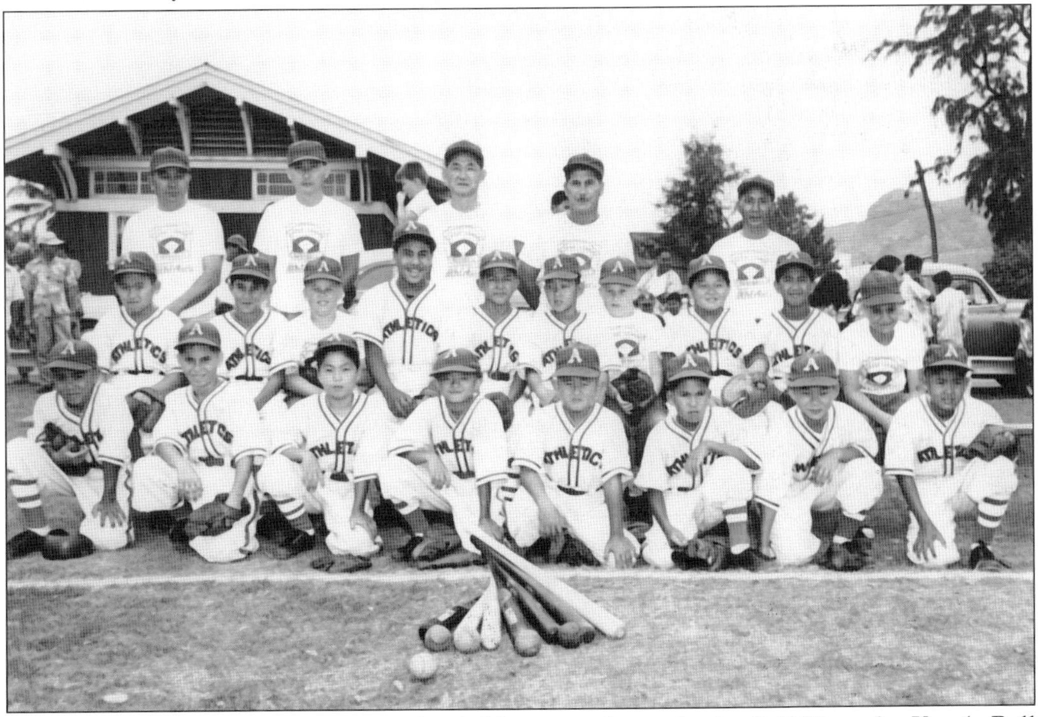

The Kawaihau Little League team, the Athletics, is shown in April 1953 at the Kapaʻa Ball Park. The coaches are in the third row. (Courtesy of the Kuboyama family.)

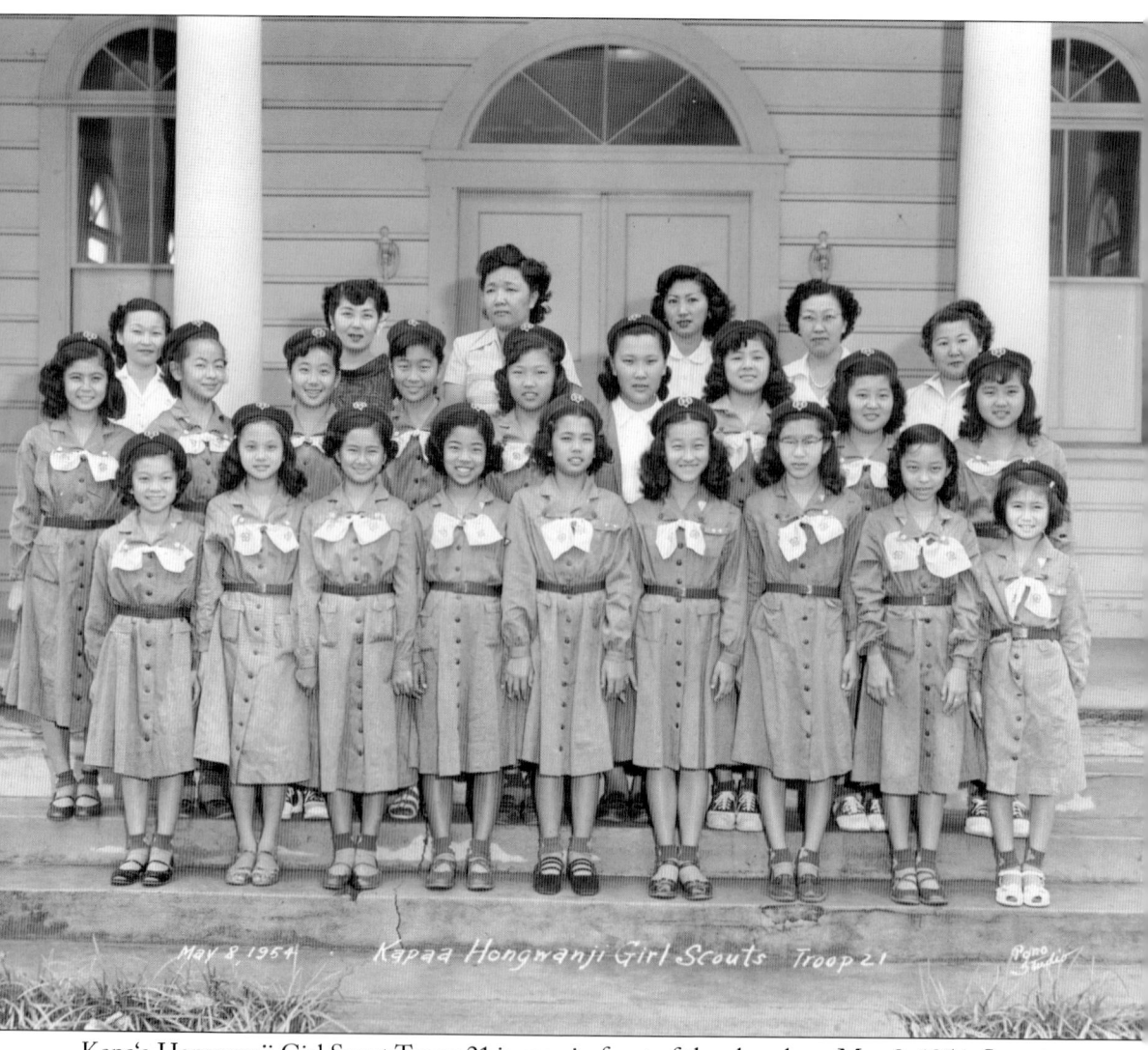

Kapaʻa Hongwanji Girl Scout Troop 21 is seen in front of the church on May 8, 1954. Scouting was a popular activity for schoolchildren, usually sponsored by various churches. The scout leaders in the third row are, from left to right, Mrs. Yonemura, Alice Yamada, Asano Saiki, unidentified, Mrs. Tanaka, and Mrs. Takesono. (Courtesy of the Kuboyama family.)

Spearfishing along the Kapa'a shoreline was a popular pastime. It was not only sport but also supplemented the family table. Frank Texeira (left) and friends proudly display their catch in the late 1940s. (Courtesy of Herman Texeira.)

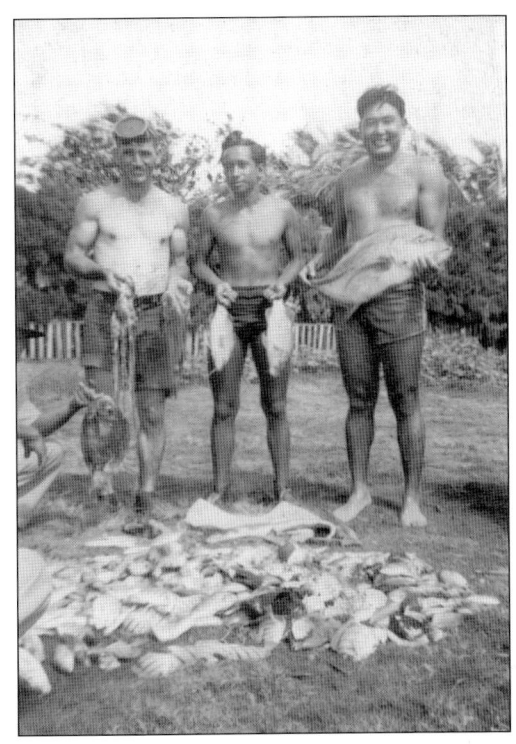

In 1975, a group of County of Kaua'i employees encountered a large marlin floundering on the shoreline. They attempted to pull the fish onto shore by its bill but decided it was too risky. They used two pitchforks from the county truck and brought in this prize. Their happiness was short-lived, as they were later reprimanded for fishing during work hours. (Courtesy of Ernest Palmeira.)

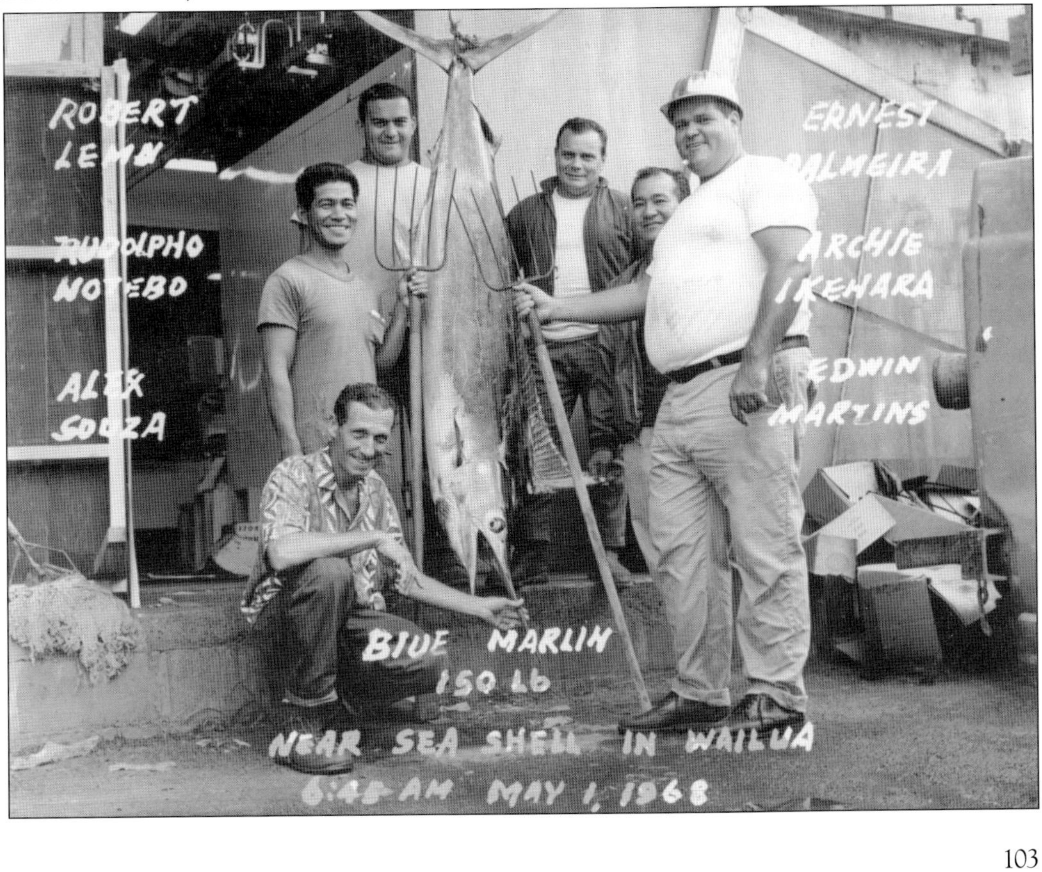

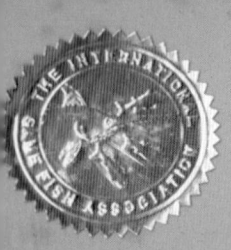

**INTERNATIONAL GAME FISH ASSOCIATION**

**WORLD RECORD**

LINE CLASS CATEGORY

All Tackle &
M-24 kg (50 lb)

SPECIES

Giant Trevally

WEIGHT

53.52 kg (118 lb)

DATE OF CATCH

July 10, 1983

PLACE OF CATCH

Wailua Beach, Kapaa
Kauia, Hawaii, USA

THIS IS TO CERTIFY THAT

**YASUO MORIBE**

HAS BEEN AWARDED A WORLD ANGLING RECORD
FOR A CATCH OF THE HEAVIEST FISH OF A SPECIES
IN AN APPROVED LINE CLASS CATEGORY,
AND THAT THE CATCH WAS MADE IN ACCORDANCE WITH
INTERNATIONAL ANGLING REGULATIONS.

IN WITNESS WHEREOF, THE UNDERSIGNED HAVE AFFIXED THEIR SIGNATURES

EXECUTIVE COMMITTEE MEMBER    PRESIDENT

On July 10, 1985, Yasuo Moribe of Kapaʻa caught a 118-pound *ulua* (giant trevally) at Wailua beach after battling the fish from the shore for seven hours. People lined the shore to watch this epic battle. The record stands today. (Courtesy of Marilyn Suzuki Haugh.)

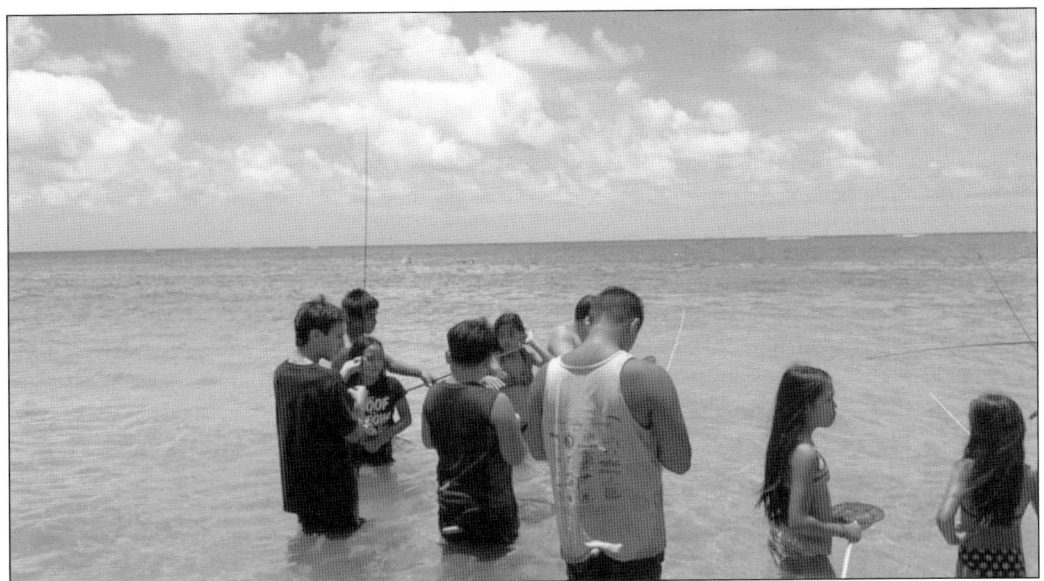

A favorite family activity during the summer months is fishing for 'oama, or baby goatfish. Schools of fish appear in the shallows inside the reef along the Kapa'a shoreline. Families spend hours fishing, picnicking, and enjoying the camaraderie of other fishermen. (Courtesy of Marilyn Suzuki Haugh.)

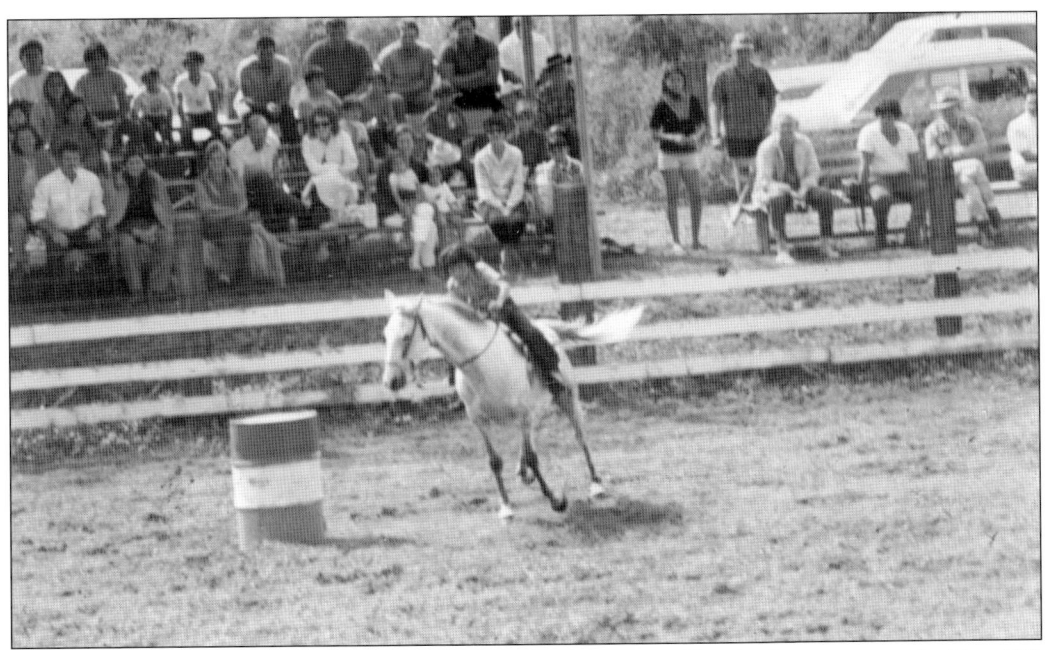

Rodeos were an important part of the ranching tradition on Kaua'i. A young rough rider, Pi'i Aiu, competes in the barrel race at the annual Fourth of July rodeo at the Kealia Arena in 1974. (Courtesy of Danita Aiu.)

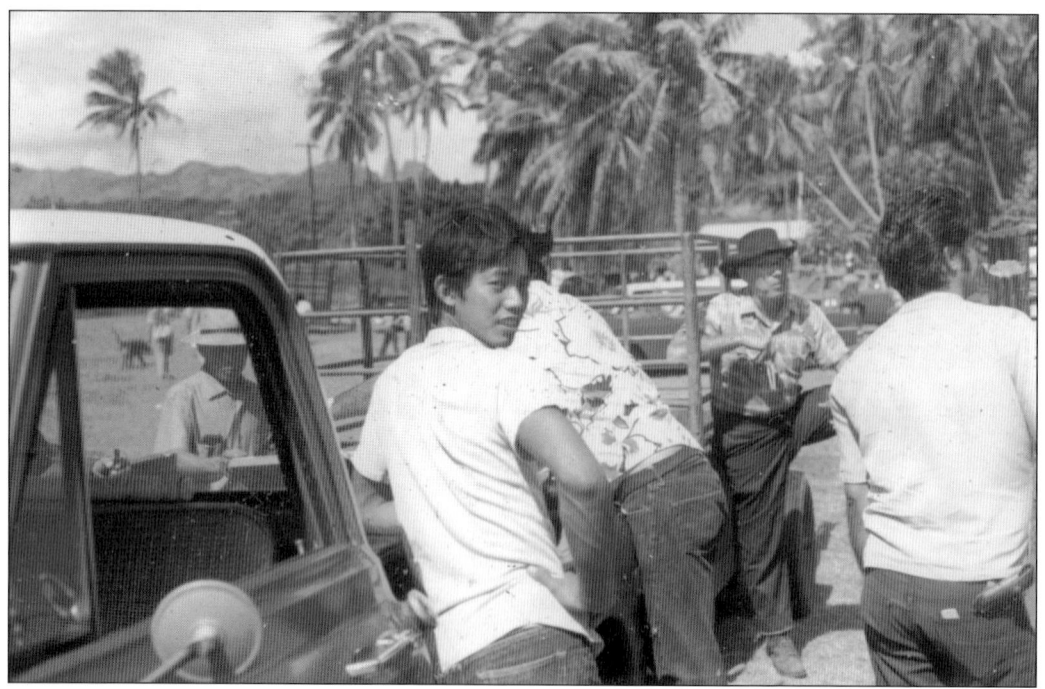

Local cowboys take a break from the annual Fourth of July rodeo in 1974. Ranchers Lincoln Ching (foreground) and Tony Arruda (back) are pictured. (Courtesy of Danita Aiu.)

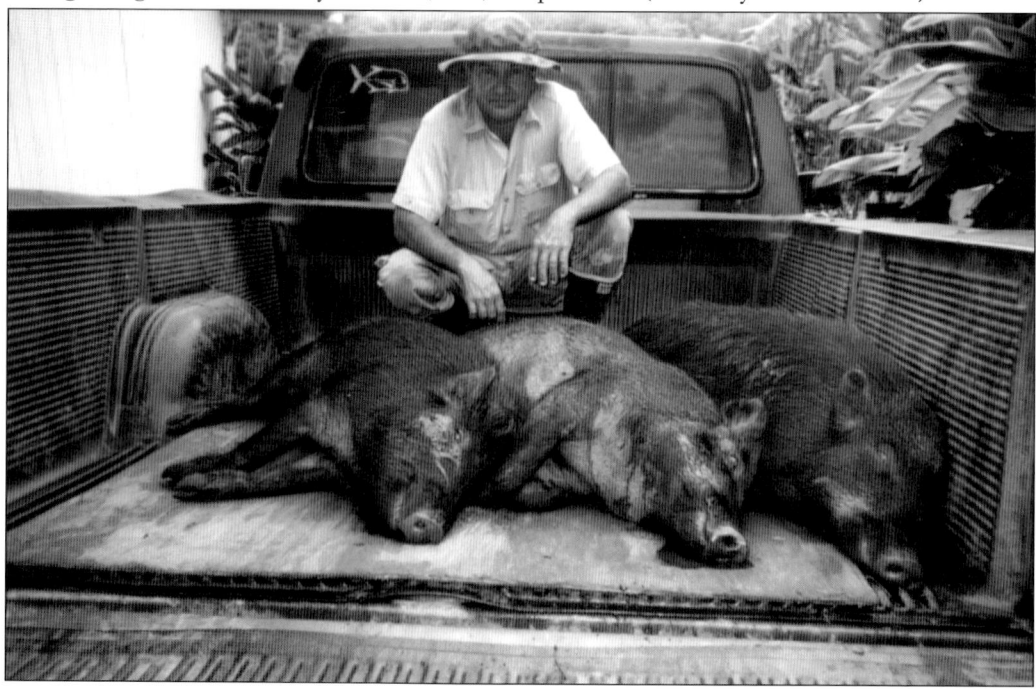

Hunting wild pigs provides an important source of food for many families. Hunters primarily use dogs to locate and chase the pigs into the mountains behind town. The meat is prepared in a number of ways, including smoking and cooking in an imu. Here, Dennis Thomas sits in the back of a truck with three large pigs from the day's hunt. (Courtesy of Dennis Thomas.)

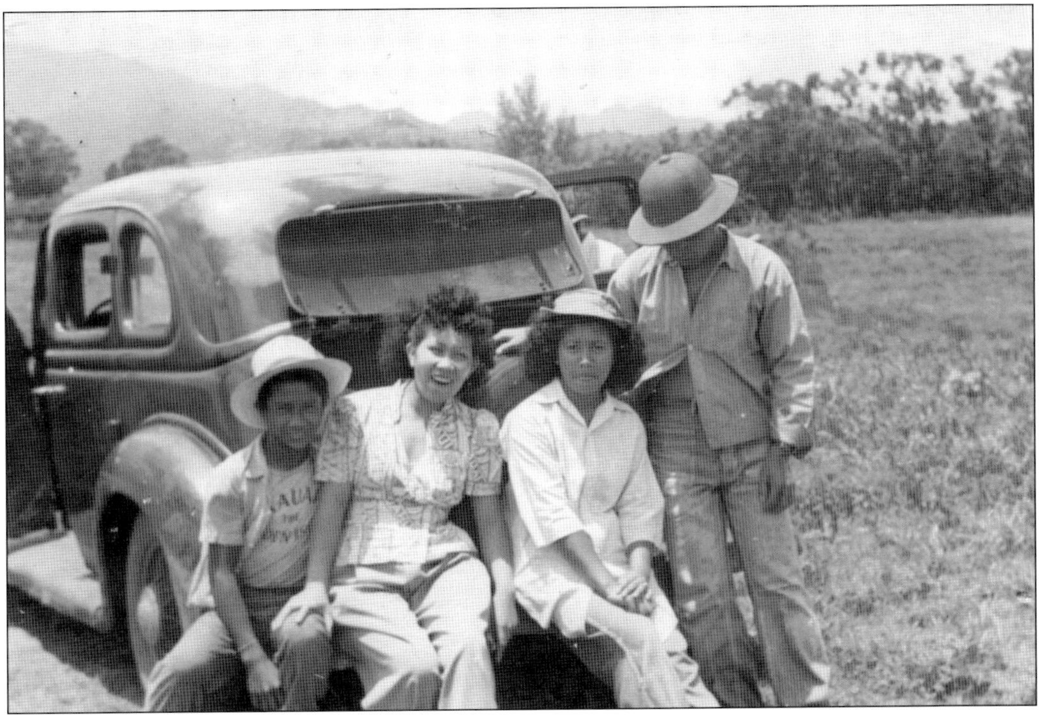

A group from Pueʻo Camp, one of several plantation camp communities in the Kapaʻa area, are enjoying an outing in 1943. Pictured from left to right are William Mande, Gladys Padre, Chrispino Laranio, and Sammy Bazin. (Courtesy of Janis Padre Plumer.)

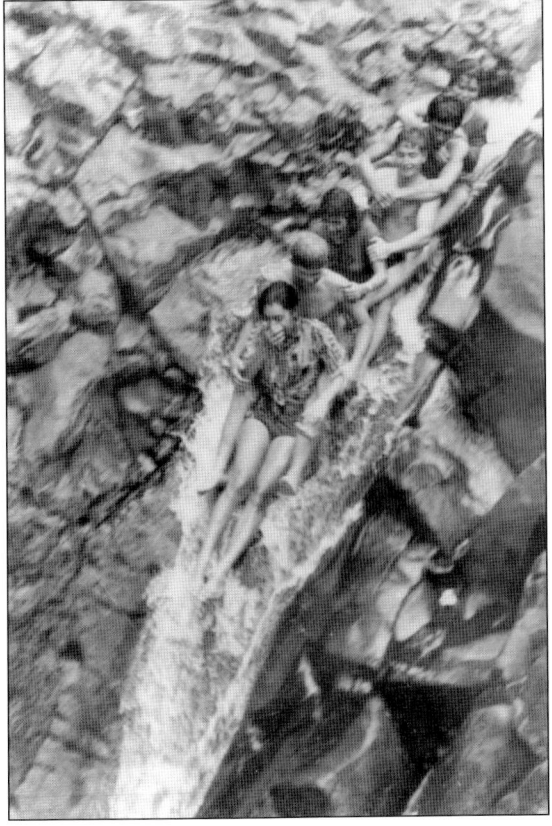

The slippery slide at Waipaheʻe Falls in the hills behind Kapaʻa was a favorite swimming hole for Kapaʻa kids. It was dangerous during periods of high rainfall but lots of fun the rest of the time. This summer of 1962 group of Kapaʻa High School boys and visiting Kamehameha School girls enjoy the exhilarating slide into the cold mountain pool. From left to right are unidentified, Russell Andrade, unidentified, Herman Texeira, Gilmore Youn, and Carolee Stewart. (Courtesy of Herman Texeira.)

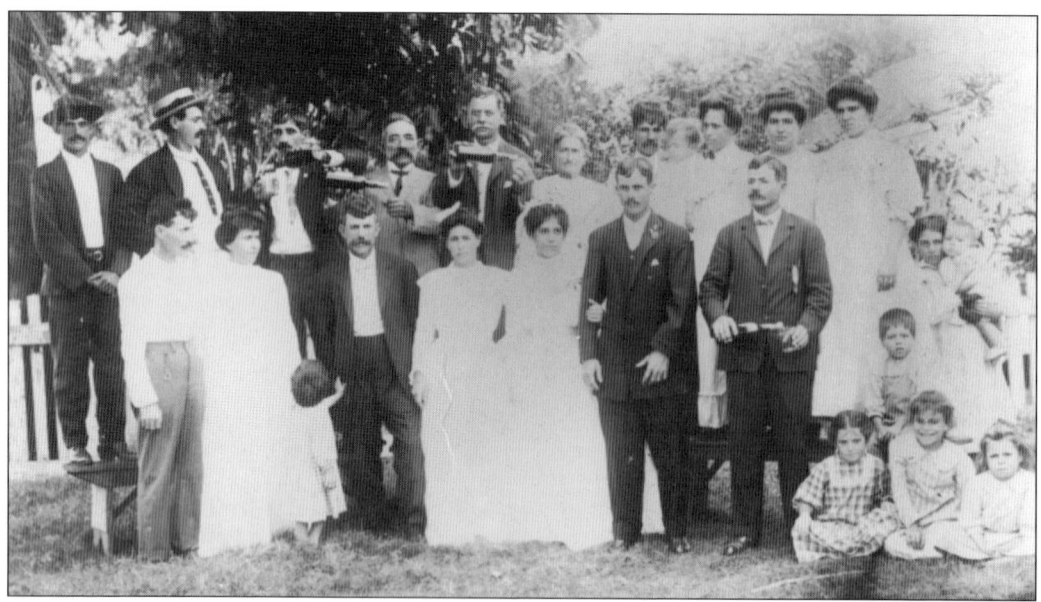

This photograph was taken in the early 1890s at the Souza family residence at Kealia Camp. It is not clear whether the bride or groom is a Souza. In the back of the bride and groom is Joaquin Souza (with the white moustache), with his wife to his right. The men in the back row are pouring from bottles, preparing for celebration. The Portuguese arrived on Kaua'i in 1880 to work at Makee Sugar Company. (Courtesy of Herman Texeira.)

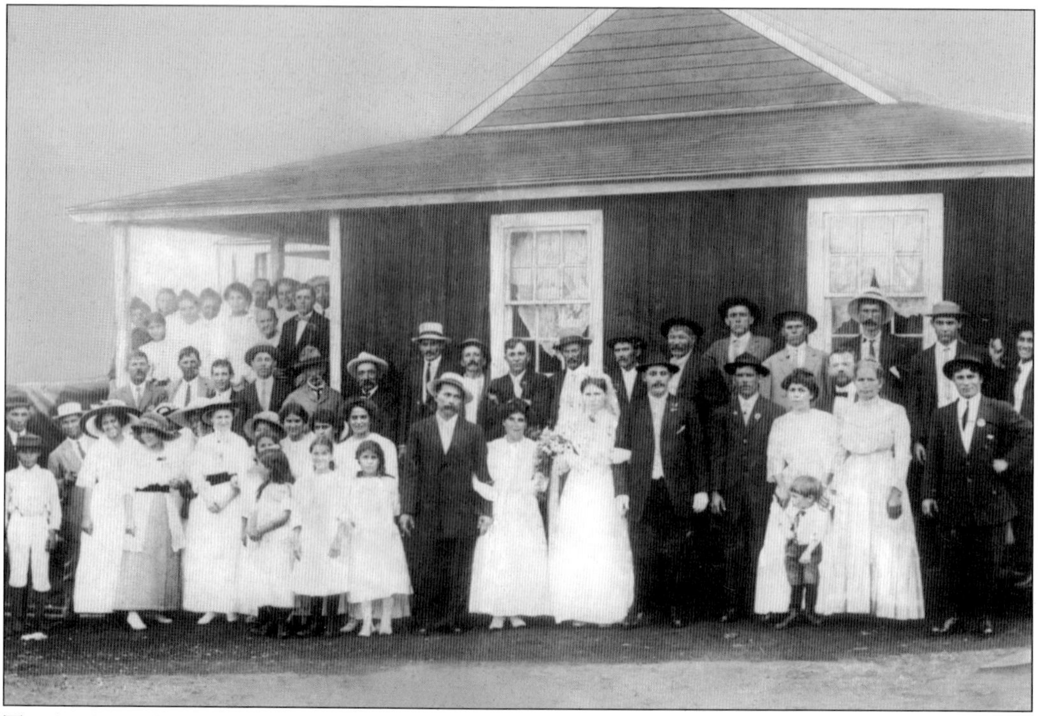

The bride and groom, Georgia Aguiar and Antone Rente, were married at St. Catherine's Church by Father Victorius on February 7, 1914. This photograph was taken in front of the family home in Kapa'a. (Courtesy of St. Catherine's Church.)

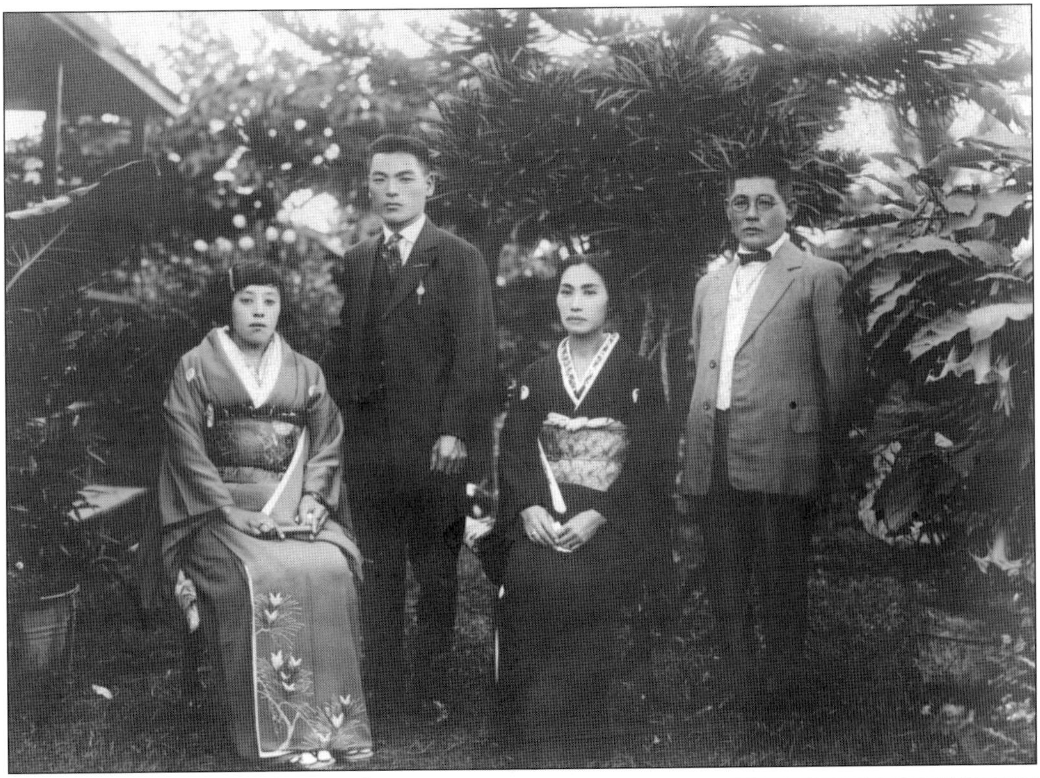

This wedding photograph was taken in 1920 at Kealia Camp, celebrating the wedding of Fumiyo Takeshiro and Enosuke Ueno Takeshiro. They are pictured in both traditional Japanese and Western attire. Pictured from left to right are Fumiyo Takeshiro (bride), Enosuke Ueno Takeshiro (groom), Toyo Takeshiro, and Jisuke Takeshiro. The photograph was taken by Y. Takemoto of Kapa'a Photo Studio. (Courtesy of Wilma Matsumura Chandler.)

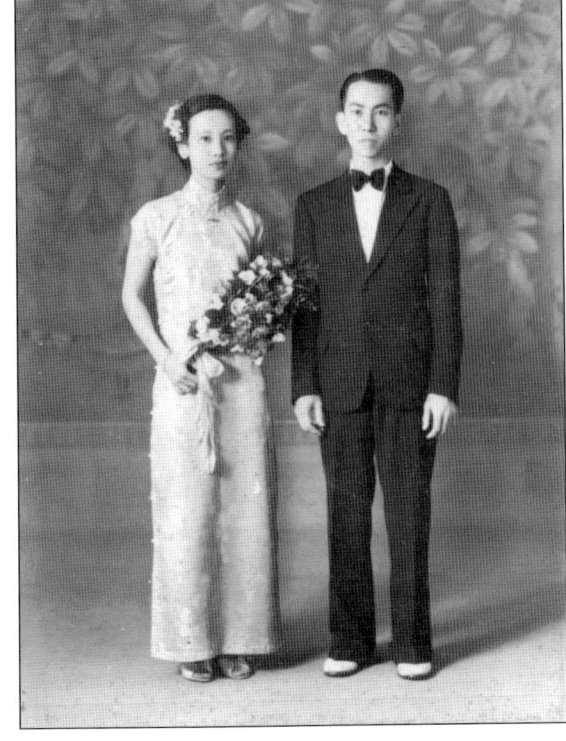

Irene Tom and Harry Hee, descendants of early Chinese immigrants, moved to Kapa'a and married in the early 1940s. Irene wears a traditional Chinese dress and Harry a modern Western suit. (Courtesy of Linda Paik Moriarty.)

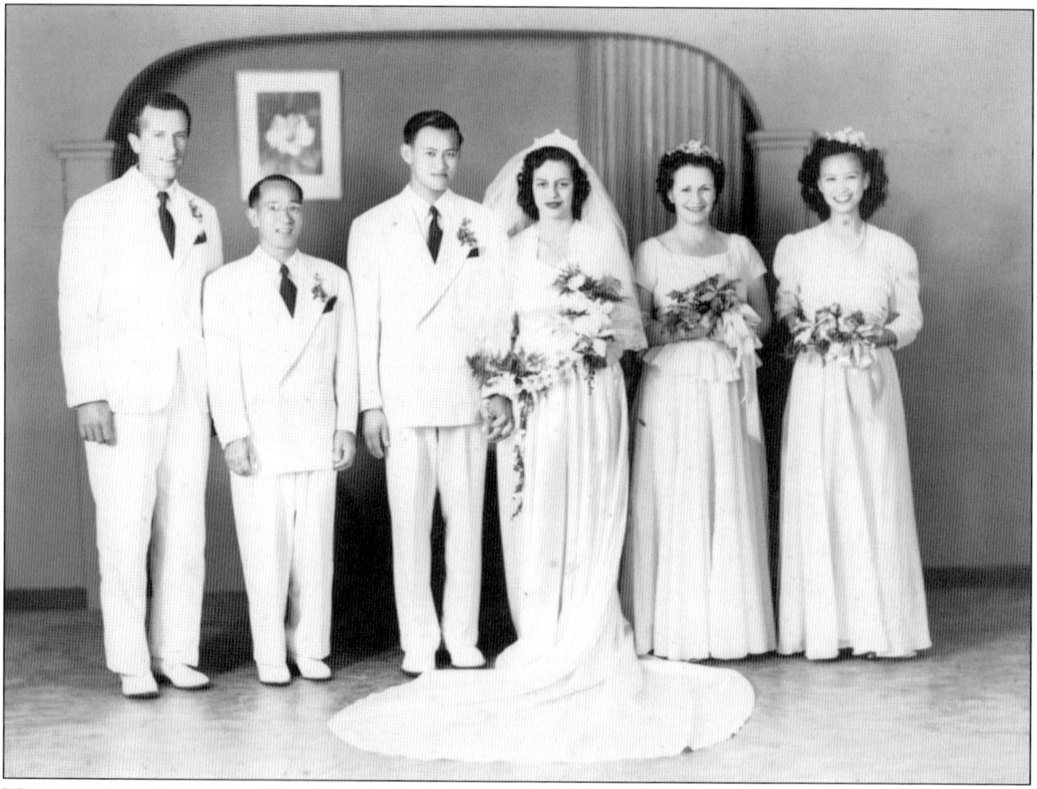

The marriage between Harold Ah Lok Wong and Mary Huddy is typical of the interracial marriages that became more common after World War II. Harold was Chinese and Mary part-Hawaiian. They were married on July 31, 1948, at St. Catherine's Church in Kealia. Their racially diverse wedding party is, from left to right, Stanford Morgan, Richard Higashi, Harold Wong, Mary Huddy, Helen Farias Morgan, and Hazel Wong. (Courtesy of the Wong family.)

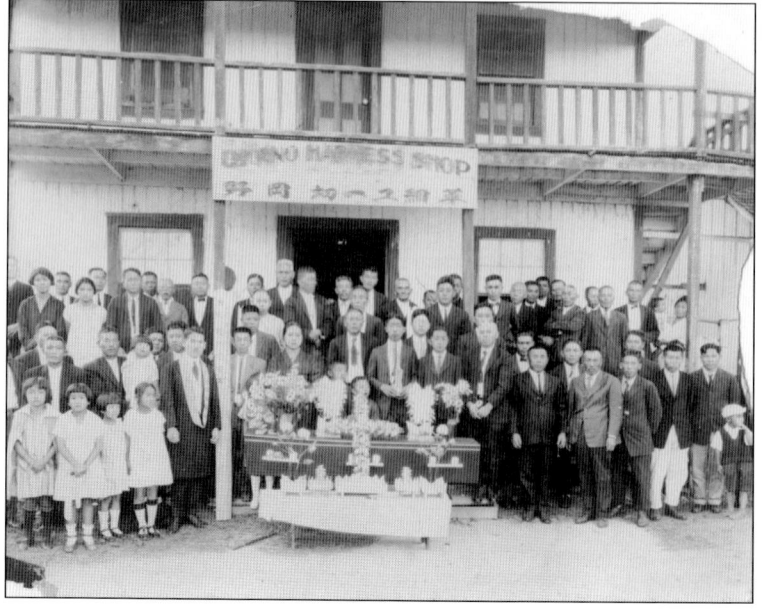

This photograph, taken in front of the Okano Harness Shop in Kapaʻa town, documents the funeral of Mataichi Okano. Japanese traditionally photograph the funeral party, which consists of family and friends. (Courtesy of Lorraine Okano Yamashita.)

# Nine

# Kapaʻa Today

In the early 1970s, Kapaʻa, a town that had thrived for almost a century as a center of agricultural production, suddenly found itself with virtually no economic foundation at all. Taro, rice, and pineapple were all gone; sugarcane fields still surrounded the town and patches of cane flourished in the hills above, but milling of the cane had moved to Līhuʻe, and it was clear that the industry itself was dying on Kauaʻi.

In the mid-1970s, from the ruins of Hawaiian Cannery near the center of Kapaʻa town, emerged the Pono Kai Resort—a 241-unit beachfront resort complex symbolizing the new direction the town was to take. Kapaʻa merchants were forced to adapt to a new visitor clientele while continuing to serve the farmers and ranchers in the surrounding hills. The old train tracks and cane-haul road gave way to a coastal multiuse path frequented by both locals and visitors called Ke Ala Hele Makalae, which translates to "the path that goes by the coast." Kapaʻa Beach Park, site of softball, football, and soccer games for generations and a tent city for troops during World War II, now doubles as a town park and a venue for numerous fairs and festivals. The largest is the coconut festival, sponsored by the Kapaʻa Business Association.

A monthly evening event, First Saturday, attracts as many as 2,000 locals and visitors to enjoy entertainment, food, and the opportunity to purchase a wide variety of locally produced products in an exciting block-party atmosphere. Yet, despite the dramatic changes, Kapaʻa retains its flavor as a Western frontier town, many of its structures built in the 1920s and 1930s. Some of the merchant families who began their businesses many decades ago are still in operation, although their merchandise is often quite different. New entrepreneurs have moved in to many of the old buildings. Of course, growth has brought problems such as bumper-to-bumper traffic. Nevertheless, in 2013, *Forbes* magazine named Kapaʻa one of America's prettiest towns.

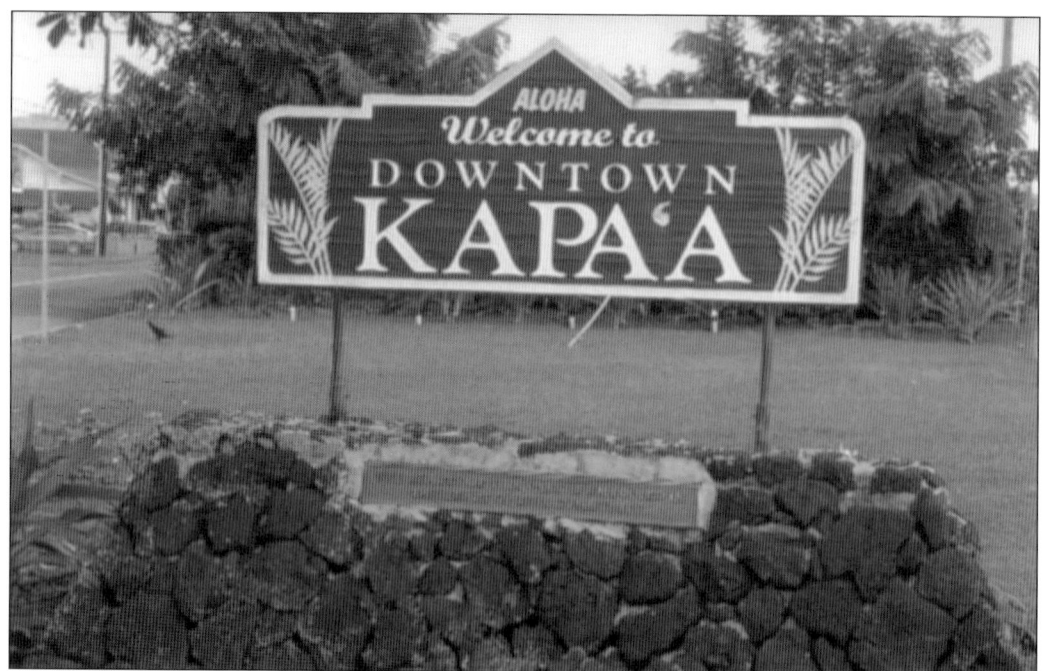

This sign welcomes everyone to Kapaʻa town. The inscription below reads "The beauty of this park is embodied in the heart of this community." As of 2010, Kapaʻa has a population of approximately 10,700. (Courtesy of Marta Miller Hulsman.)

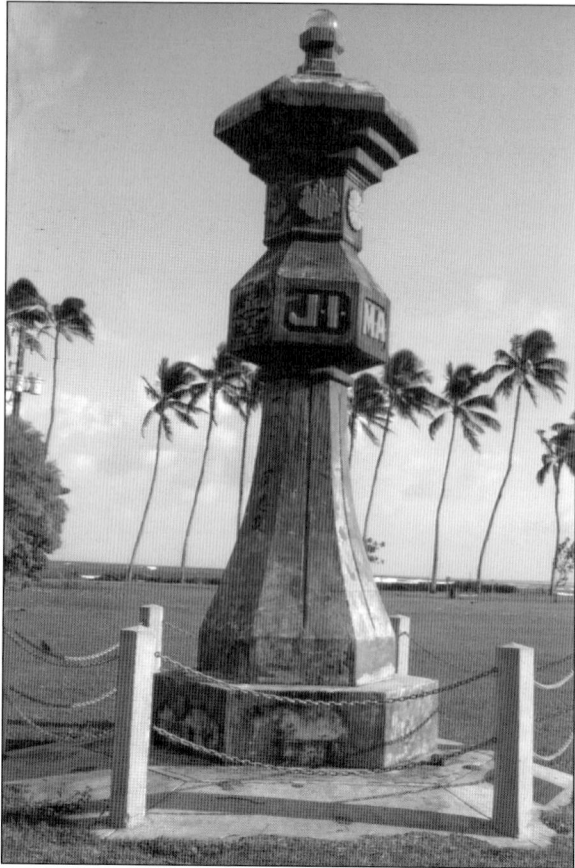

The Japanese stone lantern was constructed in 1915 by the first generation of Japanese immigrants to honor the 1912 ascension to the throne by Emperor Taisho. Buried during World War II as the result of anti-Japanese sentiment, it was unearthed in 1972, only to be buried again until 1987, when Kauaʻi Business Association partnered with Leadership Kauaʻi and the Kauaʻi Historical Society to restore the lantern to its present glory. It resides in the north end of Kapaʻa Beach Park, next to the Kapaʻa Public Library. (Courtesy of Marta Miller Hulsman.)

Established in 2001, Java Kai is probably the most popular coffee shop in Kapaʻa town. It is situated where the old Chinese-American Bank used to be. Besides coffee, it also serves breakfast and lunch. During the 1970s, it was a head shop, full of beads and incense as well as drug paraphernalia catering to the large hippie population then resident in the district. (Courtesy of Marta Miller Hulsman.)

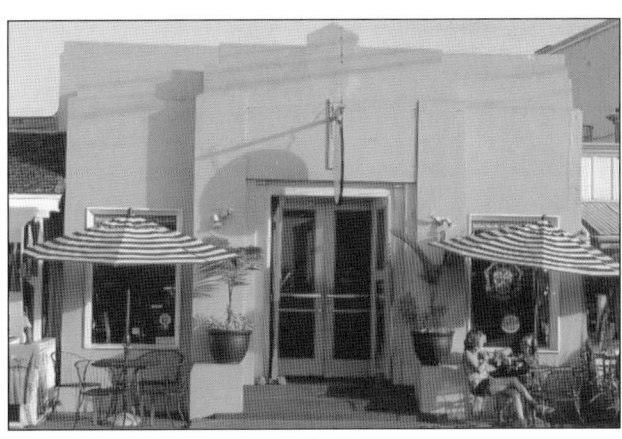

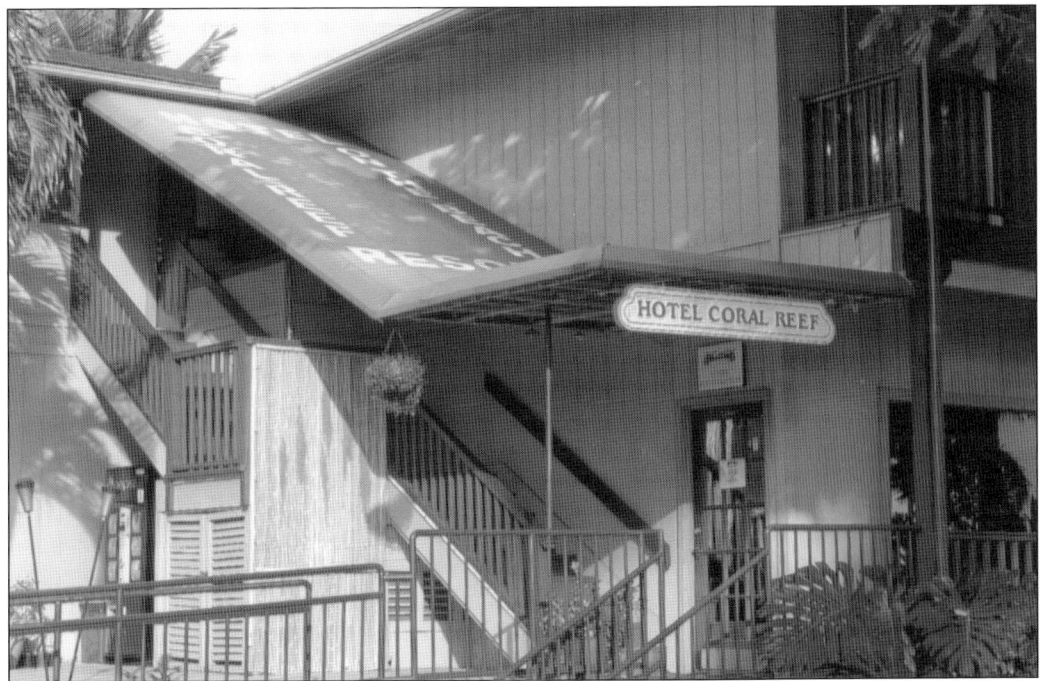

The Hotel Coral Reef, built by Ichiji Matsumura in 1956, is still in operation today. It sits next to the site of the old Kapaʻa Firehouse. For many years, it was the only hotel in Kapaʻa catering to off-island visitors. Film crews visiting the island often stay here, including the crew for the movie *South Pacific*. (Courtesy of Marta Miller Hulsman.)

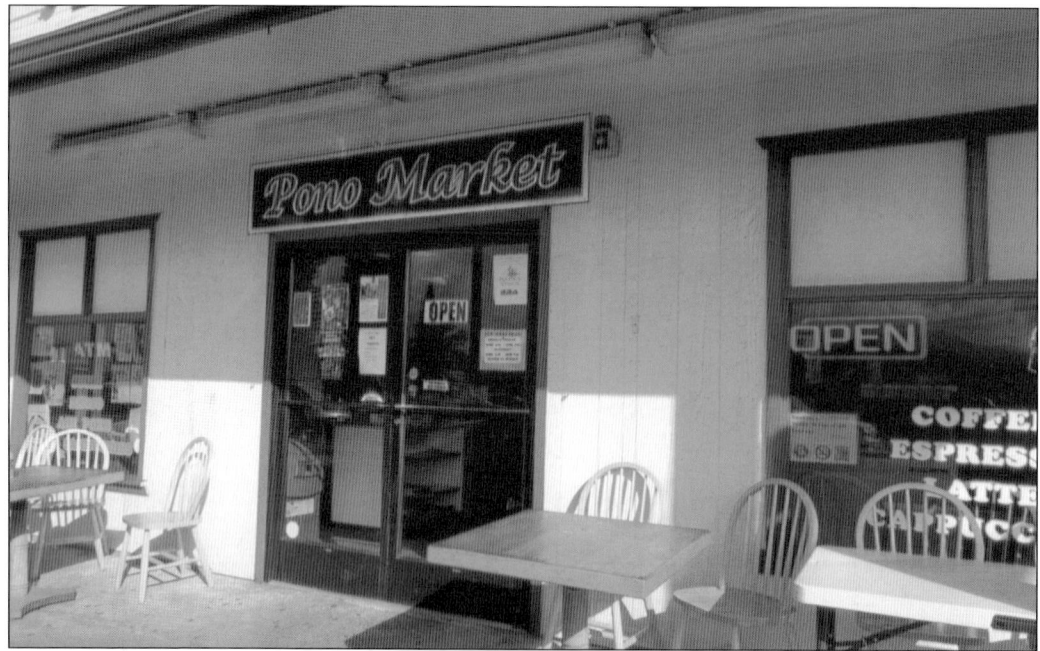

Pono Market is popular for its ethnic foods and pastries, all made on premises. It still is a family-run business. Uncle Kenneth Kubota recently established a coffee shop and ice-cream bar. Locals and visitors line up daily to grab their favorite island delight and a cup of coffee to go. (Courtesy of Marta Miller Hulsman.)

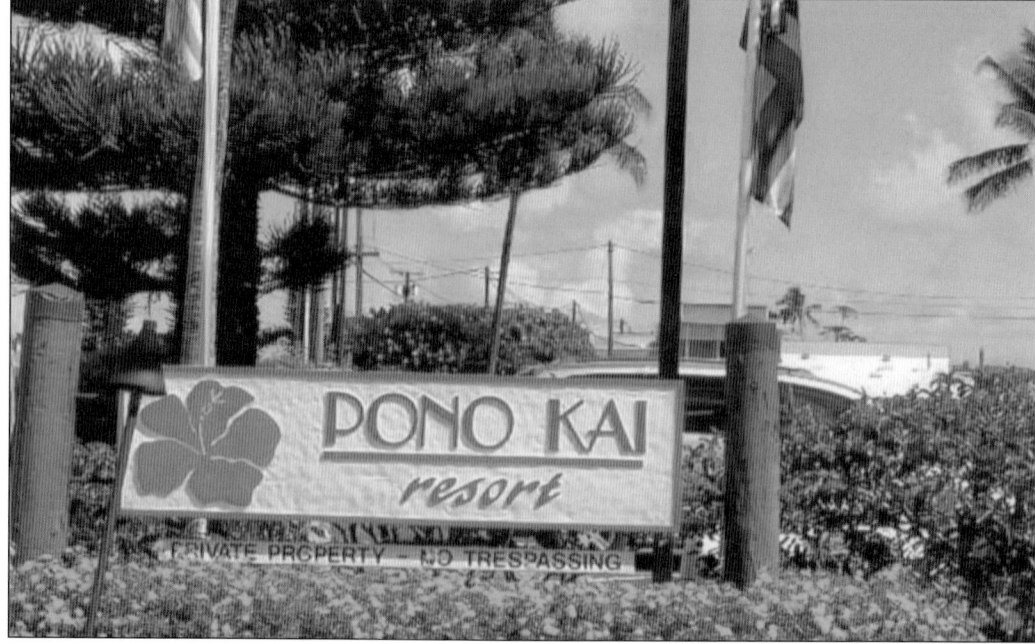

Pictured here is the entry to the Pono Kai Resort, where the old Hawaiian Canneries stood from 1915 to 1962. Pono Kai entertained its first guests in 1977 and remains the only large resort in Kapa'a town. Pono Kai Resort is a mix of timeshare and condominium units. (Courtesy of Marta Miller Hulsman.)

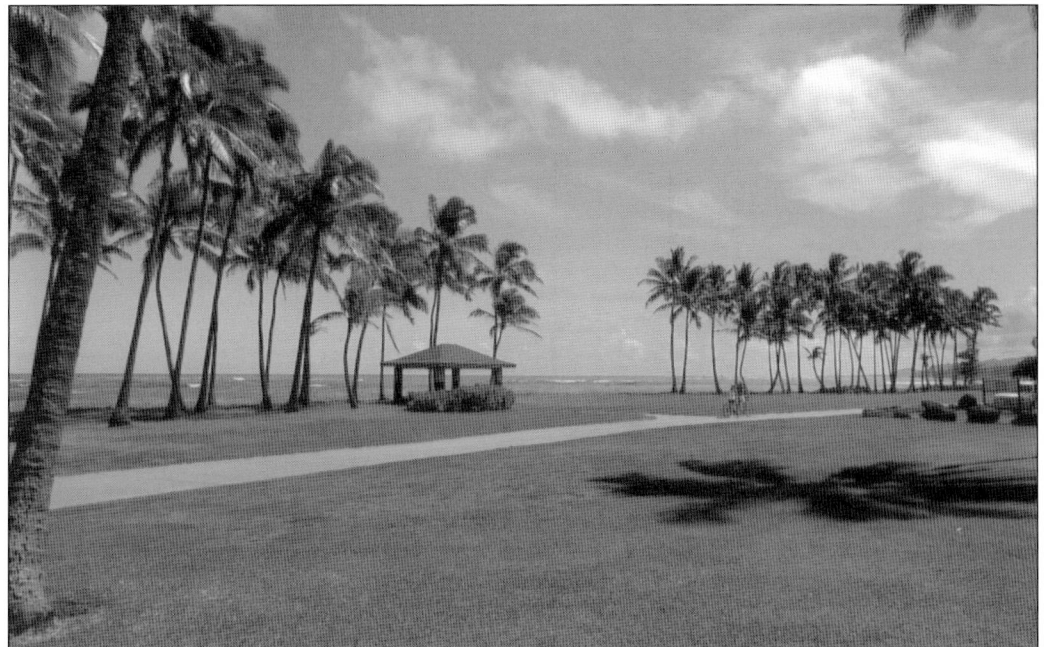

This is the multiuse path called Ke Ala Hele Makalae. Locals and visitors can enjoy a glorious bike ride, walk, or run along the ocean path with magnificent views. It was constructed by paving over what was once the railroad track and later the road used to haul sugarcane from the fields to the mill. The plan is to have Ke Ala Hele Makalae extend south into Lihu'e. As of 2012, seven miles have been completed. (Courtesy of Marta Miller Hulsman.)

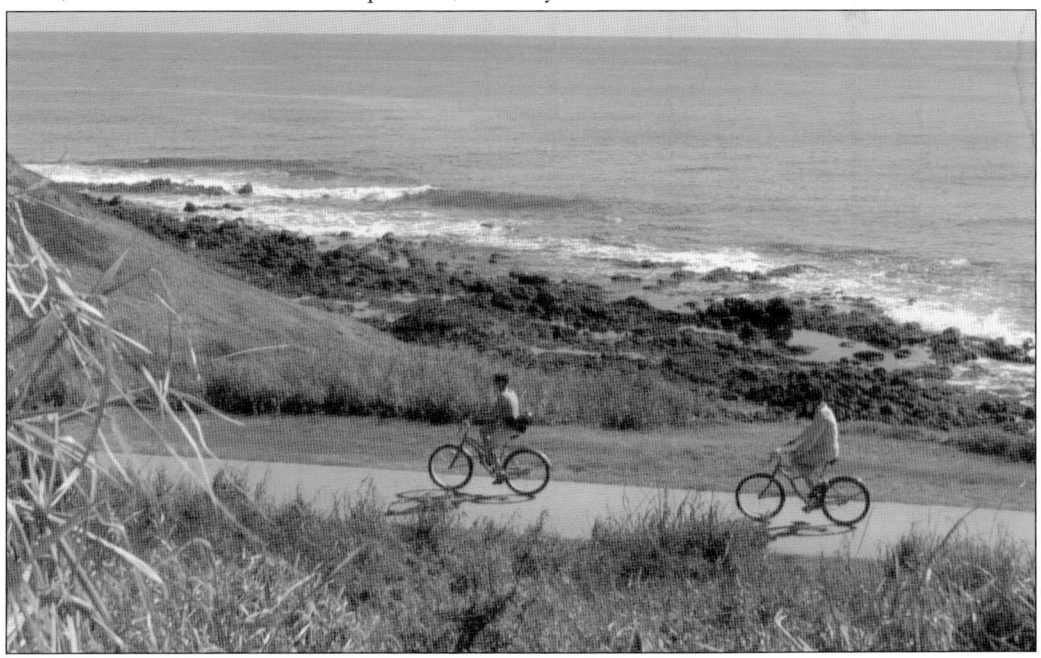

These bike riders enjoy Ke Ala Hele Makalae. It is not uncommon to observe humpback whales during whale season, along with dolphins, turtles, and endangered monk seals basking in the sun. (Courtesy of Marta Miller Hulsman.)

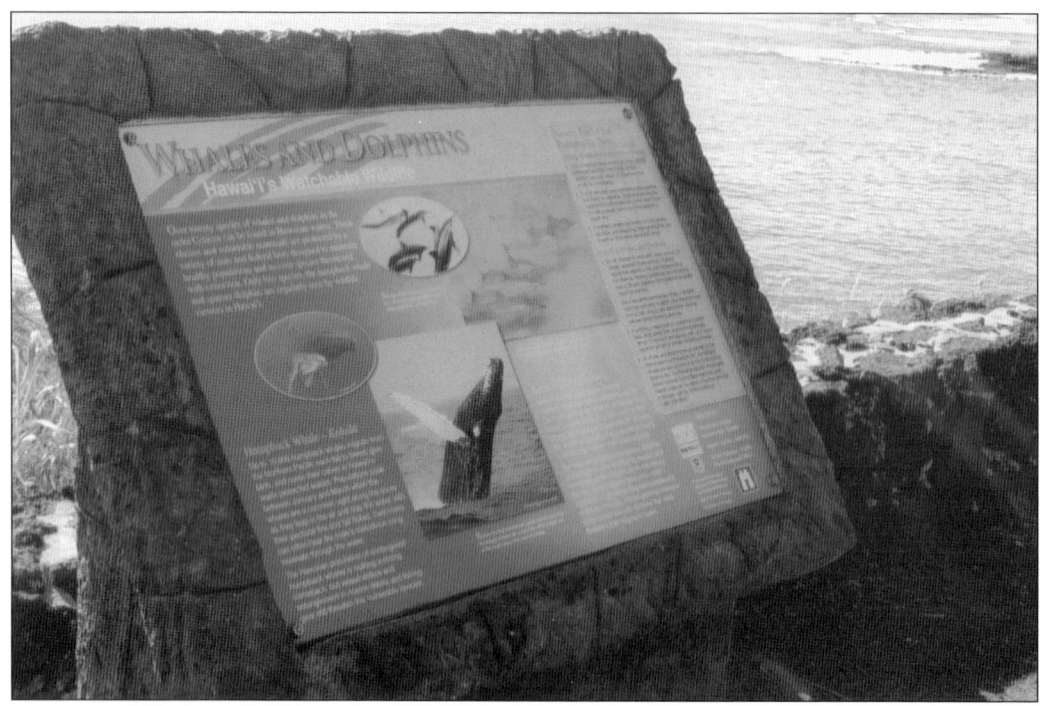

Informational signs dot the Ke Ala Hele Makalae and provide information on the town's history and coastal marine life likely to be encountered. (Courtesy of Marta Miller Hulsman.)

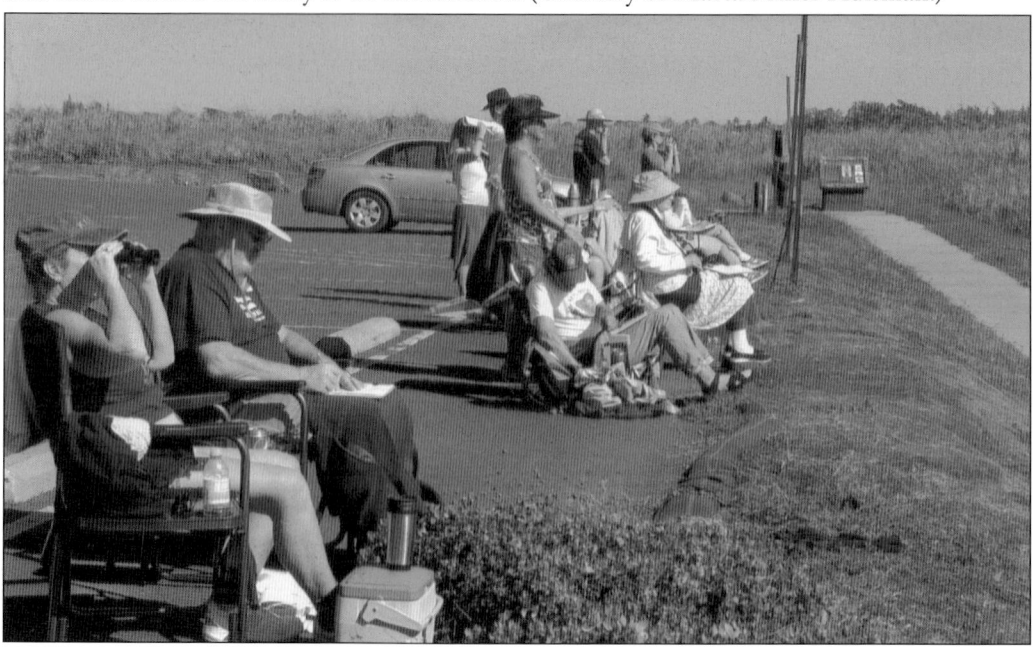

From December to May is *kohola* (humpback whale) season. These majestic gentle giants travel from the North Pacific to Hawaiian waters to breed and birth calves. Pictured here is a group of volunteer whale counters perched above Ke Ala Hele Makalae. Native Hawaiians believe kohola are *aumakua* (family guardians), so the whales are treated with great respect. (Courtesy of Marta Miller Hulsman.)

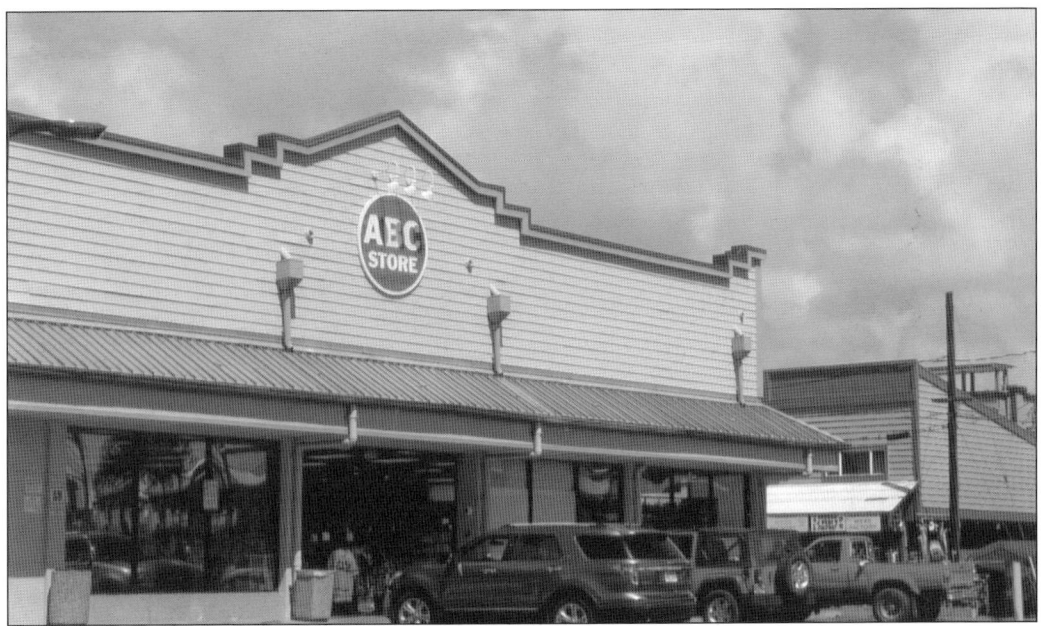

The ABC Store owned by Sidney and Minnie Kosasa got its start in the 1930s. The first ABC Store was opened on Waikīkī Beach in 1964 as a convenience store that had everything, including Hawaiian souvenirs, apparel, and foods. Today there are over 70 stores on all Hawaiian islands and in Las Vegas, Guam, and Saipan. The Kapaʻa ABC Store is situated at the crossroads where the Yoshida Gas Station used to be. (Courtesy of Marta Miller Hulsman.)

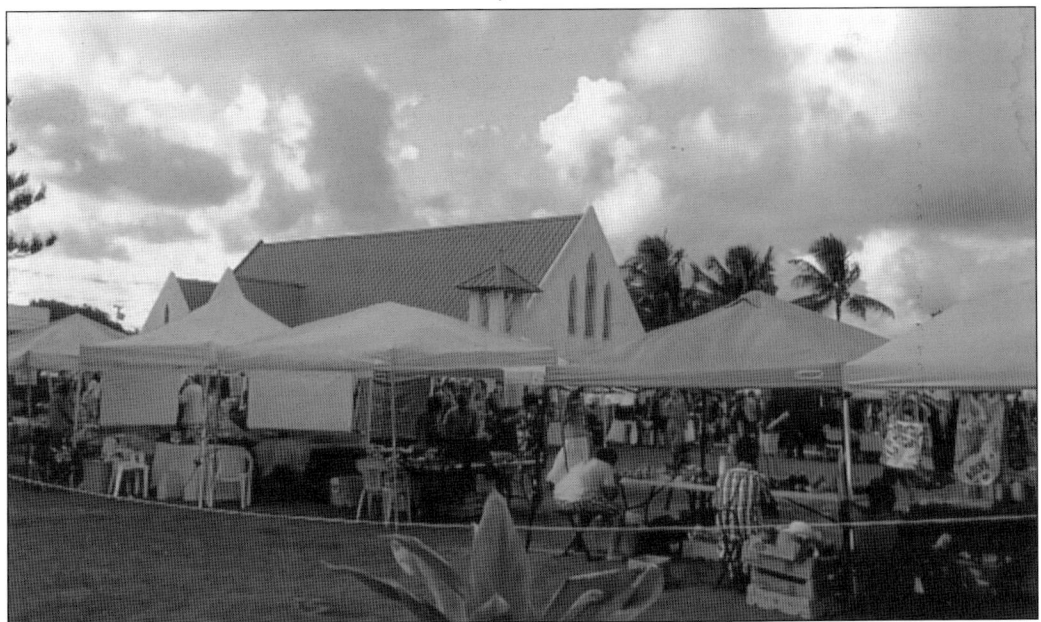

On the first Saturday of each month, Kapaʻa hosts the Old Kapaʻa Town Art Walk. Established in 2012 and sponsored by the Kauaʻi Business Association, it attracts huge crowds to Kapaʻa and creates a carnival-like atmosphere for tourists and local alike. Here, vendors set up on the lawn in front of the First Hawaiian Church during First Saturday in October 2014. (Courtesy of Marta Miller Hulsman.)

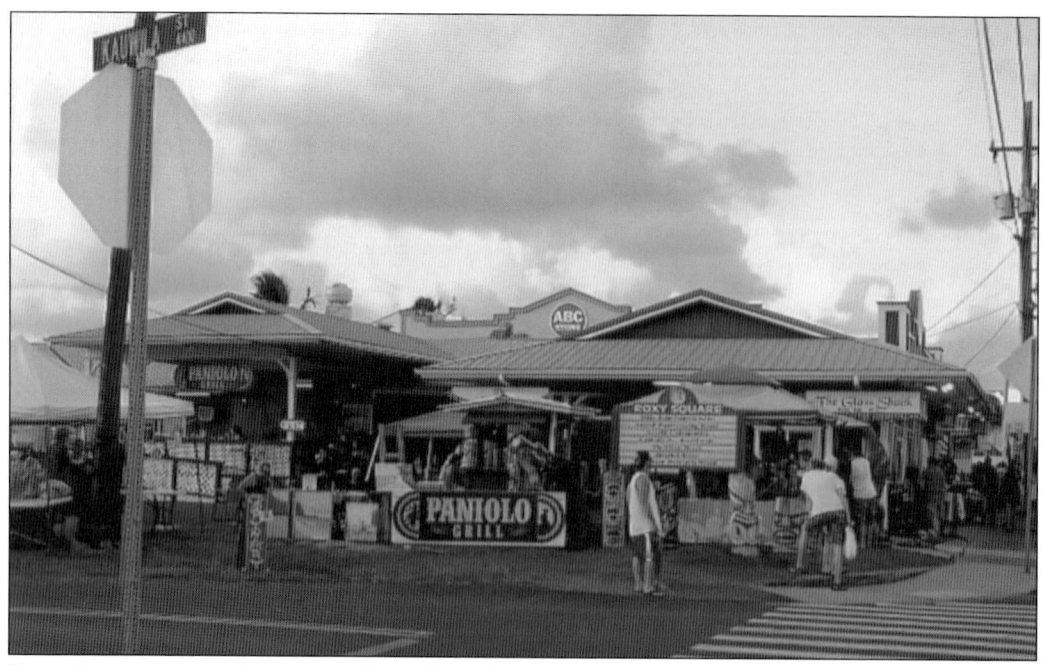

Roxy Square comes alive during First Saturday. Local artists, business owners, photographers, musicians, dancers, jewelry artisans, sculptors, and food trucks come in full force from 5:00 p.m. to 9:00 p.m. No sidewalk, yard, or alley is empty during this festive night. (Courtesy of Marta Miller Hulsman.)

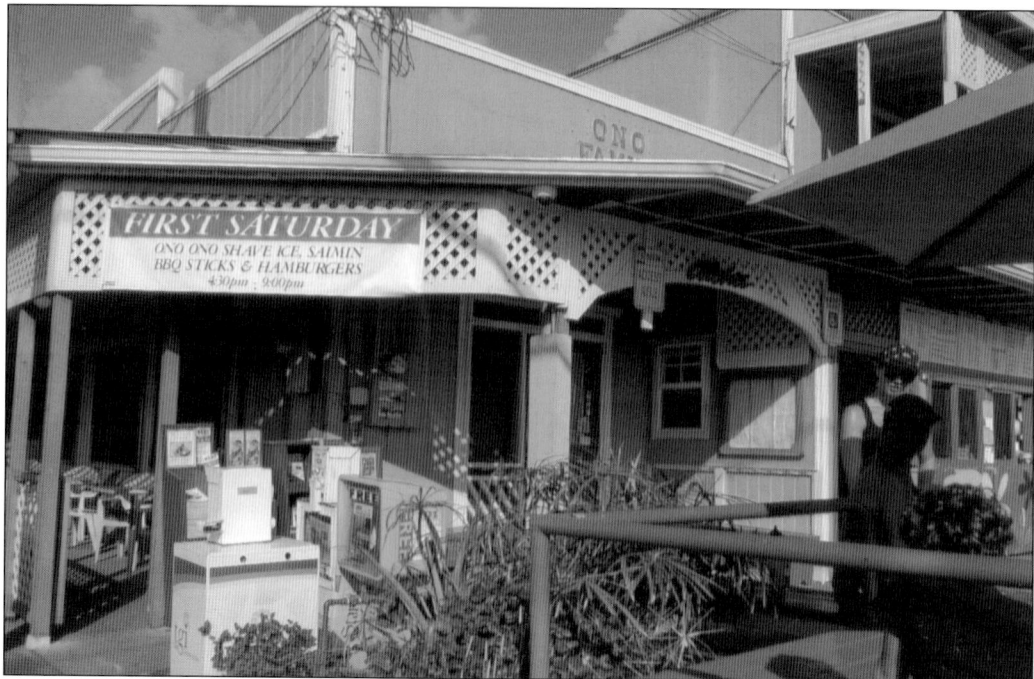

This sign advertises First Saturday in front of Ono Family Restaurant before the crowds descend for the festivities. This is the starting point for First Saturday from the south end of town. (Courtesy of Marta Miller Hulsman.)

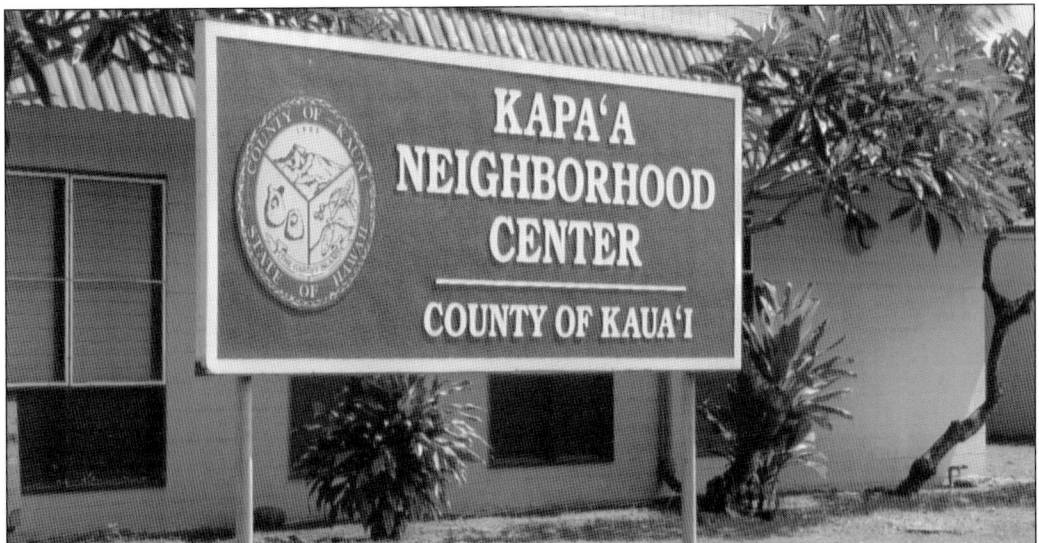

Kapa'a Neighborhood and Senior Center has been located in the north end of Kapa'a town for almost 50 years. This used to house the courthouse, jail, and police station. The County of Kaua'i sponsors the senior-center activities from 8:00 a.m. to 12:00 p.m. Monday through Friday, and residents of any age can participate. There are many classes available, like exercise, hula, ukulele, crafts, Hawaiian quilting, Japanese dance, and tai chi. These classes are free to local residents and visitors. (Courtesy of Marta Miller Hulsman.)

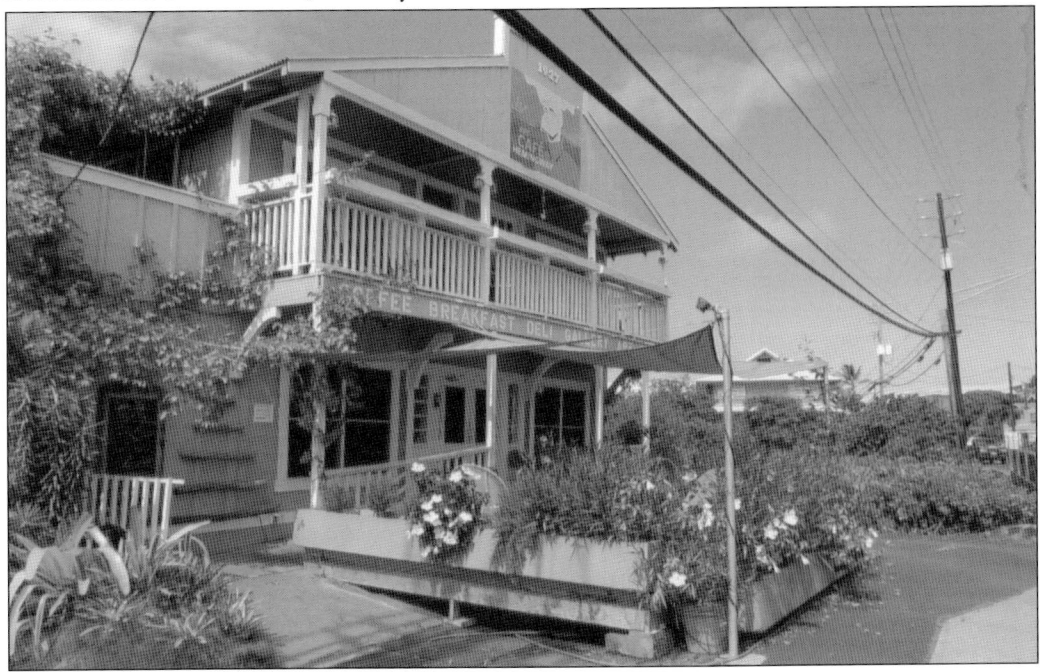

Art Café Hemingway was opened in September 2011 by owners Jana and Marcus Boemer as a new café with Old-World flavors. They used Hemingway's name because he liked to eat and drink and was a wonderful artist. All food is made by Jana from scratch using the best and freshest ingredients. They feature a new artist every First Saturday in conjunction with Kapa'a's First Saturday Art Walk. (Courtesy of Marta Miller Hulsman.)

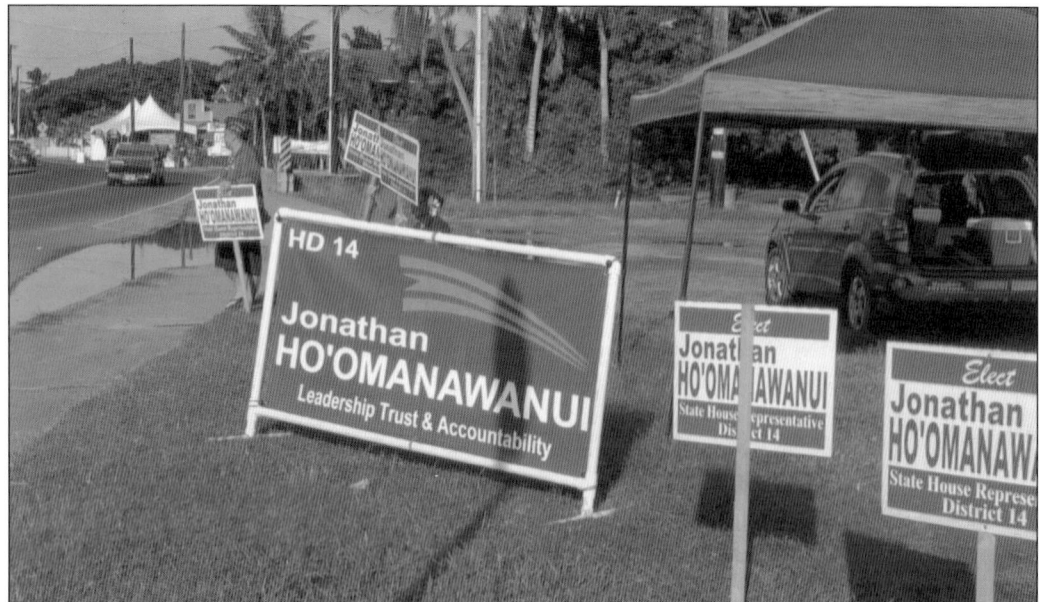

In Hawai'i during the political campaign season, volunteers at strategic locations hold and wave signs supporting their candidate. Name recognition is the game in Hawai'i politics. Visitors are surprised by this distracting practice, as sign wavers line the main roads and intersections. (Courtesy of Marta Miller Hulsman.)

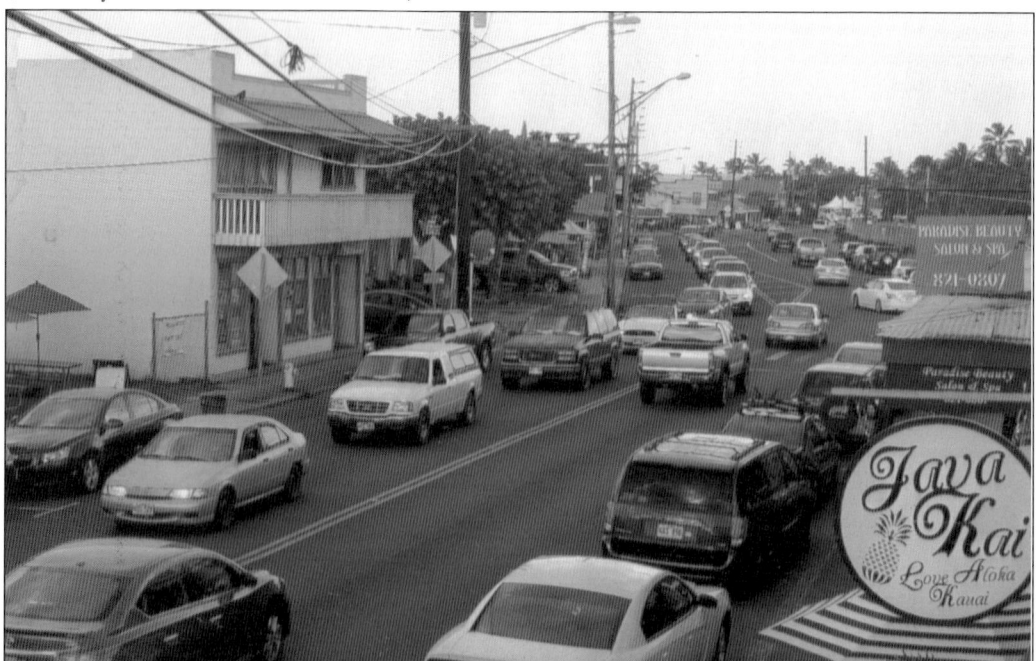

This photograph depicts the "Kapa'a crawl." Due to tourist and residential growth, Kūhiō highway is often congested and frustrating for drivers going to work, shopping, and recreating. This has been a problem for many years, despite attempts at solutions such as contra flow during rush hour, widening roads, installing roundabouts, a bypass road, and adjusting traffic signals. (Courtesy of Marta Miller Hulsman.)

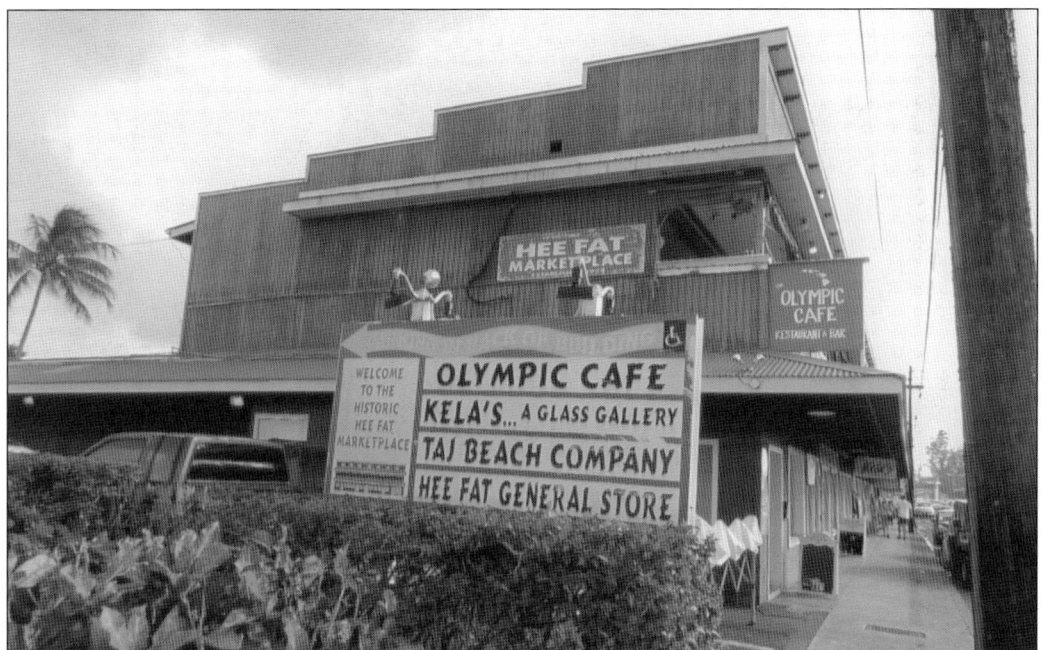

The Hee Fat Building was established by Chinese merchant Hee Fat in the 1920s. Today it houses many businesses such as Hee Fat General Store, Kela's Glass, a jewelry store, and upstairs Olympic Café. The Hee Fat General Store serves shaved ice made with all-natural ingredients. (Courtesy of Marta Miller Hulsman.)

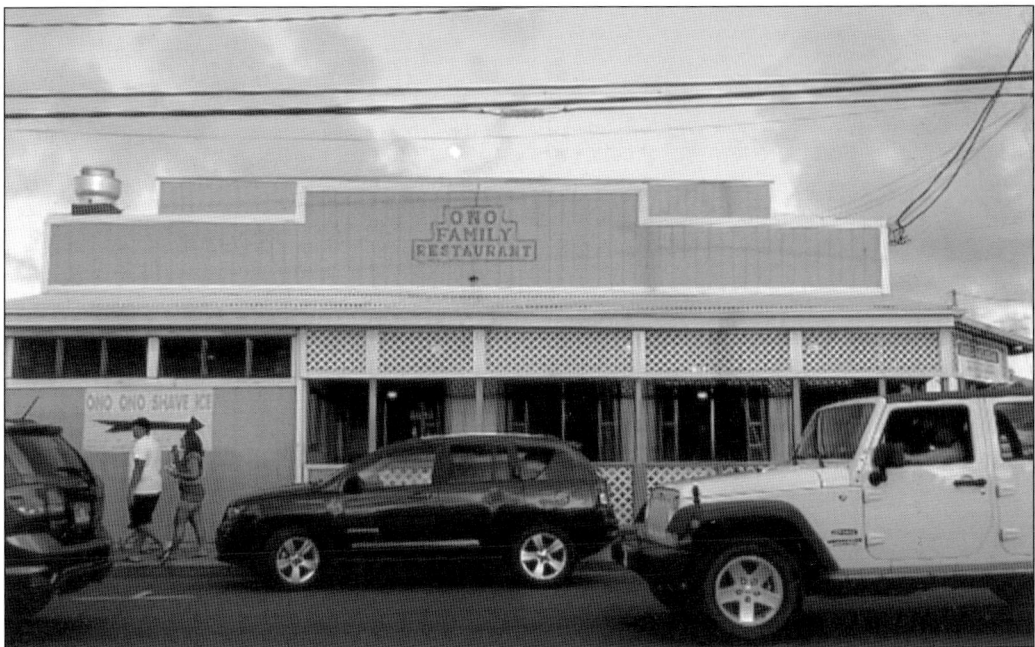

The Ono Family Restaurant and Shave Ice, owned by Kenny Ishii, has been in business for over 30 years. It offers breakfast and lunch using ingredients from local farmers, fishermen, and ranchers. Ishii believes his restaurant preaches aloha to everyone. (Courtesy of Marta Miller Hulsman.)

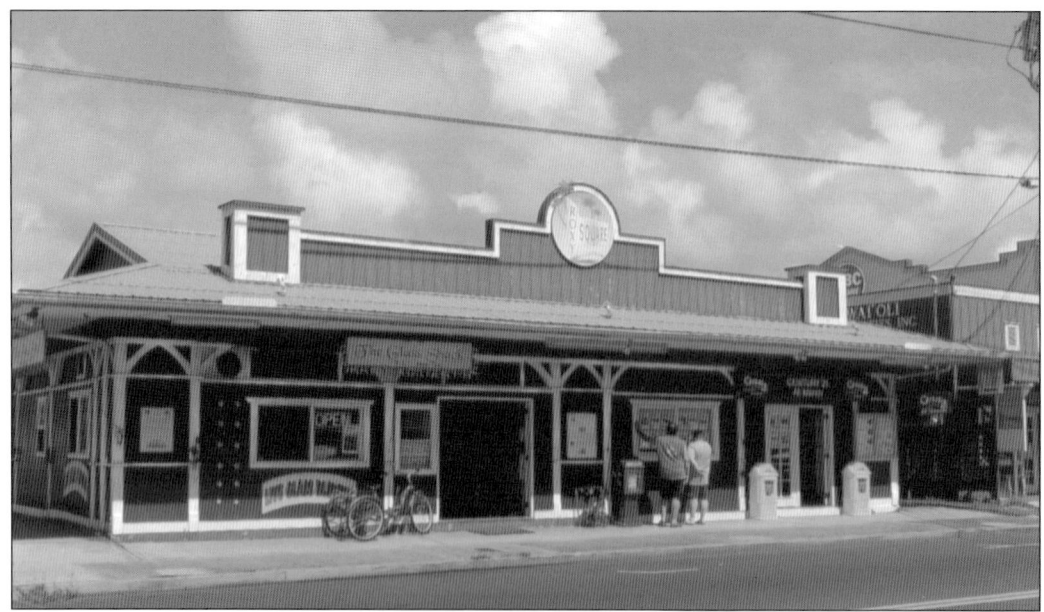

Roxy Square is on the site where the famous Roxy Theatre used to be. After the theater was demolished in 1992, Roxy Square was built by Bill Fernandez, son of William and Agnes Scharsch Fernandez, the original owners. This small shopping center was built by Bill to commemorate the memory of his parents. (Courtesy of Marta Miller Hulsman.)

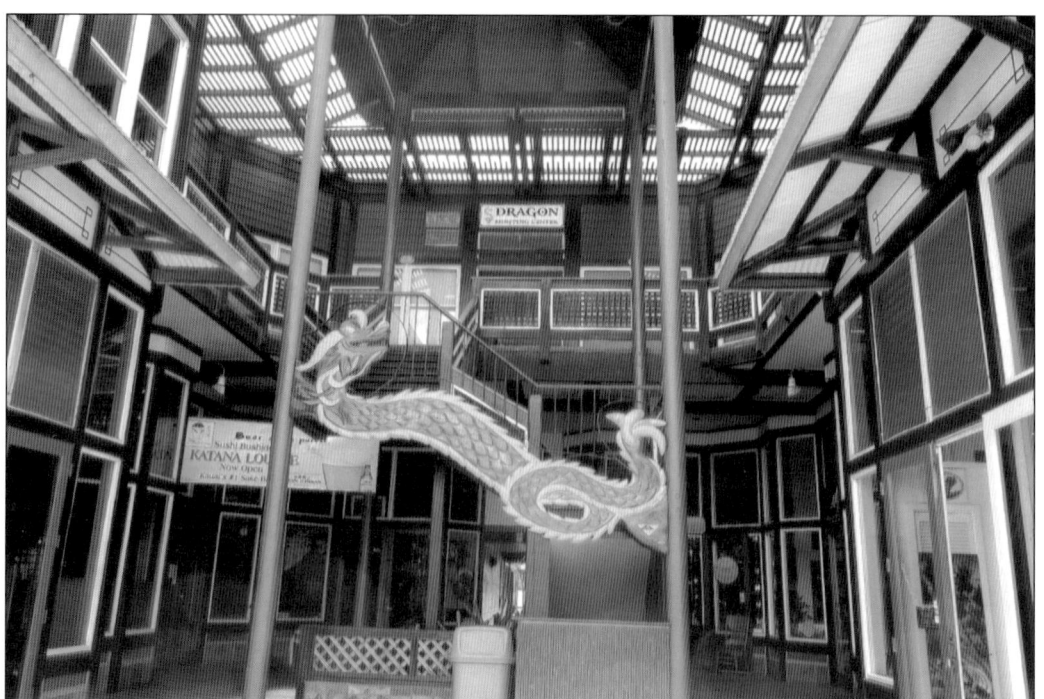

The Dragon Building, constructed in 1989, is a two-story neighborhood shopping center. It is a landmark in historic Kapaʻa town and advertises 19 tenants offering food and drink, retail shops, and classes. (Courtesy of Marta Miller Hulsman.)

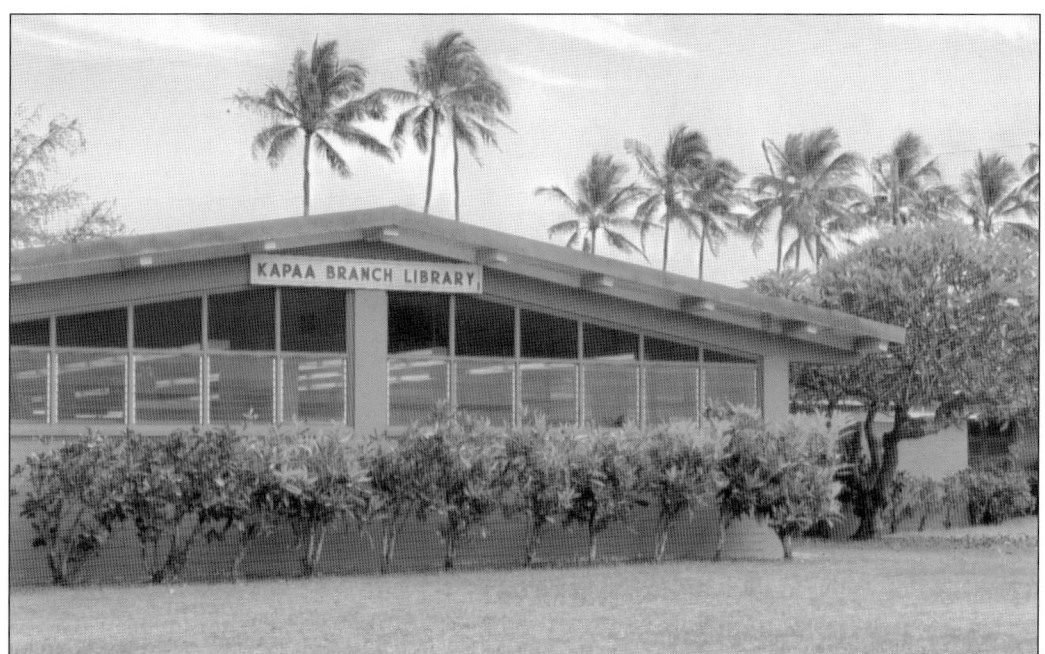

Kapaʻa Public Library, built by Kapaʻa contractor Ichiji Matsumura next to the Kapaʻa Beach Park, opened in 1955. It houses books, digital media, computers, and meeting rooms. It serves the most populated area on Kauaʻi. Matsumura also built the Coral Reef Hotel, Kapaʻa's swimming pool, and the Kauaʻi War Memorial Convention Center. (Courtesy of Marta Miller Hulsman.)

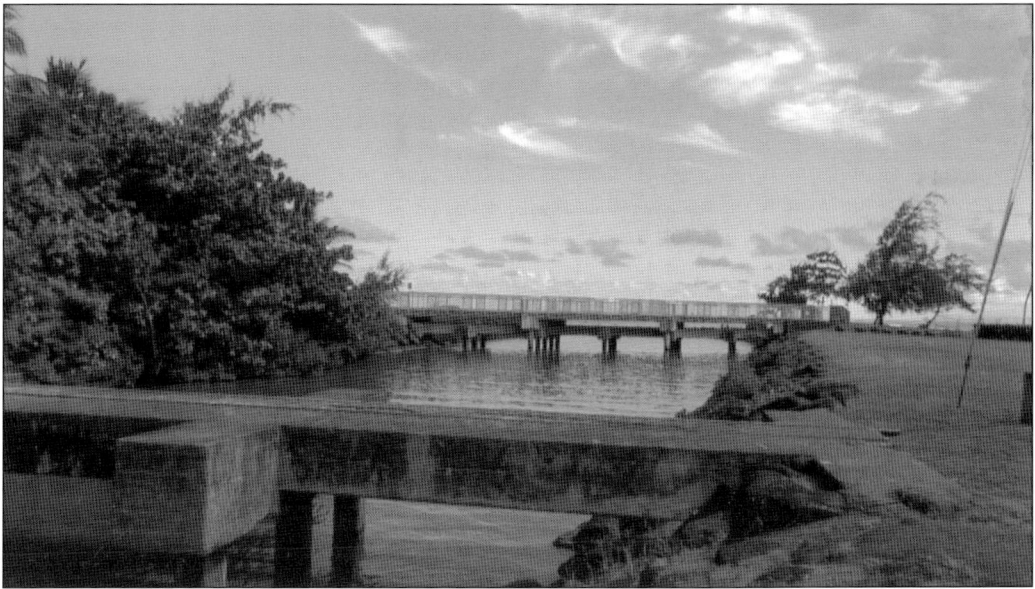

This is a photograph of the two railroad tracks that passed through town. In the foreground is the old sugarcane railroad that passed through town on Lehua Street. In the plantation days, the children would wait for the train and call out "throw cane!" The engineer always obliged and threw them pieces of sugarcane as the train passed. In the background is a bridge over Moʻikeha Canal for the Ke Ala Hele Makalae multiuse path. This was the old railroad track that delivered the sugarcane to Ahukini Landing in Līhuʻe. (Courtesy of Marta Miller Hulsman.)

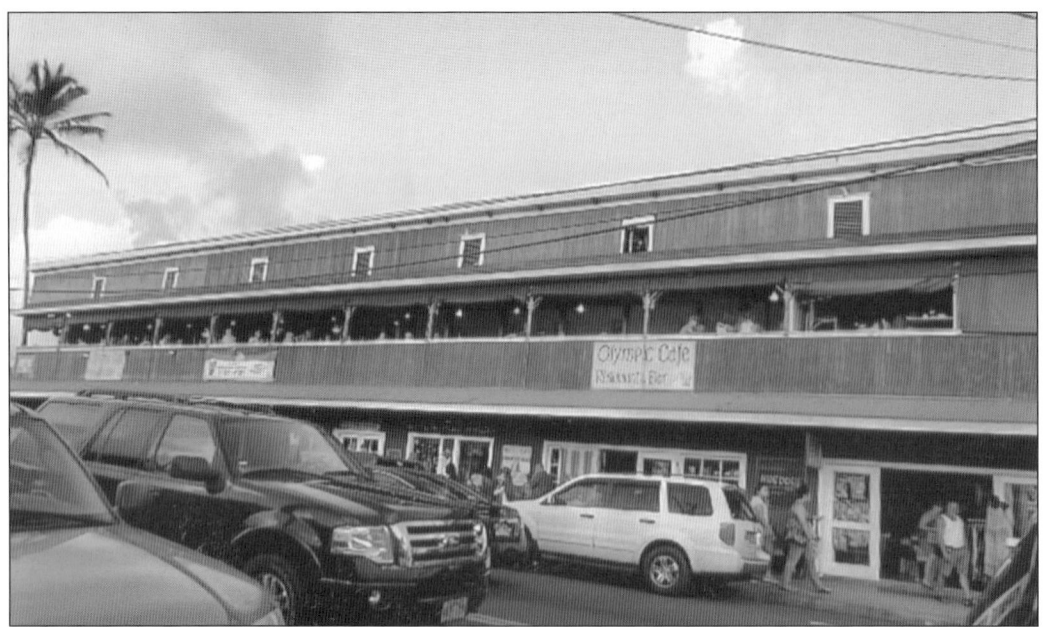

The second Olympic Café was established in 2001 and is located upstairs in the Hee Fat Building. It is known to locals as the OC, serving breakfast, lunch, and dinner. This casual restaurant and bar consistently offers huge servings at great prices. It serves mostly American-style foods combined with a few Hawaiian-style classics. (Courtesy of Marta Miller Hulsman.)

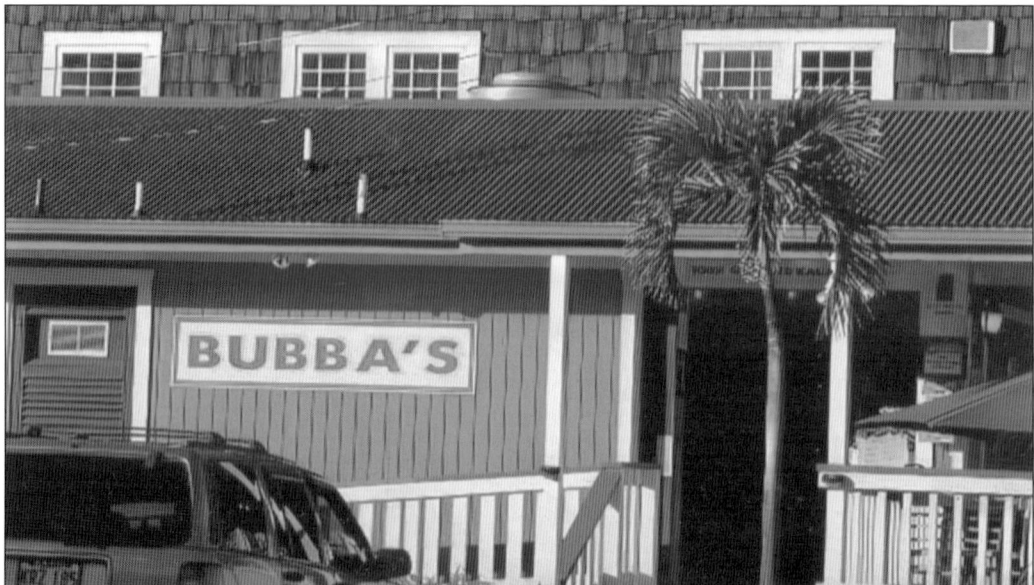

Bubba's Burgers, exclusive to Hawai'i since 1936, has three locations on Kaua'i. It opened in Kapa'a in 1989 serving the Bubba Burger, with mustard, old-fashioned ketchup-based relish, and diced onions. Owners John Greco and Debbie and Andrew Hart employ a humorous motto: "We cheat tourists, drunks, and attorneys." This is emblazoned on the front of their T-shirts, while the back reads, "We relish your buns." After the devastation of Hurricane Iniki in 1992, Bubba's generously served over 850 hamburgers free to hurricane victims. (Courtesy of Marta Miller Hulsman.)

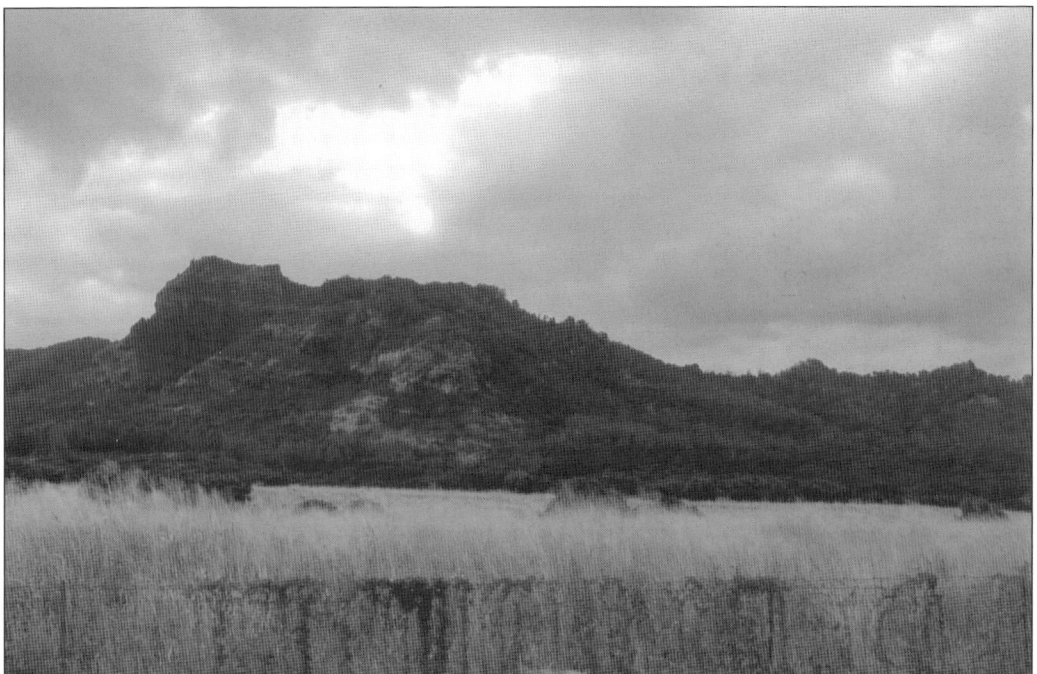

NouNou Mountain, the backdrop and symbol of Kapaʻa, is better known as the Sleeping Giant. Using imagination, it is possible to make out a human figure lying on his back. Hawaiian legends say this giant was tricked by villagers into eating rocks hidden in fish and poi. Sleepy from the meal, he took a nap and has never woken. Building codes in Kapaʻa state that no structure could be higher than a coconut tree, so that the Sleeping Giant could be seen from anywhere in town. It offers popular hiking trails that steadily climb nearly a thousand feet through forest to a picnic shelter and a lookout point. (Courtesy of Marta Miller Hulsman.)

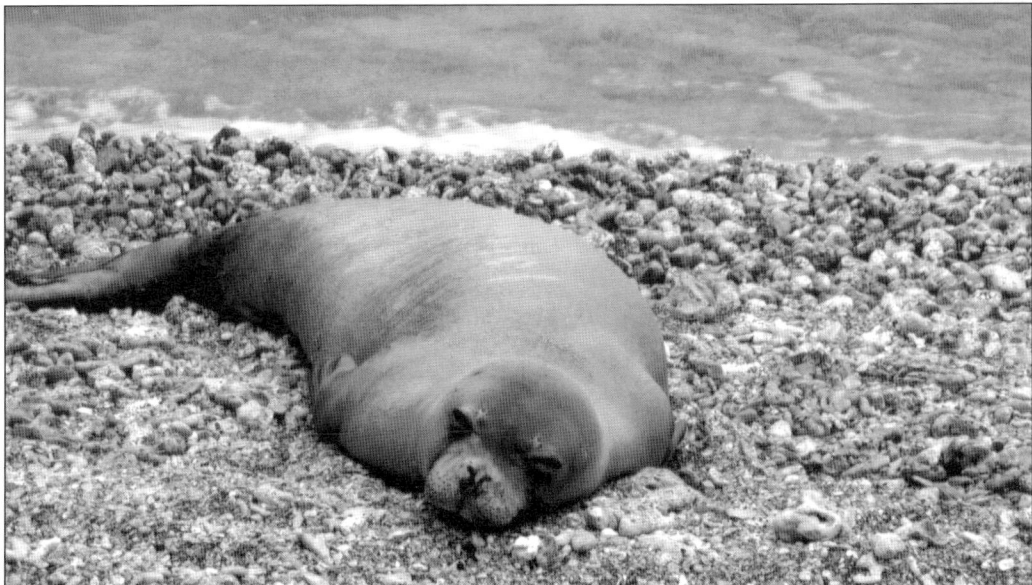

Pictured is an endangered Hawaiian monk seal basking in the sun at Kapaʻa Beach Park. (Courtesy of Marta Miller Hulsman.)

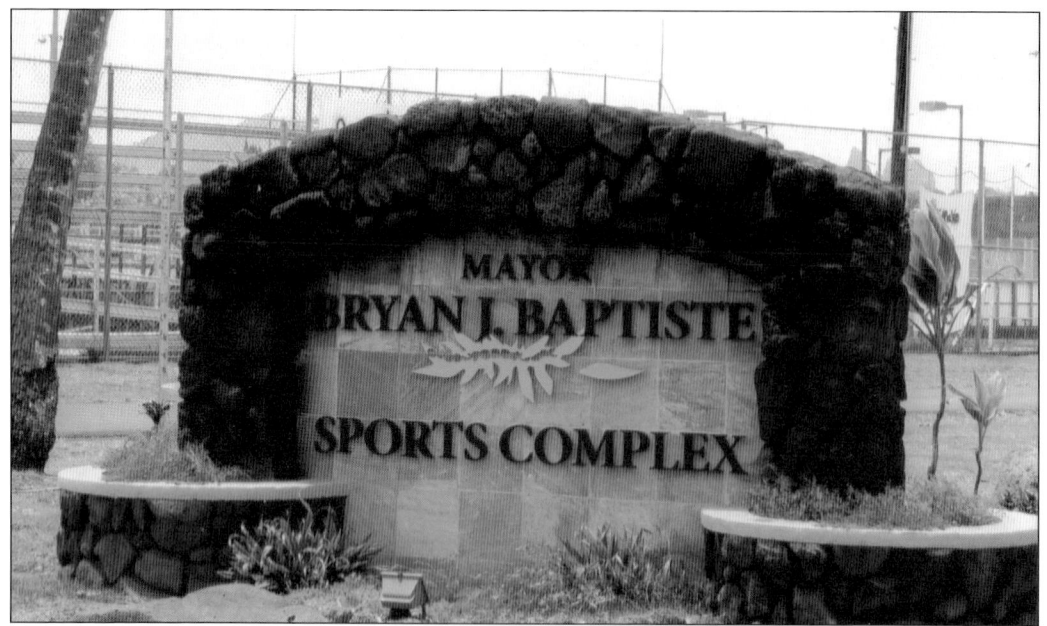

In October 2014, the Kapa'a New Town Park Facility was renamed the Mayor Bryan Baptiste Sports Complex. This was to honor the late mayor Bryan Baptiste, who passed away in 2008 at only 52 years old. It was his vision that Kapa'a High School should have its own home field. This 18-acre complex includes a football stadium, softball field, skate park, inline hockey rink, pavilion, two baseball fields, basketball courts, and tennis courts. (Courtesy of Marta Miller Hulsman.)

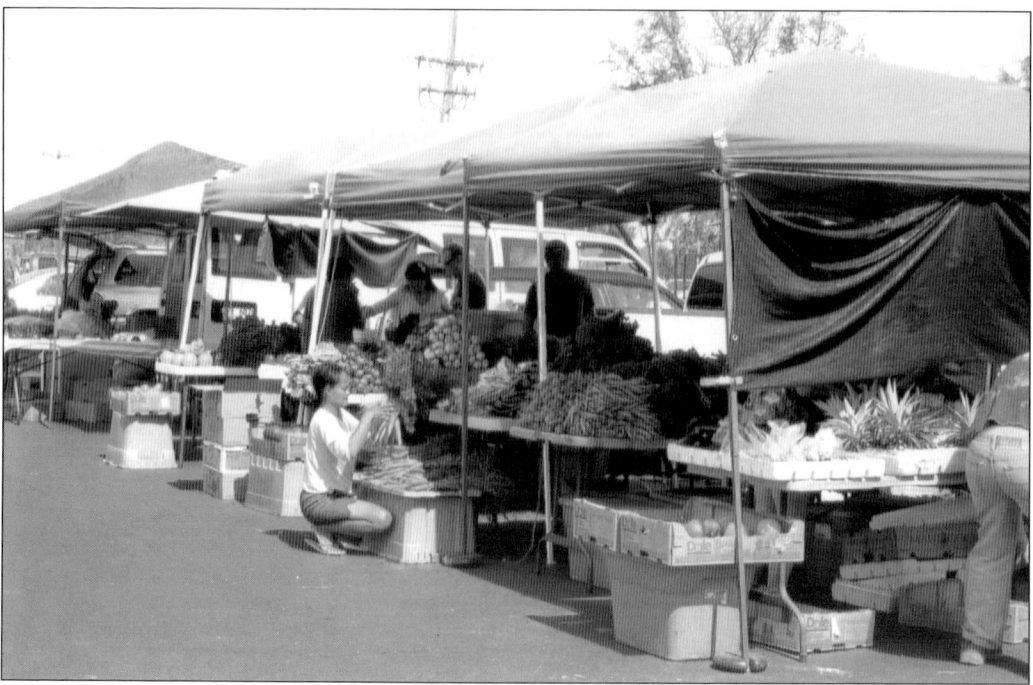

Each Wednesday afternoon, the Mayor Brian Baptiste Sports Complex opens its doors at 4:00 p.m. for the popular Farmers Market. (Courtesy of Marta Miller Hulsman.)

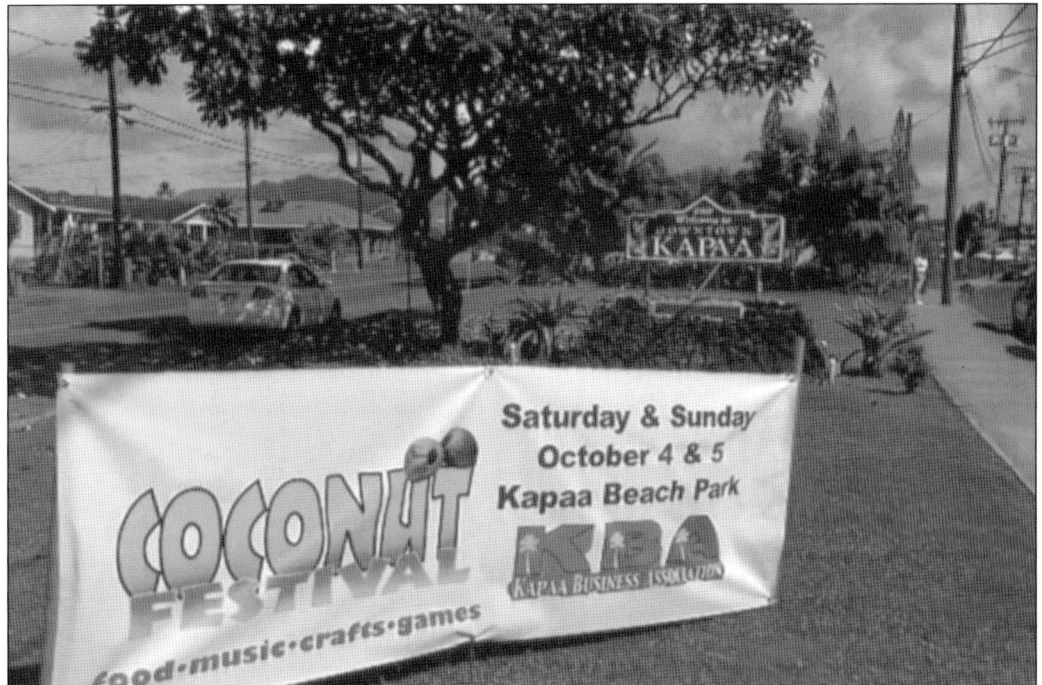

This Coconut Festival banner advertises this unique celebration. It runs for two days in October and offers coconut crafts, games, foods, and cooking contests. There is also music, hula, Taiko drumming, and a special *keiki* (children's) section. It is designed to bring families together in a safe and fun environment. (Courtesy of Marta Miller Hulsman.)

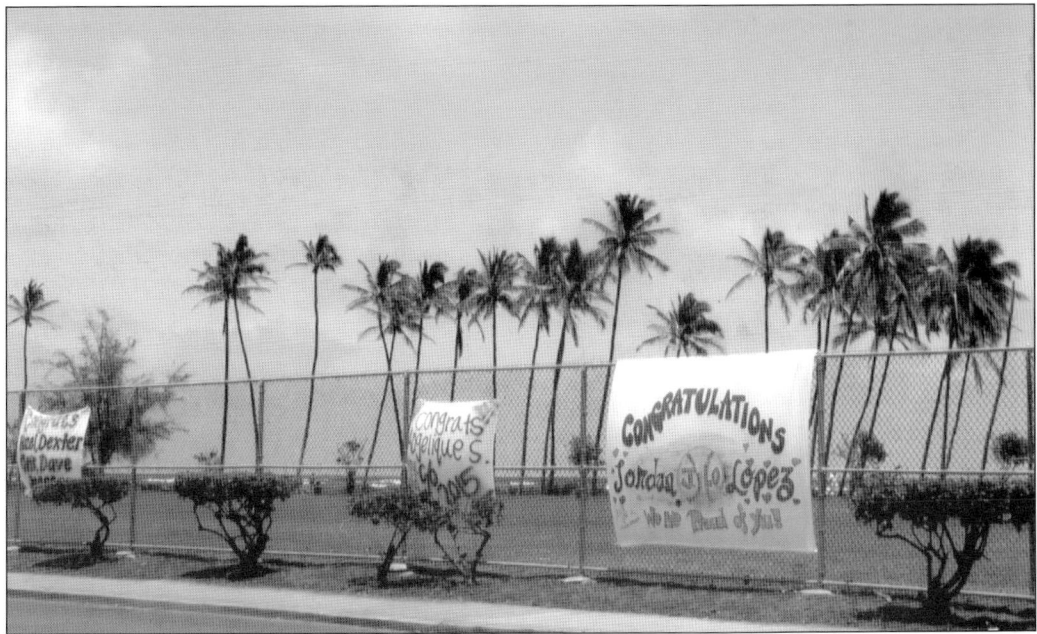

During graduation season, it is traditional for local families to festoon parks with homemade banners, celebrating and congratulating their favorite senior who received their diploma that year. (Courtesy of Marta Miller Hulsman.)

# Discover Thousands of Local History Books Featuring Millions of Vintage Images

Arcadia Publishing, the leading local history publisher in the United States, is committed to making history accessible and meaningful through publishing books that celebrate and preserve the heritage of America's people and places.

Find more books like this at
**www.arcadiapublishing.com**

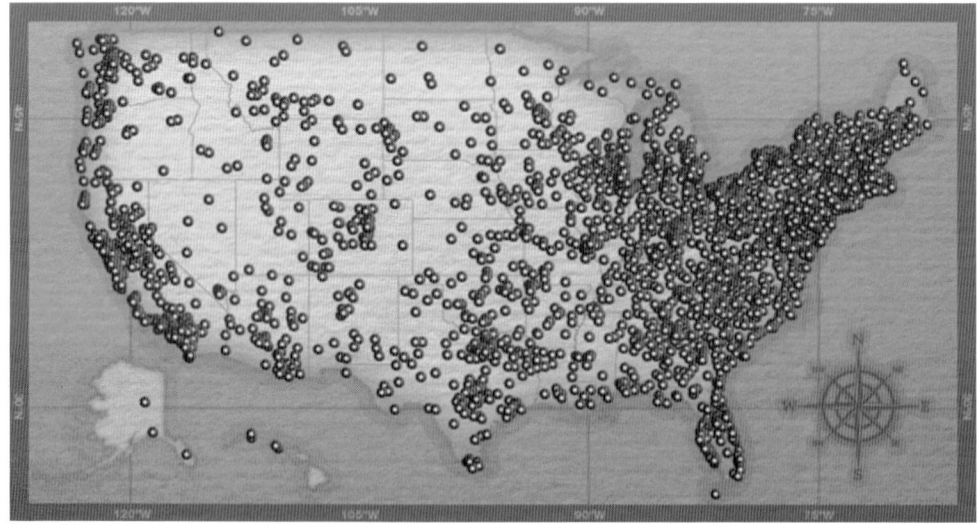

Search for your hometown history, your old stomping grounds, and even your favorite sports team.

Consistent with our mission to preserve history on a local level, this book was printed in South Carolina on American-made paper and manufactured entirely in the United States. Products carrying the accredited Forest Stewardship Council (FSC) label are printed on 100 percent FSC-certified paper.

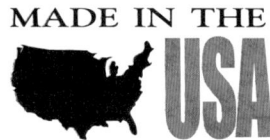